S104 Exploring science
Science: Level 1

The Open University

Exploring Earth's History

Prepared by Nick Rogers, Peter Sheldon, Peter Webb and Steve Drury

This publication forms part of the Open University module S104 *Exploring science*. The complete list of texts which make up this module can be found at the back. Details of this and other Open University modules can be obtained from the Student Registration and Enquiry Service, The Open University, PO Box 197, Milton Keynes MK7 6BJ, United Kingdom (tel. +44 (0)845 300 60 90, email general-enquiries@open.ac.uk).

Alternatively, you may visit the Open University website at http://www.open.ac.uk where you can learn more about the wide range of modules and packs offered at all levels by The Open University.

To purchase a selection of Open University materials visit www.ouw.co.uk, or contact Open University Worldwide, Walton Hall, Milton Keynes MK7 6AA, United Kingdom for a brochure (tel. +44 (0)1908 858793; fax +44 (0)1908 858787; email ouw-customer-services@open.ac.uk).

The Open University
Walton Hall, Milton Keynes
MK7 6AA

First published 2008. Third edition 2011.

Edited and designed by The Open University.

Typeset by SR Nova Pvt Ltd, Bangalore, India.

Printed and bound in the United Kingdom by Halstan Printing Group, Amersham.

ISBN 978 1 8487 3687 0

3.1

Contents

Chapter 1
Introduction

The Earth is an intensely dynamic planet, as you saw in Book 2. Unlike our nearest neighbour, the Moon, the surface of our world is not only teeming with life, but reveals its ceaseless activity in countless other ways: rough seas, surging tides, thunderstorms, waterfalls, avalanches, landslides, volcanoes and earthquakes. Nowhere on Earth is immune from change, and on a geological timescale such changes can seem hard to comprehend based on the experience of a single human lifetime. The highest rocks in the world, at the top of Everest, were once under the sea; the Earth's driest deserts will eventually be covered by ocean waters, and areas that are today almost free of geological activity may one day be prone to earthquakes and volcanic eruptions.

Certain events in the geological past have far exceeded anything known in human history. But for the pioneers of geology in the 18th and 19th centuries, the principle that 'the present is the key to the past' became the best approach to understanding the features of the Earth, and it remains the quickest way to unravel really ancient history. By looking at geological processes operating today, and what they produce, it is possible to recognise their ancient counterparts in the rock record. While fascinating in its own right, such knowledge can be of great practical value in locating resources such as oil, gas and metals.

In Book 5 you learnt about the processes of organic evolution occurring today. The fossil record is the only *direct* evidence of the course of evolution through time that we have; without it, for example, we would not know that dinosaurs ever existed. In Chapter 2, you will see how organisms can be preserved as fossils. Then, in an overview of the history of life, you will discover just how long after life's inception it took for complex animals and plants to emerge. In a sudden burst of evolution, an amazing range of animals appeared around 545 million years (Ma) ago. You will get glimpses of early life in the sea, its eventual move onto land, and its expansion into the spectacular diversity we see today.

Extinction, as you learnt in Book 5, is the natural fate of the vast majority of species that have ever lived. As you will see in Chapter 2, now and then mass extinctions have wiped clean much of life's slate, leaving survivors that have often gone on to thrive in a changed world.

The story of the Earth and its life through time is preserved in rocks, and in Chapters 3 to 5 you will continue the study of rocks begun in Book 2. Revisiting the geological specimens in the Kit will further develop the skills of observing, recording and interpreting different types of rock. Rocks and minerals are the raw materials of a technological society and without being able to extract some of the chemical elements contained in minerals, civilisation would not have progressed beyond Stone Age technology to the Bronze Age, the Iron Age and now the Age of the Silicon Chip.

Igneous rocks such as granite and basalt are formed from the cooling of molten magma, as was explained in Book 2. Different igneous rocks reflect different processes involved in the formation and crystallisation of magma, a theme of

Chapter 3. The chemical and physical breakdown of igneous rocks (or any other type of rock) produces sediments, which in turn can become sedimentary rocks, as discussed in Chapter 4. Sedimentary strata are the diaries of Earth history, containing as they do a record laid down one layer upon another, like pages in a journal. However, many such pages are missing from the diary, and recognising these omissions is part of the detective work required to assemble the story of the Earth.

In Chapter 5 you will study metamorphic rocks and the settings that produce them. When rocks are squeezed and heated, new minerals are often formed as the chemical elements in the rock rearrange themselves into more stable configurations. The older a rock is, the greater the chance that it has been subjected to high pressures and high temperatures, such as those induced during the collision of continents.

Chapter 6 explains how rocks (and their fossils) are dated, not just in relative terms – this limestone is older than that one – but also in absolute terms. You will explore the development of geochronology and why variability in the rates of most natural processes leads at best to a qualitative view of geological time. The exception is radioactivity and you will develop an understanding of the link between radioactive decay and the measurement of geological time which enables us to declare that the last volcano in Scotland erupted about 52 Ma ago (for example).

In Chapter 7 elements of the previous five chapters are brought together to give you an understanding of historical geology and the construction and application of geological maps. Maps summarise a wealth of information but reading them and translating that information into a three-dimensional understanding of a particular area or region is a fundamental skill in the Earth sciences. It is of particular value when searching for natural resources which are the subject of Chapter 8. All inorganic natural resources have geological origins, in particular metals and energy. In this brief summary you are given an overview of how energy and ore deposits form, how they relate to geological processes and how a deposit becomes economically viable.

While studying this book you will develop some fundamental skills within the context of Earth sciences that can be applied elsewhere in science. An over-arching theme of the book is that understanding the nature and history of the Earth is a multidisciplinary science that constantly involves changing scales of time and space. For example, atoms build into minerals, minerals into rocks, and rocks into continents, which themselves, like life, are continually changing. Being able to handle changing scales of time and space is a valuable skill to acquire, as is the ability to make and record observations of three-dimensional objects or features, and to interpret them and the sequence of events they reveal.

There are, of course, uncertainties in all branches of science. In Earth sciences, there are always uncertainties when reconstructing events that happened millions of years ago. Some aspects are not amenable to controlled experiments, there can be huge numbers of variables, and observations may be incomplete. This means that interpretations of complex events will have significant, albeit unquantifiable, uncertainties. Learning to deal with these uncertainties, and to be aware of the assumptions underlying any interpretation, are important skills.

'The past is the key to the future' has become today's geological cliché because of concerns over climate change (Book 1) and the effect it will have on life, human and otherwise. This book will help to equip you with some of the background knowledge and skills that, taken further, can enable Earth scientists to address these and other important issues.

Chapter 2
Fossils and the early history of life

Fossils are evidence of ancient life, and such evidence is usually found within a sedimentary rock (Book 2, Section 5.2.2). Interestingly, several early thinkers, such as the 5th century BC Greek historian Herodotus, deduced that shells now found on mountains were the remains of ancient sea creatures. Herodotus went on to reason that the rocks containing these fossils must have been formed under the sea. However, along with many other perceptive ideas held by the ancient Greeks, this theory was overlooked for about 2000 years. By the time the ideas of evolution by natural selection were being debated in the 19th century (Book 5, Chapter 14) fossils were seen as direct evidence of the course of life's evolution through time.

In this chapter, you will see how organisms become preserved as fossils, and how they can be interpreted as once-living organisms. You will then look at the fossil record of early life, and briefly explore how life has evolved from these humble origins.

2.1   Getting into the fossil record

A fossil can be part of the body of an ancient organism, such as the bones of a fish (Figure 2.1a), or the signs of an organism's activities, such as the footprints left by a dinosaur in wet sediment, now a hard rock (Figure 2.1b). In some rocks the only evidence of life may be chemicals that can only have been produced by life processes – so-called 'chemical fossils'.

Body fossils preserve something of the *bodily remains* of animals or plants, such as shells, bones and leaves, or their impression in the enclosing sediment. **Trace fossils** preserve evidence of the *activity* of animals, such as their tracks, trails, burrows, or borings. Trace fossils are often the only evidence we have of extinct organisms whose bodies lacked any hard parts.

■   Which of the following fossils are body fossils, and which are trace fossils? (i) the hair of a woolly mammoth; (ii) bite marks of the predatory fish on the smaller fish in Figure 2.1a; (iii) the moulted shell of a lobster; (iv) the footprint of a bird.

☐   (i) and (iii) are body fossils. The shell moulted by the lobster (iii) was part of its body, so it is a body fossil. Any marks made in the sediment as it struggled to shed its shell would be trace fossils. Both (ii) and (iv) are trace fossils. The bite marks of the greedy fish are a trace fossil, but the rest of the bitten fish is a body fossil.

Although the fossil record represents a very small proportion of past life, some types of organism leave a pretty good record. An organism's **preservation potential** – the chance that it has of getting into the fossil record – varies a great deal according to a range of factors, such as whether its body has any durable parts, where it lives and whether it becomes buried in sediment.

Figure 2.1   (a) Fossil fishes that were living about 50 Ma ago, revealing a clear case of greed. The larger fish overestimated its appetite and choked to death trying to swallow the smaller fish. (b) Trace fossils: the tracks of five dinosaurs that walked across what is now part of Colorado, USA about 150 Ma ago. The lateral spacing and parallel direction of the tracks suggest that these dinosaurs moved around in social groups.

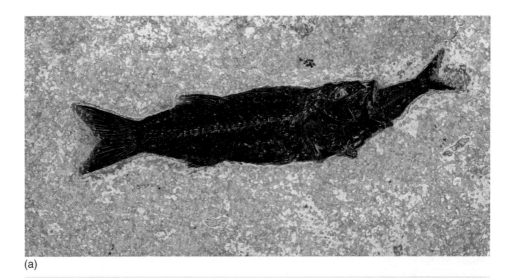

(a)

(b)

Look at Figure 2.2, which shows a scene on the coast of South Wales near St David's. Somewhere in the scene are the following organisms: (i) a rabbit in the fields above the cliffs; (ii) a flower growing in the foreground; (iii) a thick-shelled limpet attached to the rocks along the shoreline; (iv) a cockle burrowing in sand on the sea floor. Think for a moment about the chances that each has of getting preserved in the fossil record.

(i)   A rabbit certainly has hard, potentially fossilisable bones and highly resistant teeth, but if it dies a natural death its remains will probably be chewed and dispersed by scavengers, and exposed to the elements. Any remaining soft tissues will soon be eaten and decomposed by small organisms, especially bacteria. The bones and teeth may be worn down by movement in a stream, and possibly covered over by sediment. Any burial is likely to be very short-lived, however, and the remains may soon be

Figure 2.2   A coastal scene near St David's, South Wales.

exhumed by erosion during the next storm and, eventually, after many such episodes, be completely weathered away.

(ii)   The flowers growing in the foreground do not generally have durable parts and their petals, stems, roots, etc. will rot away quickly in this exposed environment. One part of them, however, has a high preservation potential — their pollen. Some of the pollen grains are likely to be blown far out to sea and settle into the sediment accumulating there. Pollen is exceedingly resistant to decay, and fossil pollen grains can be released by dissolving sedimentary rocks in hydrofluoric acid – a powerful acid capable of etching glass. The pollen grains survive this treatment, and can be studied with a microscope.

(iii)   The shell of a limpet, being hard and relatively thick, protects the animal from attack by the sea and from predators. This thick shell might at first seem to give the organism a good chance of fossilisation. However, once dead, the animal would no longer be able to cling onto the rock with its muscular foot, the shell would soon fall off the rock, the soft parts be eaten or decomposed, and the shell usually broken up by waves and strong currents along the rocky shoreline.

(iv)   A cockle burrowing in sand on the sea floor has the highest preservation potential of these four organisms. It has a hard shell, and it is already living within sediment and making potential trace fossils (its shallow burrows). Further sediment deposition may bury and further enhance the chances of preservation, though various processes such as prolonged current activity and dissolution of the shell may prevent the cockle from eventually becoming part of the fossil record.

The land tends to be a site of net erosion (Book 2, Section 5.2.2) and the sediment that starts off in rivers and lakes mostly ends up in the sea, especially the shallow seas on the edges of continents. This opportunity for long-term burial is one of the main reasons why animals from shallow marine environments dominate the fossil record, and why fossils of land-based organisms are scarce.

Question 2.1

Consider the following individual organisms, and assess their likely long-term preservation potential as fossils, taking into account the structure of their bodies and the environment they live in: (i) a garden slug; (ii) a garden snail; (iii) a whale; (iv) a jellyfish.

So, the preservation potential of an *individual organism* depends mainly on: (i) its morphology (i.e. structure and composition), particularly the presence or absence of robust hard parts; (ii) where it lives and the circumstances of its death, and especially whether or not it is buried in a marine environment where sediments tend to accumulate; and (iii) whether or not its activities are likely to produce trace fossils. Box 2.1 discusses just how good fossil preservation can be.

■ The preservation potential of any particular *species*, rather than just an individual member of it, is affected by one other crucial factor. What is it?

☐ The number of individuals in the species.

The more abundant the species, the higher its preservation potential. With animals, the fossil record is biased in favour of the most abundant ones near the base of food chains, and against scarce animals such as large vertebrates at the top of food chains. A wide geographic distribution also increases the chances of a species being found in the fossil record.

Box 2.1   Is there such a thing as perfect preservation?

Given all the factors that act against preservation, it is surprising that some extremely delicate forms of life have found their way into the fossil record; examples range from the cells lining the stomach of a 100 Ma-old fish, and the soft tissues of its last meal, to the butterfly in Figure 2.3.

Consider for a moment what must have occurred for this particular butterfly to have been preserved so well.

For a start, it had to be sealed off quickly from various agents of destruction.

■ What general kinds of agents of destruction can you think of that the butterfly must have been protected from?

☐ The butterfly must have been sealed off from: (i) some of the *biological* agents of destruction, such as scavengers that might have eaten it; (ii) *physical* agents of destruction such as strong winds or water currents that would have broken up its fragile body; (iii) *chemical* agents of destruction such as oxygen (which enhances decomposition), or solutions that might have dissolved away all its organic remains.

In fact, the butterfly came to rest on very fine-grained sediment at the bottom of a stagnant (oxygen-poor), current-free lake, and was gently covered over by a rain of further fine sediment. As we shall see in Chapter 4 very fine-grained sediment indicates weak or absent currents which would be unlikely to damage the butterfly.

■ Can you suggest another reason why *fine*-grained sediment is significant for the preservation of this butterfly?

☐ Small grains favour the preservation of delicate structures and fine details because the grains can fit closely around them.

Imagine that the butterfly had instead come to rest on a bed of gravel, and been covered over by more gravel. Apart from the fact that currents strong enough to transport gravel would break up the butterfly, the large gravel particles could not mould closely around its delicate structures, and it would soon be obliterated. The durability and preservation quality of any potential fossil thus decreases as the grain size of the enclosing sediment *increases*.

Rapid, permanent burial by fine sediment in oxygen-poor environments is one of the most favourable situations for fossil preservation. Although extremely fine details can be fossilised in the right physical and chemical conditions, there is no such thing as the *perfect* preservation of an entire organism. DNA has been recovered from various fossils up to about 400 000 years old, including frozen pieces of mammoths and other Ice Age animals and plants, but it is degraded into short fragments. It is virtually certain that *no* DNA can have survived from organisms that were alive millions of years ago, such as Jurassic dinosaurs.

Figure 2.3 A butterfly that was flapping its wings about 35 Ma ago, in what is now Colorado, USA.

Question 2.2

Consider the following species and, ignoring any effects of human predation, assess their *overall* preservation potential as a species: (i) the blue whale (population a few thousand individuals); (ii) the garden earthworm; (iii) an early species of our genus, *Homo*, with a very small population that lived in the tropics a million years ago; (iv) a common species of oyster with a thick shell.

Hard biological materials such as bones, shells and wood often contain pores (open spaces). When hard parts are lying buried in sediment, any such pores tend to be filled up with minerals that precipitate out from the water seeping through the sediment. The original biological materials (such as the cell walls of bone or wood) may sometimes be replaced by these minerals. Both the filling up of pores and the replacement of biological materials may occur in a single fossil. Neither of these processes, which are a kind of 'turning into stone', *has* to occur for something to be called a fossil; sometimes the fossil can still be composed of the original, barely altered shell or bone. A shell entombed in rock may be dissolved away at any time by percolating waters, especially acidic ones, leaving only the impression of the shell's surfaces on the adjacent rock.

■ Sharks have exceptionally durable, though porous, teeth. Suppose that there are two shark teeth on a table, each of the same size, shape and colour. One is a fossil and the other is not. How might you expect to tell the two apart, and why?

□ Pick them both up. The fossil is likely to feel heavier. Its density will probably have been increased by additional minerals that have filled up the pore spaces in the tooth whilst it was within the sediment or sedimentary rock.

2.2   Interpreting fossils as living organisms

Now that you have considered what fossils are, and how and where they tend to be preserved, the next stage is to exploit knowledge of modern organisms to interpret the biology of ancient organisms and the environments they lived in.

Although soft parts are rarely preserved in the fossil record, the form of any hard parts is always related to an animal's soft-part anatomy, the way it grows and its mode of life.

As shallow marine invertebrates dominate the fossil record, let us take two phyla that have hard parts, starting with the phylum Mollusca. (Phyla are the major divisions of animal life; Book 5, Section 3.3.) Three classes of **mollusc** are abundant and diverse, both today and in the fossil record: bivalves, e.g. cockles and mussels; gastropods, e.g. snails and slugs; and cephalopods (pronounced 'keffallo-pods'), e.g. squid and octopus. Although at first sight these animals might seem completely unrelated to each other, they actually represent variations on the same theme – the body plan (Book 5, Section 3.3) of the phylum Mollusca. All the various classes of molluscs have diverged in different directions away from a common ancestor.

In most groups of molluscs, the body secretes an external shell (such as that of a snail). **Bivalves**, as their name declares, have a shell in two parts known as valves. Except in a few bivalve groups such as oysters, the valves are of equal size and shape, one being the mirror image of the other. Growth lines are normally visible on the external surface of each valve. Each growth line represents the outer edge of the shell at an earlier stage in its life. In the case of the cockle shell shown in Figure 2.4a, these fine growth lines can be seen running parallel to the edge of the shell, cutting across the more obvious ridges that radiate away from the point where the first part of the shell was formed.

(a)

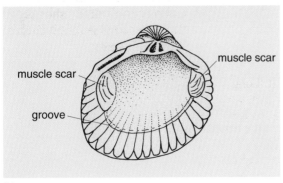

(b)

Figure 2.4   (a) A living cockle, its shell and siphons clearly visible as it lies partly buried in sand. (b) The interior of one valve of a cockle shell.

On the *inside* of each valve there is evidence that can be used to interpret the bivalve's mode of life. Although the soft parts may have long decayed away, bivalve shells have distinct areas where muscles for closing the shell were attached. The size, shape and location of these muscle scars reveal aspects of the animal's mode of life. Each valve of the cockle shell (Figure 2.4b,) has two muscle scars, between which is a thin groove that runs roughly parallel to the edge of the shell. This groove is where part of the fleshy tissue that secreted the shell was attached.

The living cockle in Figure 2.4a has two soft tubular siphons. One is used for taking in water to structures that absorb oxygen and strain off tiny food particles suspended in the water. The other siphon ejects water containing waste products. Bivalves that live in a burrow have long siphons that protrude up above the entrance of the burrow during feeding. A distinct notch in the course of the groove between the muscle scars, if present, indicates where the bivalve could retract its siphons when disturbed.

■ Imagine that you have found an isolated fossil bivalve shell, similar to that in Figure 2.5, and you are trying to interpret its mode of life. You notice it has a deeply notched groove between the muscle scars. What inference would you make from this observation?

☐ The species was probably a deep burrower.

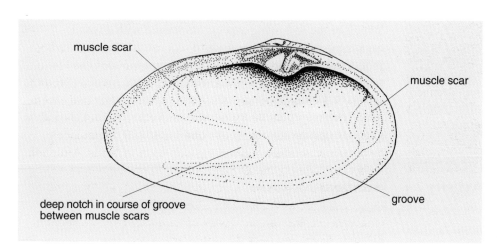

Figure 2.5   The interior of one valve of a bivalve (the common otter shell), showing a deeply notched groove between the muscle scars.

The deeper the notch, the longer the siphons that were retracted into it. Long siphons are needed if the animal burrows deeply below the sediment surface (as does the species in Figure 2.5). The cockle, by contrast, is a shallow burrower, and so its shell has no such notch (Figure 2.4b).

Echinoderms ('eck-eye-no-derms') are members of another phylum, and so have a fundamentally different body plan from that of the molluscs. Among the groups in the exclusively marine phylum Echinodermata are sea urchins (**echinoids**) and starfish. Echinoderm skeletons are made of many interlocking plates of the mineral calcite (calcium carbonate). In sea urchins, movable spines used for locomotion and defence are attached by muscles to knobs on the plates.

(a)

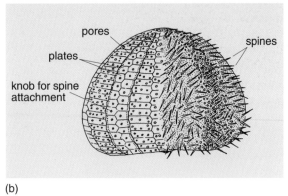

(b)

Figure 2.6 (a) A living edible sea urchin, with long tube-feet extending beyond its spines. (b) A dead edible sea urchin with its tube-feet decayed. The spines, which usually soon fall off naturally, have been removed from the left side, revealing the plates of which the skeleton is made.

Figure 2.6 shows two views of the edible sea urchin – a living animal covered in spines (Figure 2.6a), and a dead animal with its spines partially missing (Figure 2.6b). The thin tentacles projecting out beyond the calcite spines (Figure 2.6a) are soft, multi-purpose organs called tube-feet which the animal uses for feeding, respiration, locomotion and, in some species, constructing burrows. The tube-feet project through little pores in the plates of the skeleton. Most of the round sea urchins live by browsing on plant and animal growths covering rocks, whereas oval or heart-shaped ones (with a front and back end) are adapted to burrowing and usually have smaller spines. The mouth is located on the underside.

■ Which parts of sea urchins mentioned above are most *unlikely* to be found in the fossil record, but which can nevertheless be inferred to have been present because of features of the sea urchin's skeleton?

☐ The tube-feet, which are indicated by pores in the plates, and the muscles that connected the spines to the rest of the skeleton.

Question 2.3

Which of the following aspects associated with a fossil organism should make it easier to reconstruct the once-living individual, its activities, and its environment? (i) It has few relatives alive today; (ii) it left abundant trace fossils; (iii) there are several other fossil groups in the same rock; (iv) its hard parts became separated from each other after death; (v) its hard parts are complex, with many detailed structures.

Activity 2.1 Investigating fossils

We expect this activity to take you approximately 90 minutes.

In this activity you will be studying images of fossils and will develop some important skills of observation and interpretation.

Now go to Activity 2.1 on the module website for instructions on this activity.

There are no comments on this activity.

2.3 Life's long fuse to the Cambrian explosion

When beginning the study of the history of life, it is critical to be able to place important events in the perspective of geological time. Geologists have subdivided the history of the Earth into time intervals of varying duration as shown in Figure 2.7. In such diagrams, the earliest (oldest) events are placed at the bottom of the diagram, and the latest (youngest) at the top, reflecting the relative age of layers in a pile of sedimentary rocks. The way that the timescale is divided up is discussed in Box 2.2.

The major boundaries between these time intervals were chosen in the 19th century, largely on the basis of biological events recorded in the fossil record; for example, mass extinctions, when large numbers of species and genera disappeared from the fossil record, and on other events such as mountain-building episodes which left features in the sedimentary record that could be recognised over a wide area. Initially, there was only a *relative* timescale – a sequence of events – but today we can give precise dates to these in millions of years.

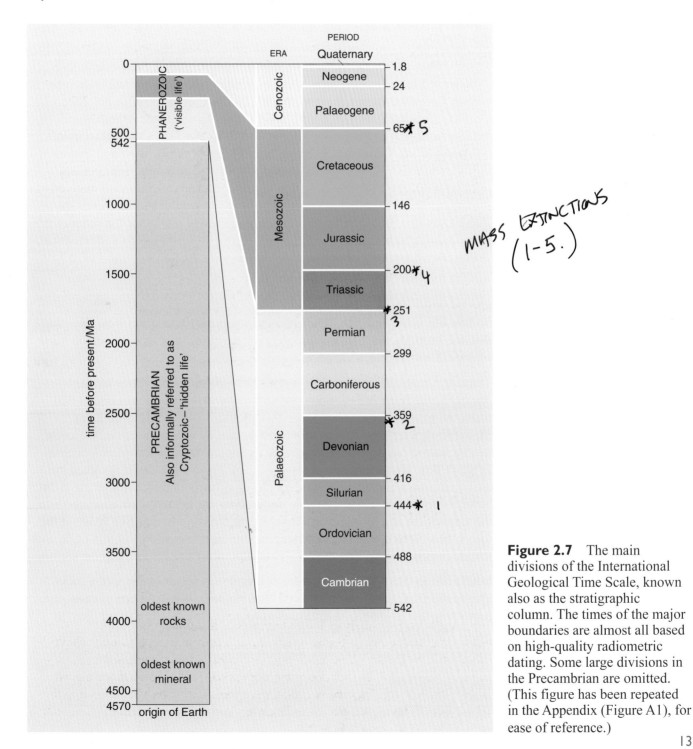

Figure 2.7   The main divisions of the International Geological Time Scale, known also as the stratigraphic column. The times of the major boundaries are almost all based on high-quality radiometric dating. Some large divisions in the Precambrian are omitted. (This figure has been repeated in the Appendix (Figure A1), for ease of reference.)

13

Box 2.2   The divisions of geological time

The broadest division of Earth history is into two intervals of very different length: the **Precambrian** and the **Phanerozoic**. The Precambrian is a vast period of time – from the origin of the Earth, 4570 Ma ago, to the start of the Phanerozoic, 542 Ma ago.

Question 2.4

What percentage of the Earth's history does the Precambrian represent?

Sometimes the Precambrian is known informally as the Cryptozoic, which is derived from Greek words meaning 'hidden life'. Phanerozoic is derived from Greek words meaning 'visible life', reflecting the obvious presence of life since the start of this time, when fossils first become abundant (Section 2.4). The Phanerozoic is divided into three eras – the **Palaeozoic**, **Mesozoic** and **Cenozoic** (meaning 'ancient life'; 'middle life', and 'recent life', respectively). Each of these eras is divided into a number of periods of unequal length (Figure 2.7). The names of periods are variously derived, ranging from the Latin for Wales, 'Cambria'; an area of Russia, Perm; to the Latin for chalk, 'creta'. You are *not* expected to memorise the order of the periods, although this would prove useful. The Palaeogene and Neogene Periods were previously placed together to form the Tertiary Sub-Era, a term which persists in the literature.

So how old is life on Earth? The oldest sedimentary rocks, from west Greenland, dated at 3800 Ma old, contain carbon in a form interpreted as evidence of biological activity, i.e. a chemical fossil.

The oldest fossil structures in the world, 3500 Ma old, come from Western Australia and South Africa. Some are so small you need a microscope to find them, but others are much larger fossils called stromatolites (Figure 2.8a). **Stromatolites** are mound-like structures formed by various bacteria. We know this because some stromatolites are still forming today in a few places, such as in Shark Bay, Western Australia (Figure 2.8b). The main bacteria involved are cyanobacteria, which produce oxygen during photosynthesis, i.e. they use light as an energy source, carbon dioxide as a carbon source, and release oxygen into the atmosphere as a by-product. The cyanobacteria live in mat-like layers at the top of the structure, trapping sediment and forming mounds 0.5–2.0 m high; each mound is mostly sediment.

In addition to these large-scale stromatolites, Precambrian sedimentary rocks also contain fossils of bacteria themselves: single cells and groups of cells, some joined together in chains. Many types of bacteria would have existed then, as today. The interpretation of microscopic material in Precambrian rocks can, however, be highly problematic, and is much debated. Nevertheless, evidence of an organic origin is often clear enough, even if the taxonomic affinities of the fossils are not. Some cyanobacteria seem to have changed remarkably little in their morphology for at least 2000 Ma. Figure 2.9 shows a comparison of living

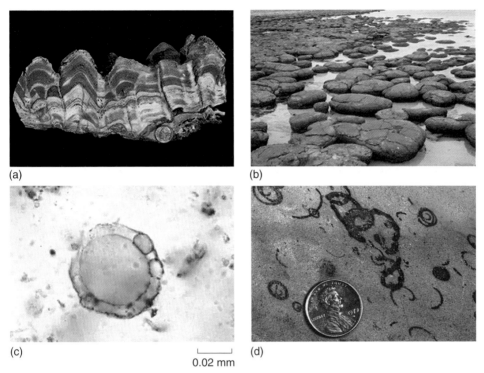

(a)

(b)

(c)

(d)

0.02 mm

Figure 2.8   (a) One of the world's oldest fossils – a 3500 Ma-old stromatolite from Western Australia in cross-section. The specimen is 20 cm across. (b) Living stromatolites in Shark Bay, Western Australia. They are about 0.5–1.5 m across. (c) A fossil cyanobacteria cell, 1900 Ma old, from the Gunflint Chert, Ontario, Canada. (d) *Grypania*, interpreted as an early eukaryote, 2100 Ma old, from Michigan, USA; the coin is ~1 cm across.

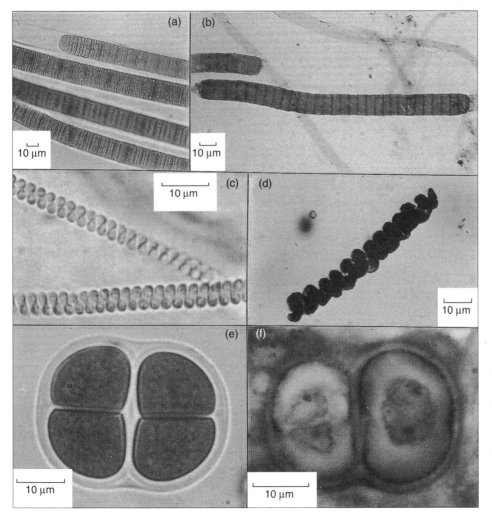

(a)

(b)

10 μm

10 μm

(c)

10 μm

(d)

10 μm

(e)

(f)

10 μm

10 μm

Figure 2.9   Comparison of living and fossil cyanobacteria: (a), (c) and (e) are from stromatolites growing today in Mexico; (b), (d) and (f) are from rocks in the former Soviet Union; (b) is 950 Ma old; (d) is 850 Ma old and (f) is 1550 Ma old.

and fossil cyanobacteria. Such cells, being prokaryotes, lack a nucleus, as we saw in Book 5, Section 4.1.

According to evidence from Precambrian rocks, the Earth's atmosphere originally lacked oxygen, but it eventually changed to being oxygen-rich, probably as a result of photosynthesis by cyanobacteria. Some oxygen may also have been formed by non-biological mechanisms, such as the breakdown of water into hydrogen and oxygen by ultraviolet (UV) radiation. It was, however, not until about 2200 Ma ago – about half the age of life itself – that oxygen in the atmosphere had built up into a permanent accumulation. Some of the oxygen (O_2) was converted into ozone (O_3), forming a protective layer in the upper atmosphere that shielded life from harmful UV radiation; previously seawater alone had this protective role.

The first eukaryotic cells (i.e. cells with DNA enclosed in a nucleus; Book 5, Section 4.1) do not appear in the fossil record until about 2100 Ma ago (though interpretations differ, and evidence from molecular biology suggests eukaryotes may have evolved much earlier). Initially, the eukaryotes were mainly slowly evolving, photosynthetic plankton, but later they diversified rapidly. The first multicellular algae (small primitive seaweeds) are known from 1200 Ma ago. It was about this time that sexual reproduction originated, enabling the production and inheritance of more genetic variation, and promoting diversification of species. Eventually, eukaryotic cells became larger, and more specialised, and with the protection from harmful radiation afforded by a thicker ozone layer, a wide variety of shallow-water environments at the edges of the oceans became accessible to eukaryotes.

One of life's largest gear-changes came when, according to the fossil record, multicellular animals made their first appearance about 580 Ma ago. Life on the Earth, for the first time, now included relatively large individual organisms with a range of specialised cells (though still lacking hard parts). This group of animals, the Ediacaran fauna (Figure 2.10, iii–vi), named after Ediacara, the place in South Australia where the fauna was first recognised, is found in many localities around the world. Some of the fossils show bilateral, segmented and radial structures and a wide range of body plans, but while some have a superficial resemblance to modern jellyfish, sea pens and worms, many seem to have left no living descendants. Ediacaran fossils are strange and hard to interpret. For example, in *Dickinsonia* (Figure 2.10a (vi)), no-one knows which end was its head, or whether it had one at all. Recent research suggests that some of these organisms, which lived in shallow seas, lived by absorbing nutrients through their outer membranes, but despite abundant fossils of their body forms, there is little evidence to indicate how the Ediacaran ecosystem, such as that reconstructed in Figure 2.10b, functioned. Most if not all the Ediacaran organisms seem to have become extinct by the start of the Cambrian Period.

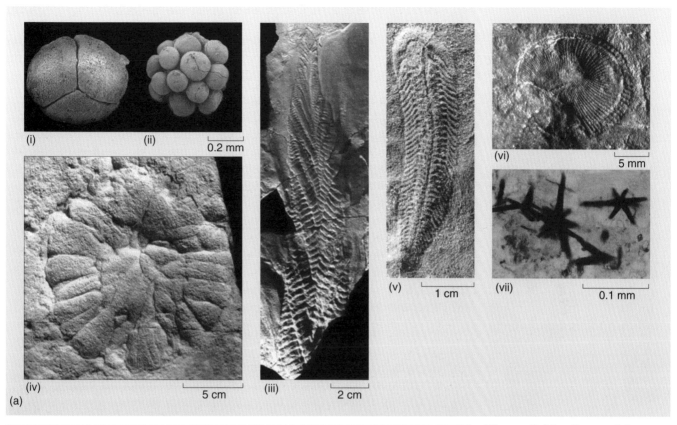

(i)   (ii)
0.2 mm

(iv)
5 cm

(iii)
2 cm

(v)
1 cm

(vi)
5 mm

(vii)
0.1 mm

(a)

(b)

Figure 2.10   Some of the earliest animals of the late Precambrian. (a) (i), (ii) Fossil embryos of uncertain affinity. (iii) – (vi) Typical Ediacaran fossils, impressions of bodies in sediment; all are of uncertain affinity: (iii) *Charnia*; (iv) *Inaria*; (v) *Spriggina*; (vi) *Dickinsonia*. (vii) Sponge spicules. (b) A reconstruction of the Ediacaran fauna. The largest organisms (the fronds attached to the sea floor) could reach about 2 m long, though most organisms were less than 15 cm in length.

17

2.4   The Cambrian explosion

One of the most important events in the history of life began at the start of the Cambrian Period. It was then that body fossils with hard shelly parts became abundant for the first time, reflecting a new-found ability of many groups of organisms to build a mineralised skeleton. (Actually, the first evidence of preservable hard parts comes from a limited range of small, rather puzzling tiny fossils, including tubes made of calcium carbonate, found in late Precambrian rocks.) A wide variety of small (1–2 mm) shelly fossils are found in the earliest Cambrian rocks (Figure 2.11). These fossils have a variety of shapes, such as tubes and cones that presumably enclosed soft tissue, as well as spines, scales and knobs. However, it is often difficult to tell whether a fossil is the complete skeleton of a single organism or an isolated part of some larger creature. The first signs of burrowing animals also appear around this time. The term **Cambrian explosion** is given to this sudden burst of evolution, when a wide variety of organisms, especially those with hard, mineralised parts, first appear in the fossil record. Thus began the Phanerozoic – the time of 'visible life' and the Palaeozoic Era.

By the middle of the Cambrian, most phyla in existence today had evolved (though life was still confined to the sea). Not surprisingly, a few entirely soft-bodied phyla living today have no known representatives in the fossil record, so we don't know when they evolved. Evidence from molecular biology, and the remarkably preserved fossil embryos in the early stages of division from China (Figure 2.10a (i), (ii)), suggests that some animal phyla diverged from each other much earlier than the start of the Cambrian explosion, but the timing remains uncertain.

The main stimulus for the acquisition of hard parts seems likely to have been the rise of predation.

■   From the information given above, which aspects of the small shelly fossils from the earliest Cambrian are consistent with a rise in predation?

☐   The appearance of features that could be used for protection, such as spines and scales, and tubes and conical shells that could protect vulnerable soft parts inside.

Natural selection, however, can only act on variation that is already there (Book 5, Chapter 14), so how did these useful hard parts ever get started? One plausible idea is that the hard parts may have originated as crystalline products of excretion. The slightest toughening of soft parts by mineral deposition would have been of selective advantage, either in defence or attack.

There is little evidence of special, widespread environmental changes that could have directly triggered the Cambrian explosion. Whatever the causes, once triggered, a wide range of ecological opportunities presumably became available for exploitation, promoting the rapid evolution of new, quite different types of

Figure 2.11   First signs of the Cambrian explosion: a variety of small shelly fossils from earliest Cambrian rocks. None is more than a few mm long.

animals. Many of the newly evolved phyla show organisation of the body into specialised areas – especially a head end with food-trapping and sensory organs, a tubular gut and limbs. There is no doubt that many Cambrian animals were equipped with adaptations for predation and were able to pursue food much more actively than could the Ediacaran fauna – such as by scuttling over the sea floor, swimming actively, and burrowing.

■ A greatly increased variety of types of trace fossils, especially burrows of soft-bodied animals, are found around the start of the Cambrian explosion. What is the significance of this finding?

☐ It reflects the evolution of much more complex patterns of behaviour, some of it probably related to the avoidance of predators.

Burrows provide evidence of biological activity even though there may be no other fossil remains. The evolution of predatory creatures with hard parts would have given soft-bodied animals prone to burrowing beneath the sediment surface a distinct selective advantage. Moreover, burrowing would also have made new food sources available, including previously unexploited buried organic material.

2.4.1 The Burgess Shale animals

High in the Canadian Rockies is a deposit of middle Cambrian age, about 510 Ma old, called the Burgess Shale. It contains the fossils of animals that lived on a muddy sea floor, and which were suddenly transported into deeper, oxygen-poor water by submarine landslides. Their catastrophic burial has given us an exceptional view of Cambrian life. Not only have animals with hard shelly parts been preserved but entirely soft-bodied forms are present as thin films on the sediment surface. Only about 15% of the 120 genera present in the Burgess Shale are shelly organisms that dominate typical Cambrian fossil assemblages (fossils that occur together) elsewhere. The shelly component was therefore in a minority, and organisms with hard parts probably formed less than 5% of individuals in the living community.

■ If the soft-bodied fossils of the Burgess Shale are taken away, all that remains is a typical Cambrian assemblage of hard-bodied organisms. Why is this important to bear in mind when trying to interpret other Cambrian fossil assemblages?

☐ The other Cambrian assemblages may also have been dominated by soft-bodied animals, even if the only fossils they now contain are of hard-bodied ones.

Another important revelation of the Burgess Shale lies in the wide diversity of animal body plans that were around in middle Cambrian time, about 510 Ma ago. There are representatives of about a dozen of the phyla that persist to the present day, including *Pikaia* (Figure 2.12c), one of the earliest known chordates (the group to which vertebrates belong; Book 5). Two forms closely related to early arthropods include *Opabinia*, which had five eyes perched on the top of its head (Figure 2.12b), and *Anomalocaris* (Figure 2.12f), the largest known Cambrian animal, which reached over a metre in length. Its extraordinary jaw consisted of spiny plates encircling the mouth, which probably constricted down on prey in much the same way that the plates of an iris diaphragm cut down the

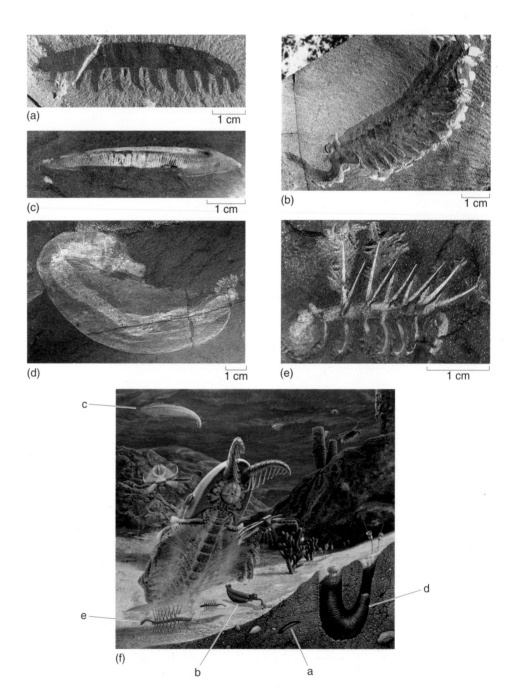

Figure 2.12   Animals of the Burgess Shale. (a) *Aysheaia*, a velvet worm; (b) *Opabinia* which had five eyes and is from an unknown phylum; (c) *Pikaia*, an early chordate; (d) *Ottoia*, a priapulid (or penis) worm; (e) *Hallucigenia*, probably a velvet worm. (f) A reconstruction of the Burgess Shale fauna, on the floor of the sea in the middle Cambrian. The labels match fossils (a) to (e). Dominating the scene is *Anomalocaris*, the largest known Cambrian predator (an arthropod); here it threatens five-eyed *Opabinia* and *Hallucigenia* below it on the sea floor. Note that the colours of organisms shown in this and other such reconstructions are conjectural.

light in a camera. About a dozen other types of fossils have been said to be so unlike anything living today and so different from each other that, had they been living now, each would have been placed in a separate phylum. With further study, however, the relationships of these puzzling animals are becoming clearer; some forms are hard to classify simply because the boundaries between major categories of animal life were still blurred shortly after the Cambrian explosion. In other words, by middle Cambrian times, there still had not been enough time for some groups to have diverged sufficiently from their recent common ancestors to be distinctly different.

Burgess Shale-type faunas have been found in over 30 sites ranging from North America and Greenland, to China and Australia. The wide range of animals they contain seems to reflect an unpruned 'bush of diversity' resulting from the Cambrian explosion. Not long after, though, extinction lopped off some of the branches, leaving phyla with the relatively distinct features that have remained to this day.

Question 2.5

Rearrange the following 9 events, listed here in random order, in their appropriate position beside the geological timescale in Figure 2.7:

- first animals (Ediacaran fauna) 7
- origin of the Earth 1
- first multicellular organisms (algae) 6
- first evidence of life (chemical fossils) in oldest sedimentary rocks 2
- Burgess Shale fossils 9
- first eukaryotic cells in the fossil record 5
- Cambrian explosion 8
- first fossil structures (including stromatolites) 3
- permanent accumulation of free atmospheric oxygen 4

2.5   Invasion of the land

It was not until about 430 Ma ago – during the Silurian Period, and more than 3 *billion* years after the origin of life – that the main invasion of freshwater and land environments by plants and animals really got going. Long before then, in the later parts of the Precambrian, some algae and bacteria may possibly have lived on land, and there is evidence that some small plants, and possibly some small animals too, lived on land in the Ordovician Period.

There were all sorts of environmental challenges to which plants and animals had to adapt to live out of the sea. For example, if a marine plant cell is directly surrounded by fresh water, the water tends to diffuse into it, causing it to burst. Alternatively, if the cell is directly surrounded by air, it loses all its water, just as seaweeds become hard and crisp when stranded above high tide and exposed to the wind and the sun. So, to survive in air, plants had to acquire an effective outer coat to keep the right amount of water in. They also had to evolve small, controllable pores (called stomata; Book 5, Figure 6.8) to enable gases to be exchanged through this coat.

To grow up off the land surface, plants had to develop groups of special plumbing cells to conduct water, nutrients and the products of photosynthesis around their structures. Without the buoyancy provided by immersion in water, adaptations in both plants and animals were needed to support a body on land against the pull of gravity. Expressed this way, it is all too easy to give the impression, quite wrongly, that such innovations could be achieved intentionally, almost as if by some directed effort. On the contrary, as in all evolutionary explanations, natural selection (Book 5, Chapter 14) would have favoured those organisms that were, *by chance*, better adapted to these new environmental challenges.

A fossil of a very early land plant is shown in Figure 2.13a. Only about 4 cm tall, it lacked roots and leaves, and sent short shoots forking upward to capture sunlight and release spores (reproductive cells) into the wind. These first land plants, which lived in swamps and on riverbanks and floodplains, provided food for the animals that, by chance, were best adapted to life on land – the arthropods, which already had an almost waterproof outer skeleton and were very

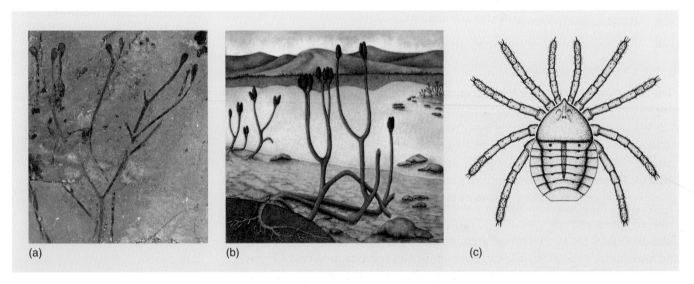

(a)   (b)   (c)

Figure 2.13   Early life on land. (a) A very early land plant, about 4 cm tall, from Silurian rocks in Wales. (b) An artist's impression of early Devonian plants, fringing a lake. They are about 45 cm tall. (c) One of the earliest known land animals – a spider-like creature (4 mm long, including legs) from Silurian rocks in England.

strong for their size. Once the greening of the land had begun, small millipedes and wingless insects were apparently tempted on to land to eat the rotting plant debris, and they and their remains were eaten in turn by predatory or scavenging carnivorous arthropods such as centipedes, scorpions and small spider-like creatures (Figure 2.13c).

So what would a typical land scene from the Silurian have looked like? A low, mossy-looking carpet of green, primitive land plants flanked the rivers, lakes and ponds. Small, early land-arthropods roved among them, unmolested by vertebrates, which were still restricted to water. Beyond, inland, was mostly bare rock and debris from weathering and erosion.

A slightly more advanced plant, about 45 cm tall, is shown in Figure 2.13b; it had an underground or surface-lying horizontal stem with tiny root hairs. The species grew beside shallow pools early in the Devonian Period in what today we call Scotland, which was then just south of the Equator. The local area was occasionally flooded by mineral-rich waters from nearby hot springs, which helped to fossilise the plants (and associated animals) and preserve them in exquisite detail.

By the end of the Devonian Period, lowland flood plains were dominated by plants sufficiently tall to be called trees, with wood, true roots, and complex branching patterns. Some of these giant fern-like trees had evolved *seeds* that protected the fertilised ovules and supplied them with a food store, giving them independence from water and allowing inland areas to be colonised. By the end of the Devonian, many features of today's land plants had already evolved, though flowers and fruits (enclosing the seed) appeared much later with the first flowering plants in the early Cretaceous Period.

2.5.1   The delayed invasion of the vertebrates

The first chordates appeared on the scene soon after the Cambrian explosion, and the oldest are known from rocks about 525 Ma old in China. During the Cambrian chordates diversified into the first vertebrates, including small, eel-shaped creatures – known mainly from their microscopic teeth – and other jawless fishes. **Vertebrates** are chordates with backbones and today include five classes: fishes, amphibians, reptiles, mammals and birds. *Pikaia* (Figure 2.12c) from the Burgess Shale was an early chordate, but not a vertebrate, as it lacked a backbone.

Although the first fishes appeared in the Cambrian, they remained rare and did not diversify until the late Ordovician. The first fish with jaws appeared in the Silurian. Fishes became increasingly diverse through the Silurian, but only became abundant in the Devonian. Furthermore, it was not until the late Devonian that vertebrates first evolved features that enabled them to live, at least partly, on land. Fossils of the first amphibians, such as *Acanthostega*

(Figure 2.14) are found in freshwater rocks of this age. Several transitional forms between fish and amphibians have been found, including *Tiktaalik* (Figure 2.14), discovered recently in Arctic Canada. The fins of ancestral lobe-finned fish (such as *Eusthenopteron*, Figure 2.14) were sturdy, with articulated bones and also thin bony rays to support fin tissue. The structure of such fins evolved, via intermediate forms such as *Panderichthys* and *Tiktaalik*, into limbs lacking rays, as in *Acanthostega*.

Acanthostega had a rather fish-like body outline, including a tail fin. Their limbs, however, show that these carnivorous animals could waddle about on land, although their lifestyle was mostly aquatic. We shall never be certain of the selection pressures that drove this transition to life on land, but plausible advantages include the escape from predatory fishes and the utilisation of unexploited food sources.

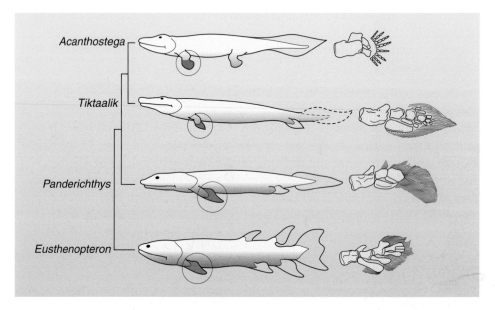

Figure 2.14   The transition from fish to amphibians in Devonian times, as shown by changes in body shape and appendages. Drawings are not to scale but all animals are between 75 cm and 1.5 m in length. The bracketed connections on the left of the figure represent closeness of relationship. Details of the forelimbs (on the right) show the progressive development of what were to become toes. The forelimbs are circled on the left. The tail of *Tiktaalik* is drawn with a dashed line as no fossil evidence for it has yet been found. (Forelimbs from Nature Publishing Group. Reprinted by permission from Macmillan Publishers Ltd., http://www.nature.com/index.html)

Amphibians remained large during the Palaeozoic Era, often reaching 1 or 2 metres in length – huge by the standards of today's frogs, toads and newts. By 350 Ma ago, in the early Carboniferous Period, the first reptiles had appeared. Unlike amphibians, which are dependent on being near lakes or ponds to lay their eggs and in which their tadpoles live, reptiles evolved a crucial adaptation – a shelled egg that did not dry out in air.

Among the huge trees of the dense late Carboniferous forest (Figure 2.15), were found reptiles, amphibians and insects such as dragonflies and cockroaches. The trees and other plants growing in these equatorial forests and in swamps trapped the energy of sunlight by photosynthesis. This energy became stored in plant debris that accumulated on the floor of the forests and in swamps (as you may remember from the discussion of the carbon cycle, Book 1, Section 7.4.3). Eventually, some of this debris was buried, compressed and converted by heat and pressure into coal; 300 Ma later the energy from Carboniferous sunlight fuelled the Industrial Revolution and the carbon dioxide liberated is now contributing to global warming.

Figure 2.15 Scene from a late Carboniferous forest. The animals in the foreground (from left to right) are a cockroach, a reptile and an amphibian.

To place these events in a better perspective, study Figure 2.16, which shows an outline of vertebrate evolution, including the branching points from which new major groups originated. As usual with diagrams depicting events in geological time, this figure should be read from the bottom (oldest) upwards.

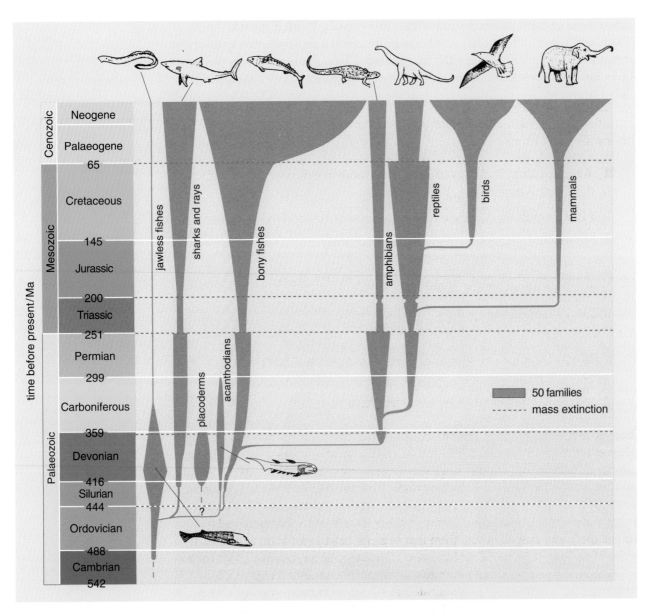

Figure 2.16   Geological ranges of vertebrates showing when various groups evolved from each other during the Phanerozoic. See text for further explanation.

The width of each group indicates its approximate diversity (as number of families); note the scale bar. The pattern of diversity change within each group summarised here is generalised and smoothed-out, and a more complex pattern is known to occur at higher resolution. Uncertainties exist over the precise timing of origin of some groups of early fish and over the evolutionary relationships between them. As in all such cases, data and interpretations are potentially subject to revision as new fossil discoveries are made, taxonomic relationships are analysed and dating methods are improved. The wide horizontal separation of some newly evolved groups from their ancestors (e.g. mammals from reptiles) does *not* indicate huge, abrupt change but is simply a consequence of the way the diagram is drawn. Placoderms were a group of jawed fishes with thick external armour, and acanthodians were slender jawed fishes with many spines.

■ Which of today's classes of vertebrates were in existence by the end of the Triassic Period?

☐ Fishes, amphibians, reptiles *and* mammals had all evolved by this time, about 200 Ma ago.

■ When were (i) jawless fishes, and (ii) amphibians at their highest diversity (in terms of number of families)?

☐ (i) In the Devonian; (ii) in the Permian.

■ In which geological period did birds first appear, and from which vertebrate group did they evolve?

☐ Birds evolved from reptiles in the late Jurassic.

There is conclusive evidence that birds, the only vertebrates that possess feathers today, evolved from dinosaurs. In Jurassic and Cretaceous times some dinosaurs possessed feathers too. Dinosaurs were a special group of reptiles – special not least because, after their origin in the middle Triassic, they became the dominant land animals for over 150 Ma. They filled almost every niche possible for large land vertebrates. They included carnivores, herbivores and a few omnivores (mixed diet), and ranged in size from that of a chicken to vast plant eaters, such as the 25 m-long, 40 tonne *Brachiosaurus*. Dinosaurs never, however, took to the air (except those that evolved into birds) or to the oceans: other large reptiles – the pterosaurs ('terro-saurs') – dominated the skies, and marine reptiles such as ichthyosaurs ('ickthy-o-saurs') and plesiosaurs ('please-ee-o-saurs') flourished in the sea (Figure 2.17).

Figure 2.17   In this coastal scene from the Cretaceous Period, a plesiosaur (marine reptile) attempts to snatch a fish from the jaws of a giant pterosaur. Many pterosaurs – flying reptiles – were far larger than the birds of the day.

2.6   Extinctions are forever

The vast majority of species that have ever existed – probably 99% – have become extinct. As you learned in Book 5 (Section 3.5.2), extinction, like death, is a normal aspect of the history of life. Extinction is the complete, global end of the line for a species; it leaves no descendant individuals anywhere. It is very important to distinguish the *local* extinction of a species from true, *global* extinction. During climate change, for example, a population may become locally extinct as it simply moves from one area into another, tracking its favoured environment. Local extinction can be a very common event on a short timescale, and over a small area, and have no long-term significance. Also, a species that has with time evolved directly *into* another species has also not become extinct in one crucial sense: it is not the end of the line. In this case the lineage has simply been sufficiently transformed for the descendants to be recognised as a different species.

At any time in the history of life some species are originating and others are in the process of becoming extinct. The fossil record shows that there has always been a normal, 'background' rate of both speciation (the formation of new species, Book 5, Section 14.4) and extinction, i.e. there has been a *turnover* of species (Book 5, Section 3.5.2). The majority of past species extinctions have been part of this 'background' rate of extinction. Early in the 19th century, however, it was recognised that, from time to time, many groups disappeared from the fossil record more or less together, never to be found again in younger rocks. It was partly for this reason that many of the boundaries between one geological period and another were constructed. Geologically rapid, major reductions in the diversity of life on a global scale are called **mass extinctions**. There have been five especially severe mass extinctions in the Phanerozoic – the 'Big Five': in the late Ordovician, late Devonian, late Permian, late Triassic, and late Cretaceous (see Box 2.3).

Box 2.3   Some casualties of the Big Five Phanerozoic extinctions.

(*Do not worry if some of the groups are unfamiliar to you.*)

1   *Late Ordovician (~440 Ma)* Many types of trilobites, brachiopods, echinoderms and corals.

2   *Late Devonian (~360 Ma)* Many marine families, especially those of tropical reef-dwelling organisms such as corals, brachiopods, bivalves and sponges.

3   *Late Permian (~250 Ma)* Nearly 60% of marine families, especially those from low latitudes. The major coral groups became extinct, and reefs were eliminated. Trilobites and water-scorpions disappeared totally. Crinoids, brachiopods, bivalves and gastropods suffered huge losses. Many groups of amphibians and reptiles perished.

4   *Late Triassic (~200 Ma)* Major losses among cephalopods, gastropods, brachiopods, bivalves, sponges and marine reptiles. On land many insect families became extinct, as did most mammal-like reptiles and large amphibians (though the extinction of these vertebrate groups does not show up well in Figure 2.16 as other reptile and amphibian families were originating at about the same time).

5   *Late Cretaceous (K–Pg boundary) (~65 Ma)* Whole groups that became extinct near (and not necessarily *at*) the end of the Cretaceous included ammonites, large marine reptiles such as plesiosaurs, and, on land, dinosaurs and pterosaurs. Groups suffering major losses included microscopic marine plankton, brachiopods, bivalves and sea urchins. Vertebrate groups *little* affected included fishes, amphibians, crocodiles, snakes, turtles and mammals. Flowering plants, including hardwood trees, suffered also, but mostly in the Northern Hemisphere.

■ Indicate with an asterisk each of the Big Five mass extinctions beside the geological timescale in Figure 2.7. Now consider the sequence of eras and periods. Which two of the Big Five extinctions would you expect to have been the most severe?

☐ The most severe extinctions were those used to mark the end, not just of periods, but of eras – the Palaeozoic Era and the Mesozoic Era, i.e. at the end of the Permian Period and the end of the Cretaceous Period, respectively.

In these two mass extinctions, the loss of marine animal species has been estimated to be as high as 95% in the late Permian and 70% in the late Cretaceous.

None of the Big Five mass extinctions seems to have been instantaneous; in most cases it probably took from about 0.5 to 1.0 Ma for all the losses to occur. Furthermore, mass extinctions are probably not discrete phenomena, completely different from other extinctions, any more than there are clear boundaries between large and medium earthquakes, or between hurricanes and severe storms. There seems to be a continuous spectrum of extinction severity from background rates at one end, through times of moderate extinction, to mass extinctions at the other. Some of the groups lost in mass extinctions were already far from flourishing. For example, the decline of trilobites was well underway before their eventual demise in the late Permian.

Can one make any generalisations about the 'victims' of mass extinctions? Well, it seems that large-bodied species tend to be more vulnerable than smaller-bodied species, perhaps because they tend to be more specialised, have smaller population sizes, and slower rates of population increase. Tropical organisms, at least those in the sea, appear to be more vulnerable than those of higher latitudes.

■ Imagine a species of marine snail that can live today only in the hot, shallow seas found immediately around the Equator. Would an increase or decrease in global temperature be more likely to threaten this tropical species with extinction, and why?

☐ If global temperature were reduced, the snails would have nowhere to go that was warm enough; they are already in the hottest environment. If, however, there were an *increase* in temperature, the snails might well, over generations, be able to migrate away from equatorial latitudes to where the water was cooler, or perhaps migrate into deeper, cooler water on the Equator. Other things being equal, tropical species may therefore be more susceptible to global cooling than to global warming. (As always, however, things are not so simple; coral reefs are currently dying off at an alarming rate due to abnormally high recent sea surface temperatures, and several coral species have become regionally extinct.)

The average duration of a marine invertebrate species in the fossil record (from origin to extinction) is about 5 Ma, though there is much variation about this mean. Interestingly, many of these fossil species, having made their first appearance, show very little change (in their hard parts at least) before becoming extinct several million years later. Continuous, gradual transitions from one species to another are rare in the fossil record. This may, however, be partly due to the lack of fossils from on land in the tropics and from the deeper sea – relatively stable environments where evolution may tend to be more gradual and continuous than in shallow marine environments.

Estimating the rate at which species are becoming extinct today is very difficult, not least because we do not know how many species there are to start with (Book 5, Section 3.5.2).

■ Mammals and birds probably provide the best data of any groups. Why do you think this is?

☐ They are particularly well-studied, being relatively large, conspicuous and mostly living on land, and in the past many have attracted attention as a human food source.

The average duration of mammal and bird species in the fossil record is much nearer 0.5–1.0 Ma than the 5 Ma for marine invertebrate species, partly perhaps because their complex social behaviour favours rapid evolution and speciation. Many large mammals and large flightless birds became extinct between 15 000 and 10 000 years ago, and there is evidence that human hunting activities, as well as climate changes, were responsible. Today, there are about 13 400 living species of birds and mammals, and at least 100 species have become extinct during the last 100 years alone through human activities. The rate of extinction is escalating, and in a few decades the average time remaining before a typical bird or mammal species becomes extinct is projected to be 200–400 years; this is approaching 4 orders of magnitude (i.e. a factor of 10^4) faster than the background rates seen in the fossil record. The loss among mammals and birds may also be broadly representative of other groups of animals and plants. Conservative estimates of current total extinction rates are more than 50 species *per day*. Many biologists believe that this general time in Earth history could appear as another mass extinction in the geological record – 'the Sixth Extinction' to add to the previous Big Five. As a warning, the fossil record shows that recovery from earlier mass extinctions is extremely slow by human timescales. The regeneration of biodiversity, and the re-establishment of communities such as reefs, typically takes 5–10 Ma.

2.6.1 The Cretaceous–Palaeogene (K–Pg) mass extinction

The mass extinction at the end of the Cretaceous Period is celebrated for wiping out the dinosaurs but they were by no means its only victims. A wide range of animals and plants was affected, and many species of microscopic organisms. The first evidence for its cause emerged from unrelated research. In the late 1970s, father and son Luis and Walter Alvarez, with colleagues from the University of California at Berkeley, tried to estimate deposition rates of ocean-floor sediment layers using changes in their concentration of the metal iridium. Iridium is extremely rare in the Earth's crust but much more abundant in meteorites. Assuming that meteoritic dust falls at a regular rate, variations in the pace at which sediments accumulate would give higher iridium concentrations in a given thickness of slowly accumulating sediment than in the same thickness of rapidly accumulated sediment. In rocks formed from deep marine sediments from Gubbio in central Italy, which ranged across the K–Pg boundary*, 10 mm

* The abbreviation 'K–T' is also often used when referring to this extinction at the Cretaceous–Palaeogene boundary; 'K' is the international symbol for the Cretaceous; 'T' stands for Tertiary (see Box 2.2)

of clay marking the boundary (Figure 2.18a) contained up to 30 times the level of iridium than in other layers. That could have been due to sediment accumulating 30 times more slowly than normal. However, the team claimed boldly that the mass extinction was due to a huge meteorite impact which supplied the iridium. Iridium analyses at K–Pg sections elsewhere gave similar results and ruled out the slow sediment accumulation model.

Publication by the Alvarez's team in 1980 opened the greatest debate in the geosciences since the discovery of sea floor spreading. Researchers flocked to the now-famous sites to sample the boundary layer, to see what else they might find. Figure 2.18 shows examples of other evidence confirming that there had indeed been an impact. It must have been huge as many sites around the world contain these anomalies (Figure 2.19a). As well as common grains of quartz showing structures uniquely formed by intense shock (Figure 2.18b), there are occasional minute diamonds formed under extremely high pressures. Tiny glass spheres formed as chilled droplets of molten rock were flung into the atmosphere by the impact (Figure 2.18c).

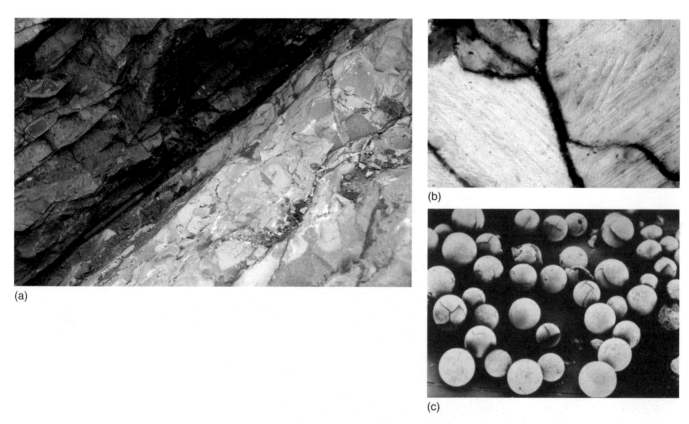

(a)

(b)

(c)

Figure 2.18   Aspects of the Cretaceous–Palaeogene boundary. (a) The clay layer at the K–Pg boundary at Gubbio in Italy, where the anomalously high concentration of iridium at this level was first discovered. A rich variety of fossil plankton occurs below the boundary, but few forms survived into the layer above it. The pencil lies along the K–Pg boundary itself, and is about 15 cm long. (b), (c) Tell-tale signs of impact at the K–Pg boundary: (b) quartz grains showing parallel lines known to result only from intense shock; (c) minute spheres (0.5–1.0 mm in diameter) that have cooled rapidly from droplets of molten rock.

The only missing information was an impact crater blasted out by the hypothesised meteorite. Eventually, geophysicists examining variations in the gravitational and magnetic fields in the southern Gulf of Mexico noticed a series of circular features about 200 km across at the coast in the Mexican province of Chicxulub (pronounced 'chick-shulub'). They indicated a large buried structure (Figure 2.19b). Drilling proved not only that the circular feature was an impact crater but also that it had formed 65 Ma ago, at the K–Pg boundary: a 'smoking gun' by any standards.

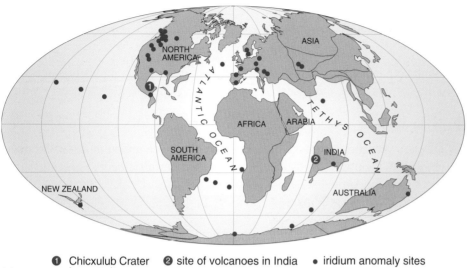

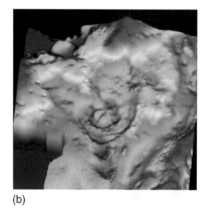

(b)

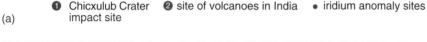

❶ Chicxulub Crater   **❷** site of volcanoes in India   • iridium anomaly sites
impact site

(a)

(c)

Figure 2.19　(a) Location of iridium anomalies at the K–Pg boundary, the Chicxulub Crater, and the site of huge volcanic eruptions in India. The reconstruction shows plate positions at 65 Ma ago, but with present-day coastlines. (b) Image of the buried Chicxulub Crater derived from variations in gravity. (c) Lava flows in the Deccan flood basalts in India, erupted at 65 Ma. The cliff section is ~500 m high.

However, there was another potential culprit. Roughly on the other side of the world from Chicxulub, in northwestern India, there are great thicknesses of basaltic lava flows that cover a huge area (Figure 2.19c). Before erosion, there may have been up to 1.5×10^6 km^3 of these flood basalts in northwestern India. They formed in 1–2 Ma at the end of the Cretaceous, when India drifted over a hot spot beneath what is now the Indian Ocean. No one has witnessed a flood basalt event, but what such an event might have done to the environment can be estimated by comparison with modern volcanic emissions.

Question 2.6

Try to imagine from your study of Books 1 to 3 what effects (a) the impact of a large (10 km diameter) meteorite travelling at a speed of 15 km s^{-1} and (b) a massive outpouring of magma, might have on global environments. Write a paragraph (about 50–100 words) for each scenario.

Although both events would make the adjective 'awesome' completely inadequate, if we did witness them, their most devastating influence would have been stealthy.

■ What would have been the effects on climate of (a) CO_2 and (b) dust?

☐ CO_2 is a greenhouse gas, so the global mean surface temperature would rise; (b) dust in the upper atmosphere increases the Earth's albedo, i.e. scattering some of the incoming solar radiation back to space (Book 1, Section 4.4) and so would result in cooling.

In the stratosphere, SO_2 forms tiny sulfuric acid droplets which also increase albedo. This would also result in global cooling.

■ What other effect might the gases have had?

☐ Both CO_2 and SO_2 dissolve in rainwater to make it weakly acidic, which would decrease the pH of ocean surface water.

The important point to note is that these three products (CO_2, SO_2 and dust) of either meteorite impact or volcanism affect the atmosphere and so spread around the world quickly – an aspect likely to favour mass extinction. A notable feature of the K–Pg extinction was the collapse of the population of coccolithophores (phytoplankton) and of planktonic foraminifera (marine zooplankton with calcium carbonate shells). That may have resulted from a decrease in pH (increased acidity) of near-surface seawater but, equally likely, less sunlight would reduce photosynthesis. Phytoplankton are at the base of the food web for the rest of marine life.

A similar scenario can be surmised for life on land, i.e. the reduced growth of land plants. Drastically reduced food, even for a few months, could trigger massive animal mortality leading to extinction by starvation. Neither dust nor SO_2 stay in the atmosphere for more than a few years; they are rained out. However, the collapse of photosynthesising organisms would have reduced the potential for the biosphere to remove CO_2 from the atmosphere. So, global warming would continue until the recovery of photosynthesising organisms.

There is little doubt that the meteorite impact or volcanism, or perhaps a combination of both, caused the K–Pg mass extinction; but there are unexplained aspects. Slower, yet important changes in the Earth system had built up throughout the Upper Cretaceous; sea level had begun to fall and global climate to cool. Some animal groups, such as ammonites, had begun to decline well before the K–Pg event. Ammonites were entirely exterminated at 65 Ma, yet families of other cephalopods, such as squid, survived. While dinosaurs perished, some reptilian groups, early mammals and birds remained. Did survival of some groups depend on good genes, or good luck? That is a tricky question, in many ways, and one that may never be resolved. It is a question that has a bearing on all evolution, including that of the primates, during the succeeding Cenozoic Era.

2.6.2   Establishing the causes of mass extinctions

Various reasons have been invoked in the past for the extinction of the dinosaurs. Frivolous or untestable suggestions include constipation and stupidity, while more scientific reasons such as disease, reduction in eggshell thickness due to stress or competition with newly evolved small mammals perhaps deserve a little more consideration.

■ Why would such suggestions be inadequate as explanations for *mass* extinctions?

□ Any proposed mechanism(s) for mass extinctions must embrace many groups, and operate over a wide area, both on land and in the sea.

■ In what ways, other than extinction, might a species respond to severe environmental change affecting its habitat?

□ A species may be able to migrate into more favourable areas, or, in the longer term, evolve adaptations to the new environment (Book 5, Chapter 14).

What kind of environmental changes, then, are so severe that large numbers of species cannot migrate away from those changes, or adapt to them? The most plausible hypotheses are those such as rapid changes in global temperature or oxygen levels – as opposed to, say, disease or predation, which are unlikely to affect many thousands of species at the same time.

In addition to the possible influence of extraterrestrial events, the Earth-bound causes most often proposed for mass extinctions include: climate change, especially greenhouse warming or cooling, and drying (drought); sea-level rise or fall; changes in oceanic circulation, leading to lower levels of dissolved oxygen in shallow waters; changes in atmospheric chemistry (especially lowered oxygen levels); and intense volcanic activity. Most of these causes are not mutually exclusive; for example, cooling and widespread glaciation lowers sea level because water is transferred from the oceans and is locked up as ice on land; volcanic activity could promote climate change and also pollute the atmosphere, causing acid rain, for example.

The only mass extinction for which the influence of a meteorite is strongly implicated (but also disputed) is that at the K–Pg boundary. Some, perhaps most, mass extinctions, may have occurred when several changes in the physical environment coincided accidentally. In the case of the one at the end of the Permian, adverse effects from huge, persistent volcanic eruptions in Siberia (causing, among other things, a drastic reduction in atmospheric and oceanic oxygen levels, and global warming) were probably combined with longer-term changes in sea-level and oceanic circulation patterns. The late Ordovician mass extinction of marine organisms was almost certainly linked to widespread glaciation, a large fall in sea level and anoxic conditions in the sea. Climate change is also implicated in both the late Devonian and late Triassic mass extinctions.

The positive and negative feedback mechanisms (Book 1, Section 6.3) in the Earth's ocean–atmosphere system, and in its ecosystems, are immensely complex. Establishing the full chain of cause and effect during extinctions, and precisely which biological attributes – or lack of them – led to the demise of a particular species, is a difficult if not impossible task, even for most extinctions taking place in the 21st century.

2.7   Evolutionary radiations

Extinction is, as we have seen, forever. But, depending on one's perspective, mass extinctions aren't always bad news. For example, the mass extinction of dinosaurs and other large reptiles at the end of the Cretaceous Period seems to have cleared the way for mammals to expand into vacated niches. And 65 Ma later it's even keeping some of their descendants employed trying to find out how it all happened.

The massive expansion of mammals in the early Cenozoic is an example of an **evolutionary radiation** – an episode of rapid and sustained increase in diversity, often involving the origin of many new groups above the species level such as orders and families. In Section 2.4 we considered the radiation of animals into many new phyla during the Cambrian explosion. The following section explores the radiation of mammals, a single class of vertebrates, during the Cenozoic Era.

2.7.1   The radiation of mammals

Mammals first appeared towards the end of the Triassic Period, about 210 Ma ago. For a long time they remained small, perhaps nocturnal, shrew-like creatures living in the nooks and crannies of the dinosaur world. Figure 2.20 shows the distribution in time of the major groups (mainly orders) of mammals from the start of the Jurassic Period, and their evolutionary relationships. Such an evolutionary tree shows the most likely pattern of branching from a common ancestor, and is based on evidence from fossils, and on the comparative anatomy and genetics of living mammals. The width of each group on the diagram gives a rough indication of its diversity. Notice that during the Jurassic and early Cretaceous a number of short-lived groups evolved, but left no descendants. The **placental mammals**, which nourish their embryos with a placenta, are much more dominant than the other two groups present today – the marsupials and monotremes. The marsupials, such as kangaroos, transfer their new-born young to pouches. The monotremes are mammals that have retained the reptilian habit of laying eggs, and they include the platypus and the spiny ant-eater; they have a poor fossil record.

■   How long had mammals been in existence before their radiation in the early Cenozoic? [*Hint*: look back to Figure 2.16.]

☐   About 150 Ma (from 210 Ma ago until about 60 Ma ago).

■   According to Figure 2.20, has the diversity of the monotremes changed much since their origin in the Cretaceous Period, and how does it compare with that of the placentals?

☐   On the diagram, the width of the bar for monotremes remains thin throughout their existence, whereas the bars for many separate orders of placentals

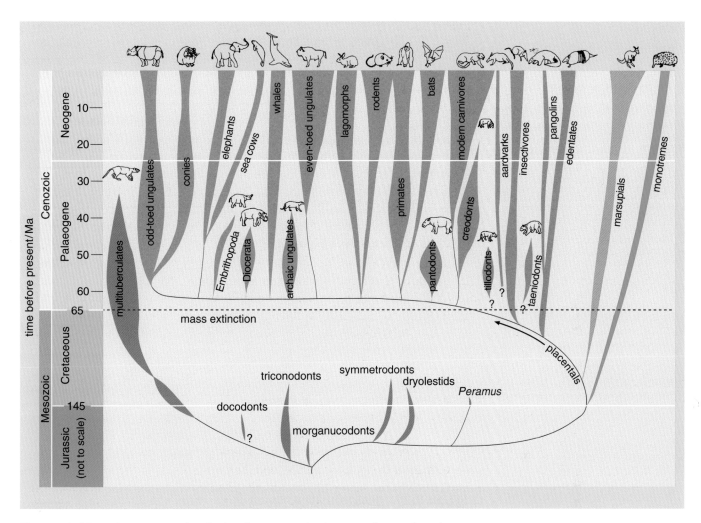

Figure 2.20   The pattern of radiation in mammals. See text for explanation.

are wider than those for the monotremes. The diversity of monotremes has therefore changed little since their origin, and has remained much less than that of the placentals.

■ How long after the extinction of the dinosaurs was it before almost all the orders of placentals had appeared?

☐ Most placentals had already appeared by 55–60 Ma ago, less than 10 Ma after the K–Pg mass extinction.

This extraordinary burst of evolution produced mammals adapted to a vast range of environments – think for a moment of today's flying bats, swimming dolphins, burrowing moles, running cheetahs, and so on. In fact, ever since the early Cenozoic Era, most of the world's largest animals have been mammals, as is true today – think of the African elephant and the blue whale, Earth's largest land and sea animals (see Box 2.4).

Box 2.4   The early evolution of whales

Whales have long been understood to be descended from four-legged land animals of the early Cenozoic Era. Modern whales lack hindlimbs entirely, but many species retain within their bodies remnants of pelvic bones and of hindlegs, visible only internally (Figure 2.21). Occasionally, modern humpback whales and sperm whales are found with externally projecting rudimentary hindlimbs. Such quirks provide convincing evidence of evolution. A variety of fossils that are intermediate between ocean-going whales and their land-dwelling ancestors have been found in early Cenozoic rocks in Pakistan and India. Some of these rather dog-like intermediates are believed to have been able both to walk on land *and* to swim with their hindlegs 50 Ma ago (see Figure 2.22).

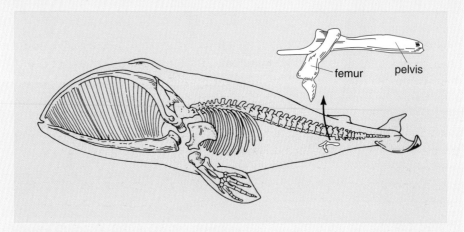

Figure 2.21   Skeleton and body outline of a whale, with internal rudimentary hindlimbs. (The long plates between the jaws are for filtering out crustaceans.)

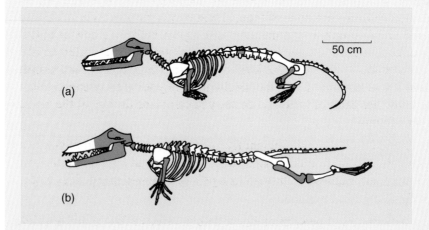

Figure 2.22   A missing link no longer missing: a fossil species about 50 Ma old from Pakistan that was part of the evolutionary transition from the land-dwelling ancestors of whales to their fully ocean-going descendants. It could probably both (a) walk on land and (b) swim with its hindlegs. The shaded regions indicate fossil parts found.

Humans are mammals of course, and apart from our exceptionally large brains, our anatomy and physiology are not much different from those of other primates, such as chimpanzees, to which we are closely related and with which, not long ago, geologically speaking, we shared a common ancestor. Our own species, *Homo sapiens*, appeared only 125 000–200 000 years ago (depending on how the origin of the species is defined). Like every other species on the planet, we are the unique product of a long string of biological events, none of which was an *inevitable* consequence of evolution. Although natural selection itself is the opposite of a chance process, it operates on what is already there, the details of which have a strong random component, such as the variation generated by sexual reproduction (Book 5, Section 4.5.2) and mutation (Book 5, Section 9.5). As we have seen, chance may also play a part on a much longer timescale, such as in the ascendancy of mammals as opposed to reptiles.

2.8 Putting things in order

Establishing the *order* of geological events is essential for understanding just about anything we might like to know about the Earth and its history: which of these volcanoes was the last to erupt? Was any oil formed before these rocks were folded? Which came first, reptiles or amphibians? In order to understand any complex situation, it is critical to unravel the *correct sequence of events* that led to it; imagine a detective trying to solve a complex 'whodunit?' without piecing together events in the order in which they actually happened. And detailed knowledge of past events can help make useful *predictions*: where should we drill for oil or prospect for silver? When is this fault likely to move causing an earthquake? How will global warming affect the melting of ice caps?

During this brief glimpse at the history of life, you have seen that evolution produces new species, and that extinction can eliminate them, sometimes in geologically brief intervals of mass extinction. Suppose it is already known from earlier work that a particular species of, say, ammonite appeared, and then died out after quite a short span of time. If that particular species is subsequently discovered in the strata (i.e. sedimentary rock layers, beds) of a new area, it can be concluded that the strata must have been laid down during the lifetime of that ammonite species. We use this kind of logic in everyday life: for example, if you find a note written in, say, the handwriting of your great-grandmother, and you know her dates of birth and death, you can place the age of the note to within her lifetime.

But how do we know when an ancient fossil species actually lived in the first place? There is no reference book to look it up in – at least not until the detective work has been done. Instead its age is determined using clues in the geological record.

There are two aspects of geological age or dating: **relative dating** and **absolute dating**. To illustrate the difference between the two, consider the statement: 'this newspaper is more recent than that one'. It's a clear indication of relative age, but says nothing about the *actual age* of each newspaper, nor the *time difference* between them. The absolute date of a newspaper is the date it was printed, such as 28 April 2010; its absolute age is then the time that has elapsed between then and now.

Imagine a pile of old newspapers accumulating day by day at home in a recycling bin. Unless the order of the newspapers has been disturbed for some reason, the oldest newspaper will be at the bottom of the bin, and the youngest at the top. The same is also true of sediments as they accumulate; generally, the deeper you go in a sedimentary sequence, the older the layers of sediment. That's sufficiently important to be given a formal name: the **principle of superposition**. Older rocks are overlain by younger rocks. An individual layer is younger than the one beneath it and older than the one above it; the oldest layer lies at the bottom (Figure 2.23). Unless the rocks have been overturned (which may sometimes happen during plate collisions and mountain-building), the 'arrow of time' will be upwards through a set of strata. In fact, sedimentary rocks provide such an important key to the past that they are sometimes said to be the diaries of Earth's history. The principle of superposition was first explicitly stated by Nicolaus Steno (1638–1687), a Dane working in Italy. Steno also realised that sediments were normally laid down in a near-horizontal position, although later they may be folded or even overturned.

Figure 2.23   A spectacular sequence of strata exposed in Utah, USA. According to the principle of superposition, the oldest strata lie at the bottom of the cliff. The clear differences in colour and other attributes from layer to layer are the result of changes in conditions during sedimentation. These will be discussed in Chapter 4.

The study of strata and their relationships in time and space is called **stratigraphy**. Sequences of strata have long been used to establish a generalised geological succession — the *stratigraphic column* – that we have already used several times in this book to show geological eras and periods. The boundaries between geological periods, and many of the subdivisions within them, have been assigned absolute dates (as in the stratigraphic column of Figure 2.7) using methods to be introduced in Chapter 6.

Question 2.7

In two of the three major types of rocks (igneous, sedimentary and metamorphic), relative dating cannot be carried out by using fossils (except in very rare cases). Which two rock types are these, and why?

To understand Earth history we need to know what happened at the same time *in different parts of the world*. For example, to get to grips with what occurred at the K–Pg boundary, we need to know which parts of the world were then mountains, which were deep sea, which were deserts and so on. The matching up of rocks of the same age from one area to another is called **correlation**.

William Smith (1769–1839), an English engineer and surveyor, was one of the first people to notice that different fossils occur in rocks of different ages, although he was not able to ascribe these differences to evolution as Darwin's key work had yet to be published. He worked on canals, roads and drainage schemes all over England, and found that he could recognise particular beds on the basis of their distinctive fossil content. For instance, he could match up certain beds of Chalk in the North Downs with others in the South Downs, because each contained a particular assemblage of fossils different from those in the similar-looking Chalk beds above and below. (The term 'Chalk' (with a capital C) refers specifically to late Cretaceous deposits of fine-grained, white limestone rich in coccoliths, the calcite plates of coccolithophores (tiny marine phytoplankton).)

William Smith then found he could correlate apparently *dissimilar* strata because they contained *similar* fossils. Widely separated limestone and sandstone beds, for instance, although quite different rock types, were sometimes found to contain certain fossils in common, so he concluded that they were laid down at the same time. Smith also found the same general succession of fossil assemblages from older to younger beds in different parts of the country. He proposed that each stage in this succession of fossils represented a particular span of geological history, and called this the **principle of faunal succession**. Using this principle, he was able to correlate widely separated outcrops of rock by the fossils they contained, and in 1815 Smith produced the first geological map of England, Wales and part of Scotland.

So, the main basis for the *relative* timescale recognised by Earth scientists is the succession of strata, which is based on the principle of superposition, combined with the correlation of fossil assemblages from successions of strata in different areas (the principle of faunal succession).

Major breaks in the stratigraphic record occur quite often, and may be widespread across large geographic areas. The absence of strata from a particular time interval in a certain region may be due either to non-deposition or to erosion of any sediment that *was* deposited. Such breaks are called **unconformities**, and recognition of them, and the missing strata they represent, is crucial in working out the geological history of an area. Such breaks were recognised by the Frenchman, George Cuvier, born in the same year as William Smith. A highly skilled observer, Cuvier systematically described the succession of fossil animals and plants in the Cenozoic rocks of France, painstakingly reconstructing the living organisms. He also noticed that many forms of life seemed to have disappeared together in a sudden catastrophe at certain levels in the strata (*not* at unconformities). These levels were later identified in other areas and recognised as episodes of extinction.

Today, the stratigraphic column is divided into **biozones** that are characterised by one or more particular fossils. The sequence of biozones in the correct order makes up the **biostratigraphic column**. A *zone fossil* is a species used to characterise a biozone in the biostratigraphic column. Ideally, to be useful, zone fossils should have a short time range (i.e. belong to a rapidly evolving group), a distinctive appearance with many easily recognisable characters, wide geographic distribution (like many free-swimming or floating marine creatures), wide environmental tolerance, and high abundance. Ammonites are an example of such a group; they are used extensively for establishing biozones in the Jurassic and Cretaceous.

■ Considering the criteria required of a good zone fossil, would you expect dinosaurs to be suitable zone fossils for the Jurassic Period?

☐ Dinosaurs are very rare as fossils, often found as incomplete remains, and restricted to land-based environments; they would therefore be unsuitable as zone fossils.

So, today, once we have correctly identified particular fossils from a rock of unknown age, we can then tell to which particular geological period – or part of it – the rock belongs, providing the succession of fossil species has already been well established. The approximate absolute age (in Ma) can be obtained by referring to an up-to-date geological timescale. The biostratigraphic column, and absolute dates, are continuously refined as new data emerge.

Activity 2.2   Matching up rocks – when it's age that matters

Figure 2.24 shows columns of rock from two localities, A and B, that are some distance apart, and indicates some of the fossils found in particular (numbered) beds. The thicknesses of different rock types making up each column have been drawn to the same scale, so, for example, bed A2 is thicker than bed B2. Note that it is usually best to consider such a geological column in chronological order, i.e. from the bottom upward.

(a) Draw dashed lines between the two columns, linking the tops and bottoms of beds that you think were probably laid down at approximately the same time, on the basis of their fossil content.

(b) Write the initial letter of the appropriate era beside the strata on the right-hand side of column A, and on the left-hand side of column B, using P for Palaeozoic, M for Mesozoic and C for Cenozoic.

Note: To work this out, you need to know the geological age ranges of the following groups of organisms:

- bivalves (molluscs) and brachiopods (members of the phylum Brachiopoda): Cambrian to present day
- corals, echinoids (echinoderms) and crinoids (echinoderms): Ordovician to present day
- trilobites (marine arthropods): Cambrian to Permian
- plesiosaurs (marine reptiles): Triassic to Cretaceous
- ammonites (marine molluscs): Triassic to Cretaceous.

(c) Where are there unconformities within the succession in each column, i.e. levels representing time gaps when no sediment was preserved for a long

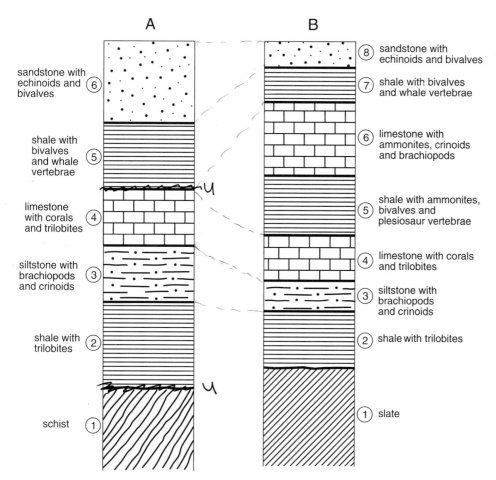

Figure 2.24 Columns of rock from two localities, A and B, with rock type and fossil content indicated.

interval? There is certain to be an unconformity where rocks of an entire era are missing between successive beds, or where the vertically adjacent rock types are such that there must be a large time gap between them. In such cases, draw a thick horizontal wavy line across the appropriate level in each column and write the letter U for 'unconformity' beside it. Where vertically adjacent beds are from different, although *successive*, eras, indicate the possibility of an unconformity between them by drawing a horizontal wavy line across the appropriate level in each column and write 'U?' for 'possible unconformity' beside it.

There are many other ways of correlating rocks that are independent of the use of fossils, although many of these methods are specific to particular situations or times in Earth's history.

■ What unusual geochemical feature of the K–Pg boundary can be used to correlate sediments deposited at that time around the world, and why is it present?

☐ The concentration of the rare element iridium is abnormally high in sediments at the K–Pg boundary, and derives from a meteorite impact. This iridium anomaly is a geochemical feature that can be identified around the world (Figure 2.19a).

■ Can you think of a potential problem in using this iridium anomaly *alone* to identify the K–Pg boundary?

☐ Meteorite impacts on the Earth have occurred at many other times, and some of these may have also introduced iridium, so that matching up iridium anomalies alone could lead to erroneous correlations.

We need to find other corroborating evidence, such as from fossils, and where possible obtain an absolute age too. The more independent lines of evidence that can be gathered, the lower the likelihood that mistakes will be made. Other means of correlating across a large area include matching up changes in global sea level and in global temperature. Ice ages, for example, produce widespread glacial deposits that can be correlated across different continents.

In Chapter 6, you will return to other ways of relative dating and, in particular, to methods of absolute dating. However, as the history of the Earth and its life is recorded in rocks, we first need to know more about the origins of rocks and the minerals of which rocks are composed – the subjects of Chapters 3–5.

Question 2.8

The following 11 items are mostly evolutionary events, here in random order. Write them in their appropriate positions on the right-hand side of the geological timescale in Figure 2.7. (You should already have marked in the events listed in Question 2.5 and indicated each of the Big Five mass extinctions with an asterisk.)

- first birds
- first *Homo sapiens*
- radiation of mammals
- start of main diversification of fishes
- first amphibians
- first flowering plants
- first fishes
- first mammals
- main invasion of the land by plants and invertebrates begins
- first dinosaurs
- first reptiles

2.9   Summary of Chapter 2

The fossil record is the only direct evidence of the course of life's evolution through time.

The preservation potential of an individual organism depends mainly on the durability of its body parts, and where it lives and dies. The preservation potential of a particular species also depends on its abundance and geographic distribution. Marine animals with hard parts form the bulk of the fossil record.

During fossilisation, the pore spaces in biological materials tend to be filled in, and the materials themselves sometimes replaced, by minerals precipitating from solutions seeping through the enclosing sediment. Fossilised hard parts such as shells, bones and teeth can often yield information about the soft parts of an organism, its mode of life and environment.

The fossil record suggests that life had begun by at least 3800 Ma ago. Life probably consisted only of prokaryotes until about 2100 Ma ago, when simple eukaryotes first appear in the fossil record. Photosynthetic bacteria produced most of the oxygen that eventually formed a permanent accumulation in the atmosphere. Multicellular algae had evolved by about 1200 Ma ago.

Only about 580 Ma ago did the first multicellular animals appear (the Ediacaran fauna). During the Cambrian explosion, starting about 542 Ma ago, animals with hard parts, and animals capable of making complex trace fossils, first appeared in a sudden burst of evolution. Most animal phyla are first represented in the fossil record at this time, though many may have diverged from each other much earlier; previously lacking shells or teeth, and possibly being much smaller, their preservation potential before then would have been minimal. The exceptionally well preserved Burgess Shale fossils reveal a very wide diversity of Cambrian animals, but it is important to remember that life was still confined to the sea.

The invasion of the land required many new adaptations, and only got going in the Silurian Period, over 3 billion years after the origin of life, when small plants (about 4 cm high) and tiny arthropods (a few mm long) first moved onto land. By the end of the Devonian Period, vertebrates capable of walking on land (amphibians) had evolved, and some plants had reached the size of trees.

The Big Five mass extinctions of the Phanerozoic were in the late Ordovician, late Devonian, late Permian, late Triassic, and late Cretaceous. The two most severe were at the end of the Palaeozoic and Mesozoic Eras. We may be living through another mass extinction now due to human activity.

While there is overwhelming evidence of the impact of a large meteorite at the Cretaceous–Palaeogene (K–Pg) boundary, 65 Ma ago, the mass extinction at this time also coincides with the rapid eruption of large volumes of flood basalts in India. Although the environmental effects of either or both of these events may have led to the rapid extinction of much of the plankton, many other groups that disappeared in the K–Pg mass extinction were already in decline, and some had become extinct well before the boundary. Establishing the causes of mass extinctions is very difficult. The most likely mechanisms include those that would affect a great many species, such as a combination of global climate change and changes in oceanic and atmospheric chemistry.

The major evolutionary radiation of mammals occurred in the early Cenozoic Era, once the large reptiles that dominated the Mesozoic Era had become extinct.

The main basis for the relative geological timescale is the succession of strata (which is based on the principle of superposition), and the pattern of succession of fossil assemblages. The resulting biostratigraphic column allows the matching up of strata deposited at the same time in different areas – an essential part of getting to grips with events in the Earth's history.

Chapter 3
Igneous rocks formed from molten magma

Some important rock-forming processes are introduced in this chapter and in Chapters 4 and 5. They also show how you can deduce the processes that formed rocks from particular features in them. Applying such deductions to rocks arranged in a time sequence (Chapter 2) helps us to understand the evolution of geological conditions at places now at the Earth's surface. Geological histories from many places form the basis for reconstructing past geography and plate tectonics, up to global scale. This broad approach has allowed geoscientists to reconstruct a graphic picture of how the Earth has worked throughout geological time.

Deducing processes that involve molten magma are considered first because, ultimately, except for tiny amounts from meteorites, all materials that now form sedimentary and metamorphic rocks emerged from the mantle as constituents of magma. Heat from within the Earth drives convection in the deep mantle, and is responsible for any melting in the upper mantle and crust. The formation of magmas, their emplacement and crystallisation involve igneous processes at divergent and convergent plate margins, and above hot spots within plates (Book 2, Chapters 8 and 9). Older crustal rocks are transformed by chemical reorganisation of their constituent minerals if pressure and/or temperature rise sufficiently. Added to these metamorphic processes is the deformation of rocks by the enormous plate-tectonic stresses to which they may be exposed. Tectonics also directly affects erosion and the supply of materials that end up in sedimentary rocks. (Both of these topics are covered in Chapters 4 and 5.)

Before proceeding, check that you remember the means of distinguishing specimens of igneous, sedimentary and metamorphic rocks from differences in their texture (Book 2, Chapter 5).

■ Describe the shapes of grains and the relationships between the grains shown in the sketches in Figure 3.1. Which sketch represents: (i) a sedimentary rock; (ii) an igneous rock; (iii) a metamorphic rock?

☐ (i) Figure 3.1c consists of rounded to angular grains and the spaces between them are filled with smaller grains. It shows a fragmental texture, typical of a sedimentary rock (Specimens 2 and 3, the sandstone and limestone in the Practical Kit); (ii) Figure 3.1a shows angular grains that are interlocking and intergrown. Moreover, the grains have no particular orientation; they are randomly oriented. This random, interlocking crystalline texture is typical of an igneous rock (Specimens 5 and 6, the basalt and granite, in the Practical Kit); (iii) Figure 3.1b also shows interlocking and intergrown grains, but elongated ones are roughly parallel. This aligned, interlocking crystalline texture is typical of a metamorphic rock (Specimen 4, the schist, in the Practical Kit).

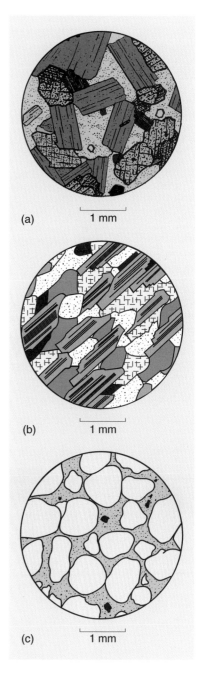

(a)   1 mm

(b)   1 mm

(c)   1 mm

Figure 3.1   Three rock textures seen through a microscope, which are typical of each fundamental division of rocks (Book 2, Activity 5.1). The different shading represents different types of mineral.

You may have seen different rock types at the coast, along road cuttings or in mountains. Without knowing what to look for, you may have been unsure how to distinguish them. In fact, rocks provide more information about their origins than this basic, threefold classification. More varieties in each of the three main categories can be distinguished, not only from textures but also from the minerals that rocks contain, and give vital clues to how the rocks formed.

In Activities 3.1 and 4.1 in Book 4 you saw the crystal structures of the minerals halite (NaCl), a natural ionic solid, and quartz (SiO_2), a natural molecular solid. You discovered that the chemical structures of minerals exert controls on their physical properties, which are easily observed. This is the point where you need to expand your knowledge of minerals and the skills needed to distinguish them.

3.1   The minerals in igneous rocks

The dominance in the outer Earth of the elements oxygen and silicon (Book 4, Section 2.1) more or less guarantees that the minerals making up the bulk of the crust and mantle must be based on silicon and oxygen in combination; they will be **silicates** of some kind. Being able to distinguish the main groups of rock-forming silicates from their observable properties will help you to understand processes in the rock cycle that create different kinds of rock. Quartz is a good place to start looking at silicate minerals (Book 4, Activity 4.1). Its basic 'building block' is a SiO_4^{4-} tetrahedron that is involved in all other silicates. Unlike quartz, the other silicates contain elements in addition to silicon and oxygen. Depending on what those elements are, the physical properties of these other silicate mineral groups differ from those of quartz because of the effect of additional elements on their molecular structure. So, the physical properties of a mineral reflect its structure and, in turn, that structure broadly conveys its chemical composition.

Activity 3.1   Igneous minerals: examining silicates

We expect this activity will take you approximately 60 minutes.

To help you with identifying minerals in Practical Kit specimens of igneous rock, this activity takes you through the structures and some physical properties of common silicates. It involves two computer-based resources: *Minerals Gallery* and *Mineral Properties*.

As you work through the four tasks, fill in the rows of Table 3.1 at the end of this activity for each silicate mineral group you examine. The one for quartz is already completed.

The physical property of mineral cleavage (or lack of it) relates to regular arrangements of weak bonding in crystal structures. Ionic crystals of halite (NaCl) have extremely regular alignments of weak bonds, and so possess excellent cleavage in three sets at right angles; they are also soft and will not scratch glass (Book 4, Activity 3.1). Molecular crystals of quartz (SiO_2) have a strong structure that links covalent Si–O bonds in a complex 3D network, based on spiral connections between SiO_4^{4-} tetrahedra and sharing of oxygen atoms between adjacent spirals (Book 4, Activity 4.1). This strength confers on quartz crystals a greater *hardness* than that of glass, and a *lack* of cleavage.

If you cannot recall these relationships, first review Activities 3.1 and 4.1 in Book 4.

Task 1   Feldspars

Open the computer-based resource *Minerals Gallery*: select feldspar and its structure tab. From the list below 'Explore the feldspar structure', start with the first option.

As well as SiO_4^{4-} tetrahedra, **feldspars** also contain aluminium atoms that bond covalently with oxygen as tetrahedral AlO_4^{5-} groups; note their −5 charge. Effectively, the similarity in size between Si and Al atoms allows aluminium to substitute for silicon, despite its different number of outer-shell electrons. In the feldspar structure this substitution is in a regular arrangement.

Move to the third option (tetrahedra joined by a 'crankshaft').

The charge difference between the SiO_4^{4-} and AlO_4^{5-} tetrahedra changes their arrangement from the spirals of quartz to a *crankshaft*.

Move to the fourth option (large cavities between crankshafts).

Three-dimensional linkage of Si–O and Al–O bonds between the crankshafts in feldspar leaves charge imbalances. These allow atoms of K, Na and Ca into the structure, to balance the charge. These metals bond to AlO_4^{5-} tetrahedra in a weak but regular fashion; such regularly aligned weaknesses define cleavage planes.

Rotate the structure and suggest how many cleavages feldspars might have.

The K, Na or Ca atoms define three marked alignments of weak bonds, two at right angles and one oblique to the others.

Now review the properties of feldspars under its properties tab. This shows various diagnostic properties of minerals (the computer-based resource *Mineral Properties* explains properties in more detail). Use it to fill in the feldspar row in Table 3.1.

Task 2   Micas

Select mica and its structure tab. Start with the third option in the 'Explore the mica structure' list.

The basic structure of **micas** is very different from the 3D framework of quartz and feldspars. SiO_4^{4-} tetrahedra in micas share Si–O bonds only at the base of each tetrahedron, to create a giant molecular structure that spreads out as a 2D sheet.

Move to the fourth option.

Aluminium also enters the mica structure but, instead of being bonded to four oxygens, each Al atom is shared by six O atoms, to give AlO_6^{9-} which takes on an octahedral (eight-faced) form. In white mica, $AlO_6{}^{9-}$ octahedra share oxygens with the corners of $SiO_4{}^{4-}$ tetrahedra to bond the silicate sheets in a 'sandwich'. In dark-coloured micas, iron and magnesium enter the structure, in octahedral combination with oxygen, to join $AlO_6{}^{9-}$ in the sandwich 'filling'.

Move to the fifth option.

Clearly, with Al, Fe and Mg being able to join with Si and O in the silicate structure of mica, there are several options for charge imbalance and the entry of yet more metals to balance them. In mica, this role is usually filled by potassium atoms, weakly bonded to two adjoining Si–O–Al (–Fe–Mg) 'sandwiches'. It is hardly surprising that micas have one good cleavage; cleaved sheets can be so thin that once they were used as window panes. Thin cleavage sheets are surprisingly strong and flexible along their length.

Now review the properties of micas under the properties tab and fill in the appropriate row in Table 3.1.

Task 3   Pyroxenes

Select pyroxene and its structure tab. Start with the third option.

The structure of **pyroxenes** is based on the linkage of $SiO_4{}^{4-}$ tetrahedra in zigzag *chains* by Si–O bond sharing. *Note*: only a part of one pyroxene chain is shown.

Move to the fourth and fifth options.

Octahedral groups of Fe or Mg and O balance charge by bonding two chains of $SiO_4{}^{4-}$ tetrahedra to form 'I-beams'. Some pyroxenes also incorporate calcium in their structure, depending on its availability in the magma.

The chain structure dominates the physical properties of pyroxenes. Although they are hard minerals, the I-beams control two planes of weak bonding and therefore two cleavages at about 90°.

Now review the properties of pyroxenes under the properties tab and fill in the appropriate row in Table 3.1.

Task 4   Olivines

Select olivine and its structure tab. As above, start with the third and fourth options and proceed to the fifth.

Olivine has the lowest silicon content of all the common igneous silicates. There is insufficient silicon for $SiO_4{}^{4-}$ tetrahedra to link up by sharing Si–O bonds, so the $SiO_4{}^{4-}$ tetrahedra exist in the olivine structure as isolated groups. Charge is balanced by bond sharing with octahedra of Fe or Mg bonded with O. The linkage between such octahedra and $SiO_4{}^{4-}$ tetrahedra fills space efficiently to give a strong set of covalent bonds in all directions.

■   Would you expect olivine to be soft and to have cleavage(s)?

☐   No, despite its very different composition, olivine is similar to quartz in its multidirectional bonding; it is strong and does not have any cleavage.

Now review the properties of olivine under the properties tab and fill in the appropriate row in Table 3.1.

Table 3.1 Main chemical and physical properties of some common rock-forming silicate minerals.

Mineral	Classification	Composition	Colour	Lustre	Cleavage	Shape	Hardness
Quartz	Silicate (framework)	SiO_2	Mainly colourless – can be coloured	Glassy	None (irregular fracture)	Prismatic	7.0
Feldspar	Silicate (framework)	Alkali $(K,Na)AlSi_3O_8$ Plagioclase, from $NaAlSi_3O_8$ to $CaAl_2Si_2O_8$					6.0–6.5
Mica	Silicate (sheet)	Pale (muscovite) $KAl_3Si_3O_{10}(OH)_2$ Dark (biotite) $K(Fe,Mg)_3AlSi_3O_{10}(OH)_2$					2.5
Pyroxene	Silicate (single chain)	$(Ca,Mg,Fe)_2Si_2O_6$					5.5–6.0
Olivine	Silicate (isolated group)	$(Mg,Fe)_2SiO_4$					6.5–7.0

Before you move on, make sure you check your entries in Table 3.1 with those in the comments on this activity at the end of this book.

Question 3.1

How might you distinguish between the two minerals in each of the following pairs using *one* mineral property that is the most distinctively different between the two (colour, shape, lustre, cleavage or hardness)? (a) Quartz and feldspar; (b) dark mica and pyroxene.

In Section 3.2.2, you will use what you have learned in Activity 3.1 to identify some of the minerals in common igneous rocks, and to use them to get a rough idea of the chemical composition of those rocks.

3.2 The diversity of igneous rocks

Book 2, Chapter 4 introduced igneous processes through their best known and most spectacular manifestation – volcanoes.

■ Which types of plate boundary involve igneous processes? Are there any igneous processes that are not obviously related to plate motions?

☐ Magmas form beneath divergent plate boundaries to give rise to new oceanic lithosphere and at convergent plate boundaries where old oceanic lithosphere is subducted into the mantle. Magmas also form within plates over hot spots which seem to be associated with mantle plumes rising from far below the base of the lithosphere and not related to plate motion.

Igneous rocks form at divergent plate boundaries from magma newly and directly derived from the mantle. They add to oceanic lithosphere through sea-floor spreading (Book 2, Section 7.3). Those formed at convergent plate margins, intimately connected with subduction, may involve melting of the overriding mantle and, if subduction is beneath a continental margin, the continental crust. Igneous rocks formed at hot spots are new additions to the outer Earth.

In Book 2, Activity 5.1 you compared hand specimens of two different kinds of igneous rock (Specimens 5 and 6: basalt and granite). This involved noting their different grain sizes and other textural features, and comparing their overall colours. Two important points you should have appreciated after completing the activity are:

- Overall grain size indicates how quickly a magma cooled and crystallised; the coarser it is, the more slowly it cooled, and vice versa.

- The overall lightness or darkness of an igneous rock stems from the relative proportions of light and dark minerals that make up the rock.

Activity 3.2   Basalt and granite: revision of Book 2

We expect this activity will take you approximately 15 minutes.

The aim of this activity is to revise the important visible properties of these rocks.

Safety warning

Read the whole of this section before starting the activity and make sure that you have read the section on 'Practical activities' in the *Introduction and Guide*.

When carrying out practical activities, you should always take care to observe the simple safety precautions highlighted in the module book. Very often, as in the case of this activity, these precautions will seem quite obvious and just a matter of using common sense. However that does not mean that you should ignore the safety instructions. The Open University has a duty to give advice on health and safety to students carrying out any activities that are described in the module. Similarly, *you* have a duty to follow the instructions and to carry out the practical activity having regard for your own safety and that of other people around you. Whenever you do practical activities you should think about the hazards involved, and how any risks can be minimised.

Important safety precautions

Take note of the following safety precautions, which apply to all practical activities:

- Keep children and animals away while you are working, as they may attempt to eat the rock specimens.

- Clear your working area of clutter. Put all food away. Ensure there is nothing to trip on underfoot.

- Always wash your hands thoroughly after a practical activity.

- Any household items used should be thoroughly cleaned before returning them to domestic use.

Precautions when handling rock and mineral specimens from the Practical Kit

Take care when handling the rock and mineral specimens not to touch your eyes. Some rock dust can be an irritant. If you get dust in your eye, wash it out with copious amounts of water for at least 5 minutes. If irritation persists seek medical help.

Equipment needed

Kit items

Rock Specimens 5 and 6

Hand lens

Non-kit items

Ruler marked in millimetres

Large steel nail

Task 1 Distinguishing rock types – rock textures

Examine the basalt (Specimen 5) and granite (Specimen 6) samples. In particular, use your hand lens to look closely at the shapes of the grains that make up each rock and how they are arranged (i.e. the texture of the samples). Also, try to prise out a few grains with the point of the nail. How do you know these samples are igneous rocks?

Task 2 Distinguishing igneous rocks – colour and grain size

(a) Observe the overall appearance side-by-side of the basalt and granite samples, and note particularly their colour and their grain size. Make a note of the ways in which they differ.

(b) Which of your observations – of colour or of grain size – might tell you about differences in the mineral content of the rocks, and which might suggest how the rocks crystallised? Which sample is an extrusive rock, and which is an intrusive rock?

Keep Specimens 5 and 6 to hand for Activity 3.3. Now read the comments on this activity at the end of this book before continuing.

The mainly fine-grained texture of the basalt suggests that it is probably an *extrusive* igneous rock, having cooled and crystallised quickly. (Note that magma sometimes cools so quickly that crystals do not develop and it solidifies as a natural *glass*.) The granite is a typical *intrusive* igneous rock, its coarse grain size signifying slow cooling and crystallisation. The overall colour depends on which minerals make up an igneous rock. The types and proportions of those minerals help subdivide igneous rocks according to the chemical composition of the magma from which they crystallised (see Section 3.2.3).

Useful as they are in deducing how rocks formed, hand specimens are mere samples from large exposures of rock. Field observations of large-scale features provide more information about how a rock formed, the processes involved and sometimes the overall conditions in which they operated.

3.2.1   More clues from igneous rocks

Volcanic cones may be the most familiar forms of extrusive igneous rocks, but they are not the only ones produced by extrusive igneous activity (Book 2, Chapter 4). Moreover, they do not survive erosion once their activity stops. The most common extrusive igneous rocks found in the geological record are those which spread far from the source of eruption. Depending on their chemical composition, magmas vary in their viscosity. Viscous ones cannot flow far as lavas before crystallising, and they tend to produce the classic (conical) volcanoes. More fluid magmas – generally of basaltic composition – move rapidly, even down gently sloping surfaces. The resulting lava flows may extend for many kilometres to form layers. How far they extend and the area which such lavas cover depend on the volume of magma produced during each pulse of activity. The biggest cover tens of thousands of square kilometres and, if many flows pile up, they form the aptly named flood basalts (Figure 3.2a) which you met in Section 2.6.1. The best-known lava flow in the British Isles crystallised from such a basalt flood, and forms the Giant's Causeway (Figure 3.2b). Its peculiar structure of regular, polygonal columns resulted from very regular contraction as it cooled after the lava had solidified.

Many of the lavas that appear in the geological record were erupted on dry land, but some show clear evidence of having erupted beneath water bodies.

■ What special feature characterises sub-aqueous lavas?

□ They contain pillow-like structures which begin to form as water chills the surface of effusing lava to form a skin. This bulges to form the distinctive pillow shape, and then breaks to release another lobe of lava. Instead of a distinct lava flow, the activity is represented by an accumulation of bulbous pillows (Book 2, Figure 7.4b).

Layers of pyroclastic material that fall from clouds of dust and ash released by explosive eruptions may blanket hundreds to thousands of square kilometres,

(a)   (b)

Figure 3.2   Lava flows produced by fluid magmas. (a) Two kilometres of individual basalt lava flows (each a few metres thick) make up the Simien Mountains in northern Ethiopia. (b) The eroded form of a basalt lava flow at the Giant's Causeway in Co. Antrim, Northern Ireland, which shows polygonal columns formed by shrinkage during cooling.

thinning outwards from the centre of an eruption. Looking superficially like sedimentary rocks, volcanic ash layers can be distinguished by their crystals of igneous silicate minerals, and often shards of volcanic glass – magma suddenly chilled after an explosive eruption.

Although volcanic eruptions show clearly that parts of the Earth's interior melt to produce magmas, *where* the magmas form is not so clear from surface observations. Magma must also find a way to the surface somehow, and that too is unclear. To find evidence that suggests how magma moves from its source to the surface, and what happens to magma that did not escape, requires observations from the geological record. Erosion may expose old *intrusive* igneous bodies that crystallised deep within the Earth. Such bodies often cut across older rocks and structures within them, proving that they did indeed form by the intrusion of magma.

Closely packed, vertical **dykes** of basalt are known feeders for the pillow lavas in oceanic crust (Book 2, Section 8.5). In continental crust, isolated dykes cut across older rocks (Figure 3.3). Some dykes occur in eroded volcanoes and suggest that they fed magma to eruptions. A sheet-like intrusion *between* individual layers of older rocks, which lies parallel to the layering, is called a **sill**. A few show intrusive relationships in detail (Figure 3.3c), but it is easy to mistake a sill for an interlayered lava flow. Figure 3.3b shows schematically how dykes and sills may be related to one pulse of magma intrusion.

Figure 3.3   Minor intrusive bodies. (a) Dark basaltic dyke cutting across shallow-dipping fractures in a light granite on the island of Lundy, southwest England (the dyke is younger than both the granite and the fractures). (b) Dykes and sills that formed at the same time and intruded older sedimentary rocks. (c) The lower contact of a basaltic sill with sedimentary strata on Salisbury Crags, Edinburgh (the image is about 1.5 m high). Proof of intrusion is visible at the centre where the featureless pale brown basalt cuts across, partly envelopes and has uplifted layered sedimentary rock. This occurrence was one of the first to be recognised as evidence for igneous intrusion, by James Hutton in the late 18th century.

■ Suggest how, apart from local cross-cutting relationships, a basaltic sill could be distinguished from a lava flow with identical composition.

☐ One distinguishing feature would be their top surfaces: weathering will have broken down the exposed top of a lava flow, whereas both the top and the bottom of an intrusive sill will be fresh, having formed in contact with existing rocks. Rocks adjacent to hot magma are baked or even metamorphosed. A lava flow would bake only those rocks below it; a sill would affect those above and below it.

Uplift and erosion of many kilometres of overlying rock can expose large igneous bodies that crystallised deep in the crust. These **plutons** (named after the Greek god of the underworld, Pluto) have volumes of tens to thousands of cubic kilometres (Figure 3.4a). At the high temperatures in the deep crust, magma cools very slowly, so that *plutonic* igneous rocks are always coarse grained. Typical plutons cut across older sedimentary rocks, and those of southwest England occur at the surface as irregular 'tors' (Figure 3.4b).

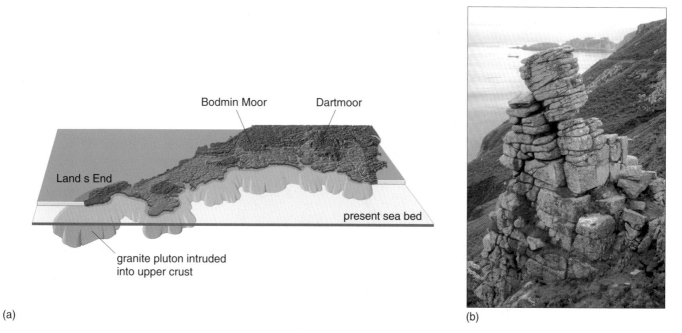

(a)

(b)

Figure 3.4   The granite plutons of southwest England: (a) showing in 3D how the surface occurrences (red) connect to a much larger body (brown) at depth; (b) exposed near Land's End in a tor.

The mainly fine-grained basalt in the Practical Kit contains a few much larger crystals; a duality of grain size that is known as a **porphyritic** texture. Such a relationship seems to contradict the notion of rapid cooling and crystallisation of extrusive igneous rocks. There is a simple explanation. Often before eruption occurs, large volumes of magma accumulate in a magma chamber (Book 2, Section 4.4), eventually to form a pluton. Entirely molten at first, the cooling magma would slowly start to crystallise. Upward movement of the partly solidified magma would carry some early-crystallising minerals with it. Intrusion of this melt plus crystal mixture at higher crustal levels in thin dykes and sills, or its eruption as lava, would involve more rapid cooling and crystallisation of the molten fraction. The solidified rock would therefore have a finely crystalline part, or groundmass, that envelops the older, larger crystals. Porphyritic igneous rocks (called **porphyries**) thereby carry some important information about the history of the magma before it solidified (Section 3.3).

Question 3.2

Figure 3.5 shows several igneous rocks which formed under different circumstances. Briefly describe the texture of each of them. How and under what circumstances do you think they may have formed?

(a)

(b)

(c)

(d)

(e)

Figure 3.5   Igneous rocks with different textures and grain sizes (note the different widths of the fields of view): (a) granite (80 mm); (b) feldspar porphyry (containing distinctive crystals of feldspar) (90 mm); (c) rhyolite (70 mm); (d) pumice (100 mm); (e) obsidian (50 mm).

3.2.2   The chemical composition of igneous rocks

Distinguishing igneous rocks, for instance the porphyry from the granite in Figure 3.5, from their different grain sizes and textures is one aspect of classification. Discovering the types and proportions of the minerals in an igneous rock is the basis for classifying rocks according to their chemical composition.

Three of the rocks in Figure 3.5 (a, b and c) are dominated by crystals of quartz, alkali feldspar and plagioclase feldspar; the other two – pumice (d) and obsidian

(e) – are glassy and don't contain crystals. Remarkably, although the five rocks look very different, they all have essentially the same chemical composition, i.e. very similar percentages of different elements. Each of them could have solidified under different physical circumstances from the same chemical type of magma.

The chemical differences of igneous rocks frequently relate to how and where magma forms. The basalt and granite in the Practical Kit have quite different grain sizes and so crystallised in quite different circumstances. But are they chemically different?

Activity 3.3   The mineral content and composition of basalt and granite

We expect this activity will take you approximately 15 minutes.

Important safety precautions

Take note of the safety precautions given with Activity 3.2.

Equipment needed

Kit items

Rock Specimens 5 and 6

Hand lens

Non-kit item

Ruler marked in millimetres

Some of the minerals you met in Activity 3.2 are present in the samples of basalt and granite in the Practical Kit. The aims of this activity are to identify the minerals in these rocks and, using the chemical composition of those minerals, to deduce how they contribute to the overall chemical composition of each rock.

Task 1

Examine Specimen 6 with the hand lens; it contains three minerals. Describe each mineral according to its average grain size, shape, colour, cleavage and lustre. Confirm that your observations match the properties of the minerals quartz, feldspar and mica in your completed Table 3.1.

Now examine Specimen 5. The finer grain size makes it more difficult to identify all the minerals. Try to recognise a few large, dark crystals of pyroxene on cut surfaces. On broken surfaces their cleavage planes glint in the light. Long, narrow, grey to white crystals of plagioclase feldspar also show good cleavages. Both minerals also make up much of the dark, fine-grained groundmass, in which the larger grains are set.

Task 2

(a) Note down the chemical formula of each mineral in the granite (see the examples in Table 3.1). Assume that the feldspar content is a combination of alkali feldspar and sodium-rich plagioclase feldspar. (You don't need to remember these particular formulae, but it is important to appreciate which elements occur in the main rock-forming minerals.)

Do the same as above for the basalt. Assume that the plagioclase feldspar is at the calcium-rich end of its composition range.

(b) The chemical formulae for the main minerals in each rock indicate the most abundant elements that are present in the rock. Assume that the granite comprises 30% quartz, 60% feldspars and 10% dark mica, and that the basalt comprises 50% plagioclase feldspar and 50% pyroxene. Try to judge which elements (ignoring oxygen and hydrogen) are likely to be more abundant in the granite than in the basalt, and vice versa.

Now read the comments on this activity at the end of this book before continuing.

Activity 3.3 revealed from their 'blends' of silicate minerals that the basalt and granite samples are chemically very different, as the magmas they crystallised from must have been. In chemical terms, basalt and granite are about as different as you can get among common igneous rocks.

Basalt contains the minerals plagioclase feldspar (the Ca-rich type), pyroxene and sometimes olivine. Pyroxene and olivine are generally dark coloured minerals. Being <u>m</u>agnesium- and iron-rich (<u>Fe</u>) silicates, they are often called **mafic** (by adding 'ic') minerals. Igneous rocks containing a high proportion of such minerals therefore have relatively high levels of magnesium, iron and calcium. They are called mafic rocks and usually appear dark. The coarse-grained, mafic igneous rock gabbro (Book 2, Section 8.5.1) has a similar mineral content and composition to extrusive basalt; it is the intrusive equivalent of basalt, and solidified more slowly from a chemically similar magma.

In contrast, **granite** contains the minerals quartz, alkali feldspar and the Na-rich type of plagioclase feldspar, and usually some mica. Pale-coloured feldspars and quartz are called **felsic** minerals (from <u>fel</u>dspar, silicon plus 'ic'). Igneous rocks dominated by them are usually pale and called felsic rocks (e.g. Figure 3.5). They contain significantly more silicon, sodium and potassium than mafic rocks. Obsidian glass is a rare exception to that general rule, being felsic but dark in colour; glass can be highly coloured by mere traces of some metals. **Rhyolite** has broadly the same mineral and chemical composition as granite. Being a fine-grained extrusive rock, it is the felsic counterpart to basalt.

Igneous rock compositions range from granites and rhyolites, which are rich in silicon and contain mainly felsic minerals, to gabbros and basalts, which have less silicon and significant amounts of mafic minerals. Variation in the mineral contents of common igneous rocks is the basis for compositional classification. The proportions of different minerals change across Figure 3.6 to signify the typical variation in mineral content of the common igneous rocks. Silicon, sodium and potassium contents *increase* from left (mafic rocks) to right (felsic rocks), while magnesium, iron and calcium contents *decrease*.

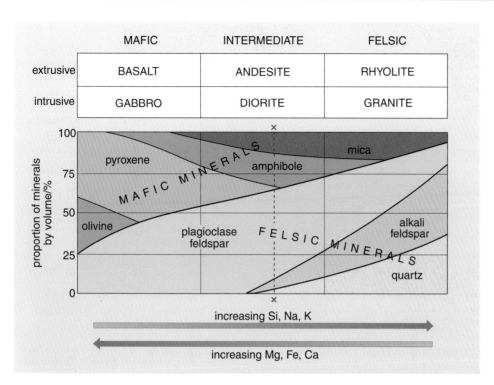

Figure 3.6 Variation in mineral content of common igneous rocks. The vertical axis shows proportions in per cent of minerals (by volume) and the horizontal axis shows the range of rock types. The arrows beneath the diagram show how the content of certain elements varies across the compositional range of common igneous rocks.

The compositions of felsic and mafic rocks in Figure 3.6 bracket those of *intermediate* igneous rocks. Fine-grained intermediate lavas are **andesites** and the coarse-grained plutonic equivalents are **diorites**. The dominant felsic mineral in these intermediate rocks is plagioclase feldspar. The dominant mafic mineral is usually pyroxene or amphibole, a chain silicate containing hydroxyl (OH^-) ions.

The line X–X shows an example of how to use Figure 3.6. The line signifies a particular 'blend' of minerals in an igneous rock: in this case, 2% quartz; 6% alkali feldspar; 54% plagioclase feldspar; 2% pyroxene; 21% amphibole and 15% mica. (You may like to check the percentage values yourself.) The rock represented by X–X is one of a variety of 'blends' constituting intermediate igneous rocks.

■ In Figure 3.6 how much can the percentages vary of: (a) plagioclase feldspar in gabbro; (b) quartz in granite; and (c) pyroxene in diorite?

☐ (a) Plagioclase feldspar in gabbro may vary from about 25% to 55%. (b) Quartz in granite may vary from 10% to nearly 40%. (c) Pyroxene in diorite may vary from about 0% to 25%.

Question 3.3

Use Figure 3.6 to answer the following questions.

(a) Which common igneous rocks contain: (i) the highest proportion of quartz; (ii) the highest proportion of mafic minerals and (iii) no alkali feldspar?

(b) How does the mineral content of diorite differ from that of granite?

(c) How do the proportions of chemical elements in diorite differ from those in gabbro?

The classes of igneous rocks are broad and divide up a continuum of chemical and mineralogical compositions in nature. Which geological processes might have produced this diversity of igneous rock? The plate-tectonic context for magmatism (Book 2, Chapter 9) opened new avenues to answering this major geoscientific question.

3.2.3   Igneous activity at plate boundaries

Igneous activity today occurs in five different settings at the boundaries between tectonic plates (Figure 3.7).

■ Describe the main types of igneous activity in relation to types of plate boundary, for example at locations A–E in Figure 3.7.

□ A is at a divergent boundary where magmas emerge from oceanic ridges to add to the oceanic lithosphere. B and E are volcanoes far from plate boundaries. They occur within oceanic (B) or continental (E) parts of plates where magmas rise from hot spots in the mantle. C and D are volcanic arcs at convergent boundaries where oceanic lithosphere is subducted into the mantle. C has developed on oceanic crust; D on continental crust.

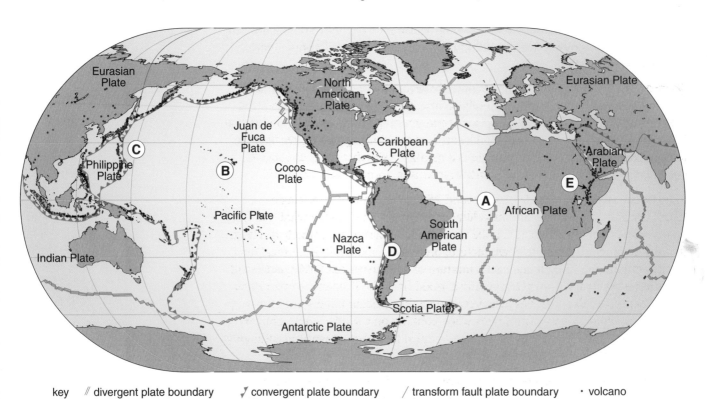

key   ⫽ divergent plate boundary   ⌐ convergent plate boundary   / transform fault plate boundary   · volcano

Figure 3.7   Global distribution of active volcanoes in relation to tectonic plate boundaries.

Each site has characteristic kinds of igneous rock. Magmas erupted at divergent plate margins (A) and hot spots (B and E) are mainly basaltic. In both cases only the mantle can have melted to produce the basaltic magma. The mantle is composed of **peridotite** and contains far more Mg-rich olivine (Mg_2SiO_4) than does basalt. Peridotite therefore contains significantly more magnesium and less calcium, aluminium and silicon than magma produced by melting it. The reason for this seemingly odd change in chemical composition will become clear in Section 3.3.

The compositions of magmas erupted at convergent plate boundaries (C and D) are much more variable than those at divergent boundaries or hot spots. Magmas of volcanic arcs range from basaltic to andesitic to rhyolitic. In *oceanic* volcanic arcs (C) the dominant compositions are basaltic to andesitic; in *continental* volcanic arcs (D) they are andesitic to rhyolitic.

■ In which type of arc are granite plutons more likely to be present?

☐ In continental volcanic arcs, where rhyolitic magmas are more important.

The diversity of magmas and igneous rocks, particularly in volcanic arcs, stems from two fundamental processes: *melting*, which generates magma (Section 3.3), and *crystallisation*, which forms igneous rocks (Section 3.4).

3.3 Partial melting processes: from rock to magma

Apart from the outer core (Book 2, Section 6.2.3), very little of the Earth is in a molten state. The lithosphere and underlying mantle are solid rock, although the asthenosphere is less rigid (Book 2, Chapter 6). Magma is produced only locally, beneath regions of igneous activity (Figure 3.7). It involves melting of either mantle or crustal rocks.

There are two features of magmas that might seem a little odd. First, they have different compositions from their likely source; for instance, basalt is produced from peridotite (Book 2, Section 6.1). Second, melting temperatures of individual silicate minerals found in igneous rocks are hundreds of degrees higher than the temperatures of magmas. An example is a quartz crystal that melts at 1600 °C, yet granitic magma, from which quartz crystallises, forms at around 800 °C.

Phoenician traders first made glass around 2500 years ago after making a discovery that helps to explain the oddity of magmas. They traded what was then a very valuable natural mineral called trona (sodium carbonate), which was used in the ancient world for soap manufacture, preserving and tenderising meat; and in mummification. They found that a mixture of 15% trona and 85% quartz sand melts at a temperature easily attained in a wood fire. The Roman historian Pliny the Elder alleged that this was discovered when Phoenician traders used trona blocks from their cargo as fire stones when cooking on a sandy beach. They were amazed when a hot liquid flowed and then cooled to a hard transparent solid, now called 'soda glass'.

When heated, trona breaks down to release carbon dioxide gas and solid but highly unstable sodium oxide. At high temperature the bonds that connect silicon and oxygen in quartz molecules vibrate strongly, allowing sodium ions to enter and contaminate the structure. At around 1000 °C the sodium ions so weaken the SiO_2 structure that it breaks down to form a sodium silicate melt. Solidified, this forms soda glass. In rock there is a similar transfer of ions between the different rock-forming minerals as temperature increases.

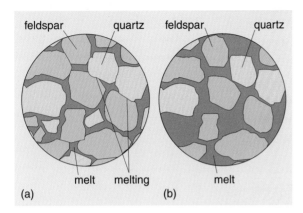

Figure 3.8   Progressive melting in rocks starts at grain boundaries where minerals are in contact: (a) 10% melting; (b) 30% melting.

As the different minerals in a rock are heated, the bonds within their structures increasingly vibrate. The chance of ions breaking free from the silicate molecules is higher at the boundaries of each mineral grain than within their crystalline structure. Therefore, rising temperature increasingly drives ions freed from one mineral to contaminate and disrupt the structure of another. That reduces the temperature at which each mineral will melt, in much the same manner as the formation of soda glass. Melting starts where different mineral grains are in direct contact with one another (Figure 3.8a). The ion-transfer process also enables several minerals to melt at the same time, although in different proportions according to each mineral's composition. Unlike the melting of single solid compounds, such as water ice or individual silicate crystals, a rock's mineral mixture melts over a range of several hundred degrees Celsius, and the proportion of melt to remaining solid minerals increases as the temperature rises (Figure 3.8b).

Rock begins melting at a temperature depending on the particular mix of minerals in the rock. For instance, felsic minerals with high Si content but with little Fe and Mg (i.e. quartz, feldspars and white mica) melt at lower temperatures than do mafic minerals (i.e. dark mica, amphibole, pyroxene and olivine), which have lower Si and higher Fe and Mg content.

The amount of water present in the rock also plays a role, by reducing the melting temperature of most silicate mixtures. Experiments show that felsic rocks made of a mixture of quartz and feldspars with water-bearing mica, start to melt at between 650 and 800 °C. Mafic rocks composed mainly of pyroxene and olivine start melting at much higher temperatures (1050–1300 °C), partly because olivine and pyroxene don't contain water.

Figure 3.9 shows the order in which common minerals in a rock tend to melt. As a rock is heated up, depending on the minerals it contains, mixtures of mainly felsic minerals melt first. At higher temperatures, mafic minerals start to melt.

Question 3.4

Referring to Table 3.2 (in the comments on Activity 3.1) and Figure 3.9, describe how, in general, the composition and internal structure of felsic minerals that melt at lower temperatures differ from those of mafic minerals that melt at higher temperatures.

One felsic mineral does not follow the trend outlined in the answer to Question 3.4. Plagioclase feldspar melts over a wide range of temperatures (600–1000 °C) because its composition varies. The more easily melted variety is sodium-rich ($NaAlSi_3O_8$), whereas the variety which melts at a higher

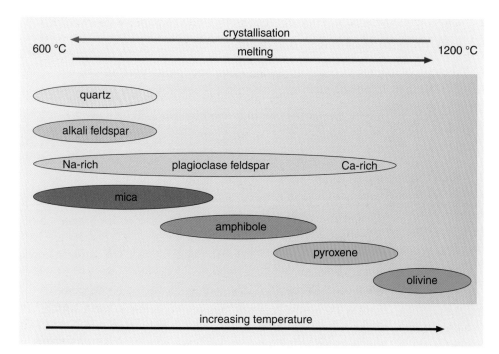

Figure 3.9   Generalised sequence of melting when a rock is heated (and crystallisation when magma is cooled) of common rock-forming minerals with changing temperature. Each mineral has a range of melting temperature.

temperature has high calcium, higher aluminium and lower silicon ($CaAl_2Si_2O_8$). It seems that the Si content of minerals, and consequently of rocks, partly controls the temperature at which they begin to melt.

When the mantle's olivine-rich peridotite begins to melt, pyroxene melts along with olivine. At this early stage, however, much less olivine melts than its proportion in the rock might suggest. So the composition of the initial magma is very different from that of the mantle – it is basaltic. The remaining solid mantle becomes even richer in olivine and so needs to reach higher temperatures to continue melting. Should that happen, proportionately more olivine would melt and the magma would become more Mg-rich and poorer in Si. However, complete mantle melting to produce magma of peridotite composition never happens because there is a limit to mantle temperature at a particular depth. This is partly because magmas move from their source and carry heat away quickly. Pockets of magma coalesce to form larger bodies which weaken the surrounding rock structure. Silicate-rich liquids are less dense than the minerals that remain solid, so magma migrates upwards. As a result, an unmelted *residue*, containing more olivine than in the original peridotite, is left behind.

Magmas are therefore produced, not by complete melting, but by **partial melting** of their source rock. This explains how basaltic magma, containing higher levels of Si and Ca, but much lower levels of Mg, is produced from peridotite. By this means, partial melting tends to create magmas with more felsic compositions than their sources.

■   Referring to Figure 3.9, how might the chemical composition of a magma formed when diorite starts melting differ from the initial rock composition?

☐   The felsic minerals of the diorite will tend to melt first, so the initial magma will be more felsic. It will be a magma of granitic (rhyolitic) composition, which is richer in Si and the alkali metals sodium (Na) and potassium (K) than the diorite (Figure 3.6).

The melting of any rocks containing both felsic and mafic minerals can be represented in a simplified way, as:

$$\text{felsic minerals} + \text{mafic minerals} \xrightarrow{\text{partial melting}} \text{more felsic magma} + \text{more mafic residue} \qquad (3.1)$$

In this way, partial melting of gabbro (equivalent to effusive basalt) can produce a dioritic (andesitic) magma; and partial melting of diorite (roughly average continental crust) can produce a granitic (rhyolitic) magma (Figure 3.10). (*Note*: for simplicity, Book 2 describes continental crust as granitic when, in fact, its average composition is closer to a dioritic or an intermediate composition.)

Melting to produce basaltic magma occurs in the uppermost mantle. Peridotite requires high temperatures to melt, which is one reason why the mantle melts in only three settings: at constructive and destructive plate boundaries and above hot spots. Dioritic continental crust also only reaches temperatures high enough to produce granitic magma under special circumstances: for example, at the base of very thick crust formed during plate collisions (Section 5.3).

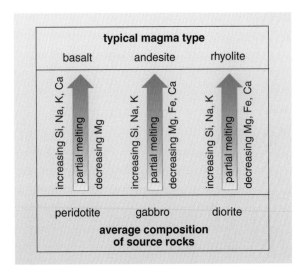

Figure 3.10 Schematic relationships between source rocks and types of magma produced by partial melting, including the resulting changes in chemical composition. Named sources represent average rock compositions. Magmas are usually referred to in terms of the extrusive rocks which form from them, e.g. basalt magma.

3.4   Fractional crystallisation processes: from magma to igneous rock

In the same way that a rock *melts* progressively over a range of temperatures, magma *crystallises* progressively over a range of temperatures when it cools. However, rapid cooling produces rapid crystallisation and a randomly oriented mass of fine-grained crystals, as in volcanic lavas and shallow intrusions. Slow cooling in a large magma chamber deep within the Earth results in gradual crystallisation; crystals grow much larger in plutonic igneous rocks. The first minerals to crystallise are those with higher melting temperatures (Figure 3.9); getting an early start, they often grow large. If the magma erupts before crystallisation is complete, a porphyritic texture forms in the rapidly cooled lava (Figure 3.5b). The large pyroxene and plagioclase feldspar crystals in the Practical Kit basalt probably formed by slow cooling in a magma chamber before eruption.

An important factor in the crystallisation of magma is the order in which different minerals appear.

■ When basaltic magma cools gradually, which minerals are likely to crystallise first?

☐ Minerals with high melting temperatures: olivine first, and then pyroxene and calcium-rich plagioclase feldspar (Figure 3.9).

Minerals that crystallise early, individually and together have a different combined chemical composition from that of the magma itself. Progressive crystallisation continually changes the composition of the remaining liquid. If crystals and liquid stay together, complete solidification will produce a rock that is chemically identical to the original magma. However, various processes can separate the magma into different *fractions* before complete solidification. A fraction rich in crystals is dominated by early-formed mafic minerals. The other, liquid-rich, fraction is a more felsic magma with few of those crystals (Figure 3.11). Such **fractional crystallisation** is another means by which chemically different magmas are produced.

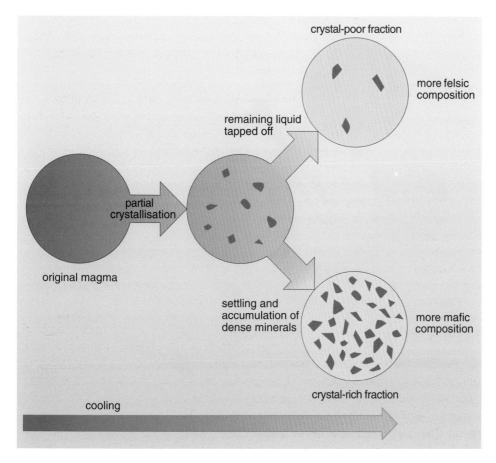

Figure 3.11   Production of different magma compositions by fractional crystallisation. One fraction is rich in accumulated crystals of mafic minerals; the other is a more felsic liquid.

How might this separation of crystals and magma occur? Crystals of some early-formed mafic minerals, such as olivine and pyroxene, are denser than basaltic magma and tend to settle under gravity. When this happens, the upper part of the magma becomes liquid-rich and more felsic than the original magma. The lower part becomes more mafic because it contains many olivine and pyroxene crystals. If the liquid fraction has a lower density than surrounding rocks, it rises to form intrusions and volcanic rocks, leaving behind the crystal-rich residue.

Such fractional crystallisation of a basaltic magma could produce intermediate (andesitic) magma. Subsequent fractionation of that andesitic magma could form felsic (rhyolitic) magma (Figure 3.12). This process helps explain the wide range of igneous rock compositions commonly found in volcanic arcs. Therefore, a continuous process of fractional crystallisation 'refines' magma originally derived by partial melting, which itself is already more felsic than its ultimate source.

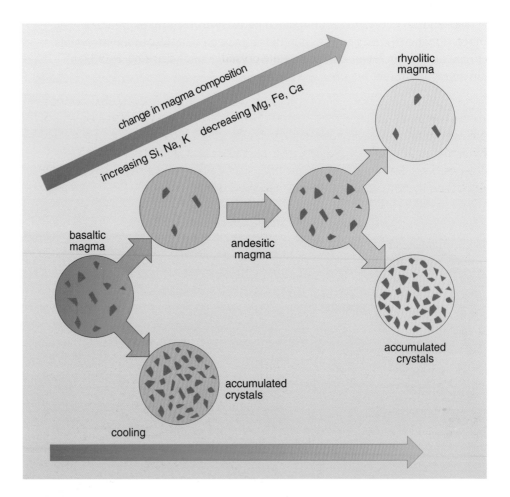

Figure 3.12 Production of progressively more felsic magma as a result of repeated fractional crystallisation. The process may be continuous or occur in stages, as shown.

■   In what kind of igneous body is fractional crystallisation most likely to happen?

☐   In a deep magma chamber, which will eventually crystallise completely to form a pluton.

There is a final point to consider: the *temperature* of different magmas. Felsic minerals melt and crystallise at lower temperatures than mafic ones. As you might expect from that general difference, felsic magmas are much cooler than those of mafic composition. Granitic magmas have temperatures as low as around 700 °C; basaltic magmas emerge at about 1200 °C; andesitic magmas are somewhere in-between.

3.5   Igneous processes and plate tectonic settings

Different magma types occur in different tectonic settings (Figure 3.7). The fundamental processes that produce magmas may account for those differences. The compositions of magmas produced by partial melting depend on the rocks available for melting (Figure 3.10) and the percentage of melting. Fractional crystallisation may produce different magma compositions depending on the starting composition of the magma (Figure 3.12) and the amount of crystallisation achieved by the time the crystals have separated from the remaining melt.

Figure 3.13 summarises types of magmatic activity in different global settings. At mid-ocean ridges, magma is mainly basaltic, produced by partial melting of mantle peridotite at relatively shallow depths. At hot spots, magma is produced by partial melting of mantle peridotite at greater depths. Although basaltic compositions dominate in both settings, other compositions can be produced by fractional crystallisation in shallow magma chambers.

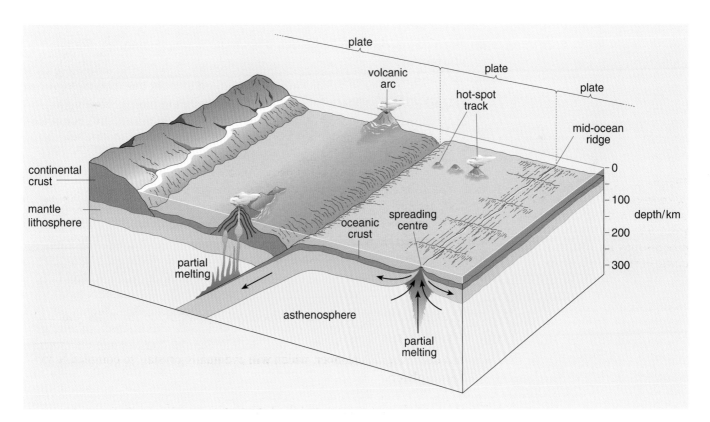

Figure 3.13   Composite diagram showing the typical nature of magmatism in various plate-tectonic settings that correspond with locations A, B and C in Figure 3.7. At a divergent plate margin partial melting of the mantle generates basaltic magma. Partial melting of mantle at a convergent plate margin forms an oceanic volcanic arc from basaltic and andesitic magmas. Basaltic magma generated by partial melting of the mantle at hot spots forms oceanic volcanic islands.

69

Magmatism in volcanic arcs (Figure 3.13) is more complicated; volcanic rocks there vary in composition from basalt to andesite to rhyolite. Not surprisingly, plutonic intrusions of gabbro, diorite and granite are exposed in older, eroded arcs. However, in oceanic arcs, basaltic to andesitic magma compositions tend to dominate, whereas more andesitic to rhyolitic compositions occur in continental arcs. Which processes might explain this?

In volcanic arcs, the partial melting of peridotite that generates basaltic magma is assisted by water released by dehydration of subducted old oceanic lithosphere. Andesitic magmas, that are characteristic of oceanic arcs, form by fractional crystallisation of this basaltic magma. In continental arcs (D on Figure 3.7), it is not quite so simple. From Figures 3.10 and 3.12, you can see that andesitic to rhyolitic magma compositions that dominate continental arcs may be produced in one of two possible ways: by partial melting of gabbroic to dioritic source rocks; or by fractional crystallisation of basaltic to andesitic magmas. There might even be a combination of both. Indeed, basaltic magmas that melted at temperatures around 1200 °C do form parts of continental arcs, and must have been produced in the mantle beneath, and continental crust is of dioritic composition – more felsic than the gabbroic crust of oceanic arcs.

■   What do you think might happen if hot basaltic magma intrudes dioritic crustal rocks?

☐   If the temperature of the dioritic rocks is raised to more than 600 °C (Figure 3.9), the felsic minerals in them could start to melt, producing a granitic magma in a deep magma chamber, which will eventually crystallise completely to form a pluton.

Intrusion of basaltic magma into the dioritic crust beneath continental volcanic arcs could form rhyolitic magma by partial melting, if sufficient heat was available to raise diorite above its melting temperature. There would also be a good chance, at around the same time, that the cooling of basalt magma in a magma chamber might generate andesitic magma by fractional crystallisation. Another possibility is mixing basaltic and rhyolitic magmas to produce intermediate, andesitic magmas. Regardless of how andesitic magma might have formed, its fractional crystallisation in crustal magma chambers could also account for rhyolitic magmas. A range of processes can thus account for magmatic complexity in continental volcanic arcs, although methods of telling them apart are beyond the scope of this module. Similar complexities characterise the production of magma at newly formed divergent margins on the continents (E on Figure 3.7).

3.5.1   Clues to ancient igneous processes

You have seen how distinctive types of igneous rock are produced in certain tectonic settings today. So the occurrence of the same rock types in the geological record hint strongly at the presence of equivalent settings in the past. However, the geological record on land, which is the most accessible place to study old rocks, may be biased.

■ Which are more likely to be preserved in the geological record on land – igneous rocks of volcanic arcs or the ocean floor?

☐ The rocks of volcanic arcs are more likely to be preserved in continental crust, as they are less likely to be subducted than those of the ocean floor (Book 2, Chapter 9).

Volcanic arcs are preserved in the geological record either because they formed along a continental margin that is still active (e.g. the Andes), or because they were tectonically accreted to continents (Book 2, Section 9.4), as seems to be the destiny of the island chains of the western Pacific. More rarely, ocean floor rocks also become accreted onto continents.

Some rocks forming the island of Anglesey off the coast of North Wales include basaltic pillow lavas (Figure 3.14a) together with gabbro and serpentinite (Book 2, Section 8.5). They originated as oceanic crust around 800 Ma ago, and perhaps indicate the site of an ancient divergent plate boundary. North Wales also has a 470-Ma-old range of basaltic, andesitic and rhyolitic volcanic rocks, which probably originated in a volcanic arc during the Ordovician Period (Figure 3.14b).

(a)

(b)

Figure 3.14 Ancient igneous rocks showing characteristics distinctive of different tectonic settings: (a) 800-Ma-old basaltic pillow lavas on Anglesey, North Wales, which formed as oceanic crust; (b) 470-Ma-old rhyolitic lavas in Snowdonia, North Wales, showing banding produced during eruption. These rocks are evidence of a former volcanic arc.

3.6 Igneous processes in the rock cycle

Basaltic magma, and other magmas derived from basalt by fractional crystallisation, originate from the mantle as a consequence of partial melting. They therefore constitute new additions to the Earth's crust and are the primary materials from which all other rocks in the crust are ultimately derived. Except in cases of extreme uplift and erosion in continental collision zones or where oceanic lithosphere has accreted to the continents, mantle rock in bulk never sees the light of day. It participates in the rock cycle through its magmatic products. In this 'second-hand' way the mantle has the most profound effects on the rock cycle, being the ultimate source of the rocky material found at the surface, and of the carbon on which life is built. The continental crust itself has grown over four billion years mainly by the accretion of oceanic volcanic arcs (Book 2, Section 9.4.2), made from mantle-derived igneous rocks and their derivatives.

Having crystallised at temperatures as high as 1200 °C, and being made up of silicate minerals, most of which don't contain water or hydroxyl ions, igneous rocks that reach the surface are not in equilibrium with their surroundings. Minerals formed at high temperatures are highly prone to weathering, and the resulting debris is a major source of material that ends up in sediments (Chapter 4). In the case of igneous rocks ultimately derived from mantle melting, that material is a new addition to the rock cycle.

Figure 3.15 expresses these fundamental relationships between igneous processes and the rest of the rock cycle. Chapter 4 begins with the surface processes that operate on exposed crystalline igneous rocks to involve them in the 'upper' part of the rock cycle.

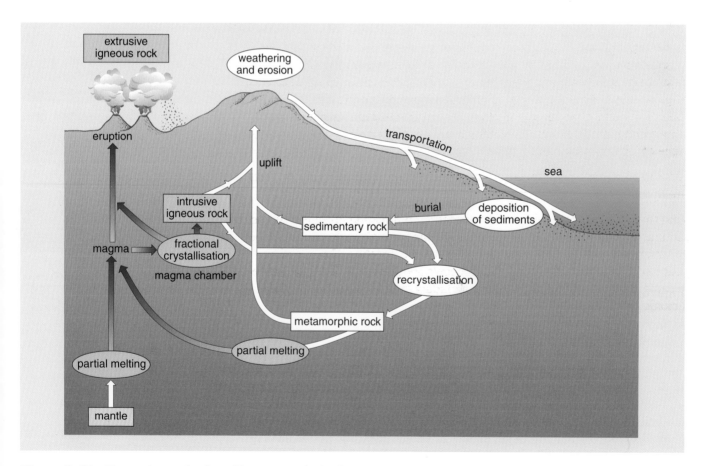

Figure 3.15   Formation and roles of igneous rocks in the rock cycle. This is based on Figure 10.2 in Book 2, with the igneous components highlighted.

3.7 Summary of Chapter 3

Igneous rocks are distinguished by their textures, which feature randomly oriented, interlocking and intergrown crystals.

There is a diversity of igneous rocks because of different magma compositions and crystallisation histories. Usually, large bodies of intrusive rock are coarse-grained; layers of extrusive rocks are fine-grained. Magma chambers form plutons; offshoots during the upward rise of magmas form sheet-like dykes and sills.

The fundamental differences in magma composition are often reflected by the presence of different minerals in igneous rocks. Mafic rocks (such as gabbro and basalt) are rich in mafic minerals (especially pyroxene). Felsic rocks (such as granite and rhyolite) are dominated by felsic minerals (especially quartz and feldspar). The amounts of mafic and felsic minerals are more equally balanced in intermediate rocks (such as diorite and andesite).

Magmatic activity today is concentrated at mid-ocean ridges, over hot spots and along volcanic arcs, both in oceanic settings and along continental margins.

Partial melting produces magmas that are more felsic in composition than their source rock. Fractional crystallisation produces magmas that are more felsic in composition than the original magma.

Partial melting and fractional crystallisation processes operating in different circumstances account for the production of different types of igneous rock in different tectonic settings. Peridotite mantle partially melts to produce basaltic magma beneath mid-ocean ridges, ocean islands and volcanic arcs. The partial melting of peridotite mantle and dioritic crust beneath continental arcs, with subsequent mixing of magmas and fractional crystallisation, together produce a range of igneous rocks, including andesites and rhyolites.

Particular associations of igneous rock types in the geological record can help to reveal past plate-tectonic settings.

Your study of this chapter involved: comparing information given in diagrams and graphs, and by rock hand specimens and the minerals in them; describing and interpreting that information; applying it more widely, and summarising your findings. You have also applied concepts about magma-related processes to explain variations in igneous rocks, including their relationships to global tectonic processes.

Chapter 4
Sedimentary rocks – records of changing environments

Igneous processes are mostly hidden at depth, except where magmas erupt on to the Earth's surface. Discovering what the deeper processes might be involves interpreting evidence preserved in old igneous rocks. Yet there are not many fundamental igneous processes that form and transform magmas. By comparison, processes that create accumulations of sediment are extremely varied. Furthermore, since they operate at the surface, you can see and understand some of them in action: sand or pebbles shifting on a beach; boulders and mud accumulating after a landslide; sand, silt and mud moving and settling in a river or estuary (tidal river); sand blowing over dunes in a desert or along the coast and salts accumulating along the coast or in lakes when the conditions are hot and dry. Many, but not all, modern sediments are accumulations of fragmentary material derived from exposed older rocks of all kinds. They result from weathering and erosion, followed by the transport and eventual deposition of the liberated materials (Book 2, Section 5.2.2). Others are made up of minerals that have precipitated from seawater or lake sediments (e.g. evaporites) or the remains of dead animals and plants (e.g. chalk and coal) that once lived on the surface of the Earth or in the oceans. Sedimentary processes span the entire planet, from the highest mountains to the deepest ocean floor, and cover a great range of environments.

Over time, the soft and loose sediments become hardened so that they form cliffs, for example, or can be mined like coal. Their origin as unconsolidated sediments usually shows clearly in their fragmental texture (Figure 3.1c). In moderately extensive exposures, another characteristic feature of sedimentary rocks stands out: usually they show some kind of layering. These layers can have developed on a range of scales, from millimetres to tens and, rarely, hundreds of metres. Some represent marked changes in the style of deposition which may produce sedimentary rocks of different kinds (Figure 2.23), often after a break in deposition. These constitute beds or strata (singular, stratum) which may also vary in thickness. Each bed often consists of several thinner layers of the same kind of rock. Figure 4.1 gives a flavour of the variety of sedimentary layering.

Finally, it should be emphasised that sedimentary rocks are of great economic value. All fossil fuels – natural gas, petroleum and coal – originate in sedimentary rocks; many building stones, such as sandstone and limestone, have a sedimentary origin; and a number of mineral deposits, such as ironstones and salt deposits, were formed in sedimentary environments. Thus sedimentary rocks provide a record for the evolution of life and the environment and are a storehouse of many of the mineral resources that are essential for a modern technological society.

(a)

(b)

(c)

Figure 4.1   Field exposures of different kinds of sedimentary rock (vertical extent of image in parentheses). (a) Beds of rounded cobbles and pebbles, separated by beds of sand (2 m). (b) Horizontal beds of sand, in which minor layering within the beds is at an angle to the horizontal (20 m). (c) Beds of fine-grained silt and mud (40 cm).

From the examples in Figure 4.1 (and others you may have seen), you will be aware that there is a wide diversity of sedimentary rocks. Before discovering what these rocks can reveal about the environments in which they formed, you first need to appreciate what they are made of and understand how to classify them.

4.1   Sedimentary materials

Although some sedimentary rocks form by chemical means (Section 4.3.2), most are made of discrete grains. The sizes of these grains span a vast range, from the finest of wind-blown dusts, measured in micrometres, to house-sized blocks moved by tsunamis, floods, glaciers, or landslides. Different size ranges are given familiar names (Figure 4.2). Muds (including clay- and silt-sized particles) feel smooth when squeezed between fingers and are very fine-grained. Sands feel gritty and are granular. Pebbles are grains larger than peppercorns; cobbles are larger than a tennis ball; and boulders are larger than a football. Granular sediments are classified primarily in terms of the grain-size ranges shown in Figure 4.2.

Few materials on Earth are more familiar or common than soil. So some simple but informative tests on a soil sample will be a good introduction to sediments and sedimentary processes.

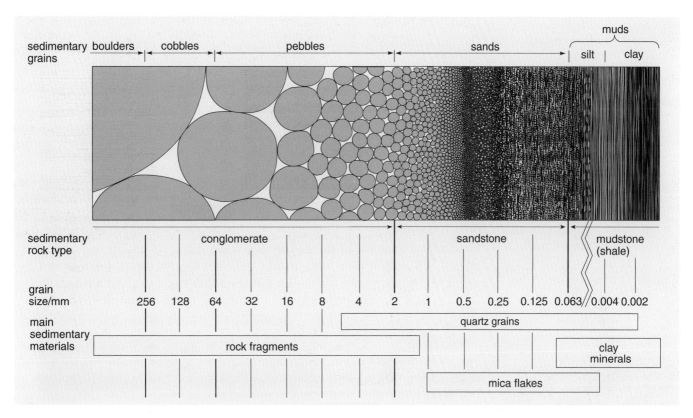

Figure 4.2   Classification of sedimentary materials and corresponding rock types according to grain size. Typical materials found in sediments are also indicated. Note that the scale is not linear; successive divisions represent a halving of grain size, with a break between 0.063 and 0.004 mm.

Activity 4.1   Examining sedimentary materials in soil

We expect this activity will take you approximately 60 minutes (spread over 24 hours).

In this activity you will investigate how a mixture of sedimentary grains in a sample of soil settles in water. You will also investigate differences between the sedimentary grains.

Important safety precautions

Take note of the safety precautions given with Activity 3.2.

In addition, you should note the following precautions which are specific to this activity:

- Soil can contain harmful microorganisms. You are strongly advised to cover any cuts and abrasions with plasters and to wear rubber gloves when collecting and handling the soil. As with any practical work, when you have finished wash your hands using a bactericidal soap if you handled samples without gloves.

Equipment needed

Kit item

Hand lens

Non-kit items

Clear glass jar with a tight-fitting lid

Old spoon and fork

Ruler marked in millimetres

Paper tissues

Sufficient garden soil to fill about one-third of your glass jar

Task 1

First, collect a sample of soil and break it down with a spoon. Remove any large stones (>10 mm), leaves, roots, worms and other organic debris. Fill a jar to a depth of about one-third with soil, topping up with water to about three-quarters full. Let the soil soak and break up for some time (up to an hour if it is dry).

Tighten the lid and shake the jar vigorously for about a minute. Then let the jar stand, and observe what happens for a few minutes.

Record your observations, noting especially what sort of material you see settling in the jar and the condition of the water. Then leave the jar to stand for at least two hours (preferably overnight).

Task 2

After the jar has been standing for at least two hours, make notes on what you can see in the sediment at the bottom. Describe any variations in the grain size (use the terms in Figure 4.2), or in the colour of the sediment. Is the water clear?

Draw a sketch of the jar and its contents, with labels based on your notes.

Task 3

Taking care not to disturb the sediment, pour off the water.

Use a spoon to sample different layers of sediment, from top to bottom – four or five samples will be sufficient. Scrape off the top layer, and retain a small amount of sediment on a tissue. Then excavate another layer and retain some, and so on until you have a sample of material from the very bottom. Be sure to make a note of the order of the samples.

Examine the samples closely with the hand lens, noting the size, shape and colour of the grains present at each level. (*Hint*: for the coarsest grains, it will help to clean any fine-grained material from them by carefully adding water to them in a saucer and swirling it for a few minutes with a fork.)

Now look at the comments on this activity at the end of this book.

Activity 4.1 showed that you can distinguish individual sediment grains in terms of three features: shape, size and mineral composition. The same three features distinguish the grains in sedimentary rocks.

- *Grain shape:* shape can vary from very angular to well-rounded (you will learn more about this in Activity 4.2). A hand lens reveals the shape of sedimentary grains of sand-size or larger. A high-powered microscope can reveal the shapes of finer grains.

- *Grain size:* **mudstones** and **sandstones** are named according to their grain sizes (Figure 4.2). A rock containing grains larger than 2 mm is a **conglomerate** if the grains are well-rounded, but a **breccia** if the grains are angular; the reason for this difference will become clear later.

- *Composition:* any material that can survive weathering, erosion, transport and accumulation – rocks, minerals and the hard parts of organisms – may become a sedimentary grain. Pebbles and larger grains are usually made of rock fragments. Sand grains are mostly composed of minerals (especially quartz) or the broken shells of organisms. Muds contain very fine grains, especially clay minerals, but also silt (mostly fine quartz) and organic matter. However, many minerals found in igneous rocks, such as olivine, pyroxene and feldspars, occur only rarely in sediments; you will see why in Section 4.2.1.

The processes that form and shape grains operate at the Earth's surface and so can be observed directly. The character of sedimentary grains therefore conveys information about the origins of the sedimentary rocks that contain them. Added to that is the form of the layers in which they are deposited (Section 4.3).

4.2   Sedimentary processes

In the upper part of the rock cycle, weathering and erosion break down all kinds of existing rocks, including older sedimentary rocks (Figure 4.3). These processes liberate fragmentary material, which is transported until it settles out under gravity and is deposited as sedimentary layers.

Most sediment grains are transported across the land surface by flowing water, strong winds and glaciers (Book 2, Section 5.2.2). Once sediment reaches the sea, shoreline wave motion and tidal currents carry materials, as do gravity-driven flows of sediment – water slurries where seabed slopes are steep. Some organisms create sediment particles by secreting hard parts from ions dissolved in water (e.g. the shells on a beach). Intact or as broken fragments, such organic material may mix with inorganic grains in a sediment. Where they are the only kind of grain, such organically derived grains are buried and form limestones (Section 4.3.3). There are also sediments which are not fragmental, having formed directly from dissolved ions by chemical means (Section 4.3.2).

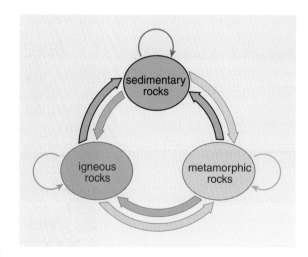

Figure 4.3   Formation of sedimentary rocks in the rock cycle. The three blue arrows indicate the routes through which sedimentary rocks can be formed from any kind of rock by weathering, erosion, transportation and deposition.

4.2.1   Surface rocks and the weather

Existing rocks break down to yield fragments that end up in sediments through several weathering processes, which can involve both physical and chemical processes. Rocks disintegrate and decompose when they are exposed to heat and cold, rain and surface water, chemicals exuded by plant roots, and even an atmospheric gas – carbon dioxide – dissolved in water.

Physical weathering directly breaks rocks into fragments but geological processes that affected solid rock far beneath the surface can also help. When rocks are buried or formed at depth, pressure tends to compress them – not much, but enough to cause them to crack when the pressure is released. This is demonstrated in a spectacular and dangerous fashion in deep mines. In active mine workings the newly exposed rock sometimes explodes spontaneously in a rock burst. Erosion and uplift very slowly shift rocks that were once deeply buried to the surface, so their compression is released imperceptibly. Yet that still produces cracks, called **joints**, which you will see in one form or another in any exposure of solid rock. Joints allow water to penetrate deeply into exposed rock.

■ What happens if water in a crack freezes?

☐ When water solidifies, it expands (by about 9%). Ice forming in cracks and joints therefore exerts a force tending to wedge the rock apart.

A burst water pipe during cold weather makes us uncomfortably aware of the magnitude of that force. It is also responsible for breaking up road surfaces in winter. Figure 4.4 shows the result of this simple process on jointed rock exposed on a mountain top; this is the result of year-in year-out, day-and-night freezing and thawing, possibly over several thousand years.

Figure 4.4 Slabs of rock on a mountain top broken apart by frost action. Note the skyline, which shows how the accentuation of vertical joints by ice forming in them produces the typical jaggedness of cold mountainous areas – the slabs in the foreground have toppled from the area of exposed rock. (The person just above the patch of snow on the left shows the scale.)

■ Which other physical process might result in expansion and contraction?

☐ When solids are heated they expand slightly and they contract as the temperature falls.

Heating and cooling also produces forces in rock, directly at the surface. Solar radiation can heat rock to uncomfortable temperatures, even in climatically frigid areas such as Antarctica. Radiation emission from the surface at night cools the rock. So, on a 24-hour basis, thermal expansion and contraction continually stress any rock exposed at the surface. Each kind of mineral responds differently to heating and cooling. So, differential forces act at boundaries between different minerals, particularly in coarse-grained rocks. Eventually the forces begin to split the minerals from one another, allowing water to seep along the grain boundaries. Freezing and thawing then liberates grains of each of them.

■ Which property of minerals is likely to assist breakage?

☐ Some minerals have one or more cleavage planes; the planes of weakness within their crystal structure that allow them to break apart more easily.

Easily cleaved minerals, such as mica, feldspar and calcite, are more susceptible to breakage by physical weathering processes than quartz, which has no cleavage planes.

Physical weathering, by breaking rocks into fragments, increases the exposed surface area of different minerals so that they become more susceptible to chemical attack. Physical weathering accelerates **chemical weathering** which is dominated by two processes: the action of acids and oxidation, often operating together. Rainwater is slightly acidic, because it dissolves carbon dioxide:

$$H_2O(l) + CO_2(aq) = H^+(aq) + HCO_3^-(aq)$$
$$\text{rainwater} \qquad \text{acidic solution} \tag{4.1}$$

The pH (Book 4, Chapter 11) of rainwater is not particularly low (5.2–6.5) but that is sufficient to attack many minerals chemically. Stronger acids are produced by vegetation, particularly when it decays in the soils of the humid tropics. However, there is another potent and widespread source of hydrogen ions. Crustal rocks contain on average about 0.04% sulfur. That is not very much but, since sulfur cannot enter silicates, it forms sulfide minerals in its own right; the most common being iron sulfide or pyrite (FeS_2) (you can view this in the computer-based resource *Minerals Gallery*). Pyrite is present in many rocks but usually in tiny amounts. However, its effect on chemical weathering can be dramatic because it readily oxidises when exposed to water containing dissolved oxygen to produce sulfuric acid:

$$2FeS_2(s) + 7O_2(aq) + 2H_2O(l) = 2Fe^{2+}(aq) + 4H^+(aq) + 4SO_4^{2-}(aq)$$
$$\text{pyrite} \quad \text{oxygen} \quad \text{water} \quad \text{iron ions} \qquad \text{sulfuric acid} \tag{4.2}$$

The reaction is exothermic (Book 4, Section 9.2) and proceeds spontaneously when pyrite is exposed to oxygen. Once they reach the surface, rocks containing pyrite and those nearby are exposed to highly acidic conditions because of this vigorous reaction.

The most 'pristine' minerals to encounter surface conditions are the silicates in igneous rocks. Some are more prone to chemical attack by hydrogen ions than others. Quartz resists because of its strong framework structure (Book 4, Chapter 4). Olivine and pyroxene have structures containing metal atoms bonded weakly to their isolated and chained silicate tetrahedra (Section 3.1) and are particularly susceptible to chemical weathering. Feldspars and micas fall somewhere in between. They are less stable than quartz because a variety of metal atoms weakly connect the silicate tetrahedra in their framework and sheet structures respectively but they are more resistant than mafic minerals.

Igneous minerals are stable when igneous rocks crystallise at very high temperatures (Chapter 3), and most of them are anhydrous, i.e. contain neither water nor hydroxyl ions. When they meet the cool, wet, acidic conditions of the Earth's surface, all except quartz are unstable and eventually succumb to chemical attack. During weathering, hydrogen ions help to break free their loosely bonded metal atoms. When this happens their structures collapse to form clay minerals, which are hydrated aluminosilicates (e.g. kaolinite or 'china clay' – $Al_4Si_4O_{10}(OH)_8$) with a mica-like, platy structure that is stable under acid conditions. A good example is the breakdown of alkali feldspar ((K,Na) $AlSi_3O_8$) by acidic water:

$$\text{alkali feldspar(s)} + H_2O(l) + H^+(aq) = \text{kaolinite clay(s)} + Na^+(aq) + K^+(aq) + SiO_2(aq) \quad (4.3)$$
$$\text{acidic rainwater} \qquad\qquad\qquad \text{soluble ions} \qquad \text{silica}$$

The end products are the hydrous clay mineral kaolinite, along with K^+ and Na^+ ions and SiO_2 dissolved in water. Much the same happens to olivine and pyroxene, plagioclase feldspar and micas. The products are various clay minerals and dissolved metal ions, according to the composition of the original igneous mineral.

■ Alkali feldspar is a major constituent of granite, along with quartz and mica. If chemical weathering of granite proceeds to completion, what are the solids that remain?

☐ Just quartz and clays.

The effects of climate on weathering are illustrated in Figure 4.5. Figure 4.5a clearly shows interlocking, random crystals of different minerals that are fresh and shiny, whereas image 4.5b, although showing signs of a typical igneous texture, is a crumbly reddish material.

(a)

(b)

Figure 4.5 Effects of climate on the chemical weathering of granite: (a) an exposure in cool, wet southwestern England (the camera lens cap is about 70 mm across); (b) an exposure in a hot, humid part of Africa (the shiny coin is about 20 mm across).

■ How might high rainfall and high temperatures influence chemical weathering reactions such as Equation 4.3?

☐ Intense tropical rainfall provides copious amounts of acidic water. High temperature encourages abundant vegetation, whose rapid decomposition produces more acidity, and heat speeds up chemical reactions (Book 4, Chapter 10).

When quartz-free igneous rocks – that is, most intermediate and all mafic varieties (Figure 4.5) – are completely weathered in this way, almost the only solids left are clays. Chemical weathering is more rapid in warm, wet, tropical climates than in more temperate ones, and extremely slow to non-existent in cold climates. Indeed, rock can be weathered to depths of tens of metres in tropical climates. Hence, exposed rocks in the cool climate of northern Europe are often quite fresh (Figure 4.5a). In contrast, rock exposures in the humid tropics are often almost completely weathered (Figure 4.5b).

The end products of the weathering of igneous rocks are:

• physically broken rocks and chemically stable minerals, mainly quartz

• newly formed clay minerals which are stable at the surface

• soluble ions.

Note that, although quartz is the most stable common mineral, small amounts of silica (SiO_2) do enter solution as a result of chemical weathering of other minerals (Equation 4.3).

This weathered mixture is more easily picked up by an agent of transportation than simply cracked, fresh rocks. Its exposure to flowing water, wind or, in frigid conditions, a glacier, leads to mechanical removal or **erosion**. Once charged with moving debris, each transporting agent can become a means of eroding unweathered rock. Pebbles carried in rivers, sand grains carried by strong winds and fragments jutting from the base of a moving glacier can pound, blast and scrape more debris to wear away the surfaces over which they pass. The transported fragments are also broken down as they move along, to become smaller and more rounded.

Rates of erosion vary immensely, partly depending on topography because gravity is the dominant force in water and glacial erosion. Erosion can slowly wear away rocks over long periods of time, or it may be associated with sudden, catastrophic events. You may have witnessed the scouring of a river bank during a flood, the collapse of a sea cliff by storm-wave action, or rock debris sliding down a steep slope after heavy rain.

4.2.2   Sediment transport

Whether sedimentary grains can be transported or not depends partly on the energy supplied by the transporting medium so that grains can be moved.

■ What form of energy is this and on which properties of the transporting medium does it depend?

☐ It is energy due to movement, or kinetic energy (E_k) (Book 3, Chapter 3):

$$E_k = \tfrac{1}{2}mv^2 \tag{4.4}$$

Kinetic energy varies with the speed of movement (v) and the mass (m) and, therefore, the *density* of the transporting medium.

A grain's resistance to motion, which varies with its shape, size and density, also governs transportation. The video sequence *A Story in Sand* (Activity 4.2) shows what happens when sediment, containing a range of grain sizes, is dropped into flowing water. The larger grains settle to the stream bed, their mass being too great for them to be transported. Under the influence of the water current, smaller grains roll or bounce along the stream bed, and very small grains are picked up and carried along in suspension.

Activity 4.2   Sedimentary grains, transport and sorting – a story in sand

We expect this activity will take you approximately 60 minutes.

Important safety precautions

Take note of the safety precautions given with Activity 3.2.

Equipment needed

Kit items

Rock Specimen 2

Hand lens

Non-kit item

Large steel nail

First, watch the video sequence *A Story in Sand*. It shows how physical and chemical weathering of granite, in a humid climate, produces grains available for transport by water and wind; and the types of sediment that these processes deposit. Make notes based on the questions in Task 1.

The rest of the activity involves making deductions about the origins of sediments and sedimentary rocks (including the sandstone sample from your Practical Kit) from simple observations and measurements.

Task 1

(a) Which processes break down exposed rocks to produce sediment grains?

(b) What are the three ways in which grains move downstream in flowing water?

(c) How do typical river sediments differ from typical beach sediments?

(d) How do the shape and surface texture of wind-blown grains differ from grains deposited by water?

Task 2

Draw a histogram (as demonstrated in *A Story in Sand*) to describe the grain-size distribution of a sample of sand. (The sieving data for this sediment are given in Table 4.1.)

First, calculate the total mass of sediment, and then express the mass retained by each sieve as a proportion of the total mass, in per cent (enter your results in Table 4.1).

Table 4.1 Grain-size data from a sieving experiment with a sand sample.

Sieve size/mm	Mass in sieve/g	Proportion of total mass/%
4	1.0	2.1
2	1.4	2.9%
1	4.8	10.1
0.5	7.1	14.9
0.25	14.5	30.4
0.12	9.4	19.7
0.06	7.3	15.3
pan	2.2	4.6
Total	47.7	100

On Figure 4.6 plot a histogram showing the grain-size distribution of this sample of sand, using the mass percentages that you entered in Table 4.1. The height of each vertical bar on the histogram should correspond to the mass percentage in a particular sieve. By convention, each bar should be drawn to the left of the sieve size it represents. For example, the bar for the 0.5 mm sieve should be drawn between 0.5 mm and 1 mm. This is because the 0.5 mm sieve retains all grains with sizes between 0.5 mm and 1 mm (the size of the grains that just pass through the next largest sieve).

Is the sediment sample well-sorted or poorly sorted?

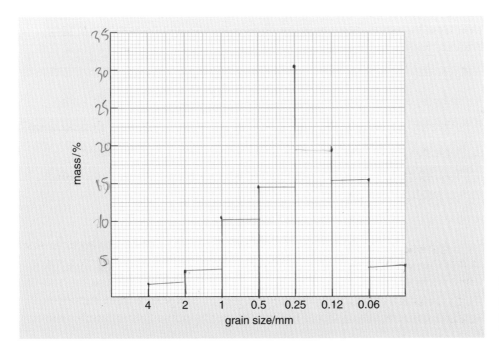

Figure 4.6 Graph paper for plotting a histogram of the sieving experiment data in Table 4.1.

Task 3

Histograms represent visually the grain-size distribution in a sediment. Different environments of deposition result in different forms of distribution; in the video sequence you saw histograms of desert sand and beach sand.

(a) From your notes on the video, suggest which histogram in Figure 4.7a corresponds to the grain-size distributions for river, beach and desert dune sands, and explain why.

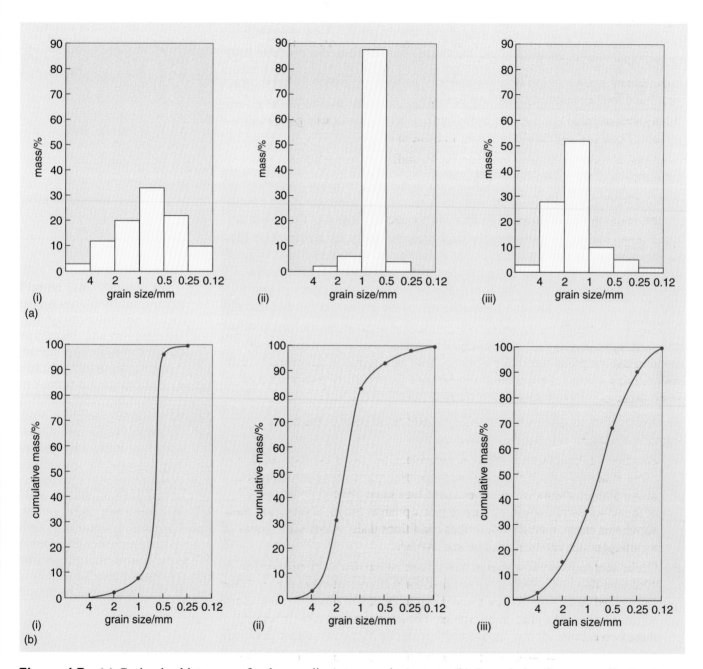

Figure 4.7   (a) Grain-size histograms for three sedimentary environments. (b) Cumulative frequency distribution diagrams, featuring equivalent sediment grain-size distributions to those in part (a). Note that grain sizes in the histograms decrease from left to right.

Cumulative frequency distribution diagrams (as you saw in *A Story in Sand*) are an alternative means of representing sediment grain-size data.

(b) Which cumulative frequency distribution diagram in Figure 4.7b matches which histogram in Figure 4.7a?

Task 4

The video sequence showed sand grains from a beach and from a desert.

Try to scrape some grains from the sandstone sample (Specimen 2), first with a fingernail, then using a steel nail.

How difficult is it to remove grains from the sandstone compared with the igneous samples (Activity 3.2)? Why do you think that is?

Prise several grains onto millimetre-squared graph paper (Figure 4.6), and use your hand lens to examine them.

What kinds of grain can you see, and roughly what is the range of grain sizes present? (You will use this information in Section 4.2.3.)

Now look at the rock through your hand lens, and describe the shape and the arrangement of the grains.

What medium would have transported them?

Place a few drops of water on the surface of the rock.

What happens to them, and what does that suggest about the rock? (Make a note for use in Section 4.4.)

Now look at the comments on this activity at the end of this book.

Activity 4.2 showed that the ability of wind or flowing water to pick up, transport and deposit sediment grains depends largely on both the speed of the flowing medium and the grain size of the material. The behaviour of different grain sizes with varying speed of flow is shown in Figure 4.8. This graph is explained in some detail in the video sequence *A Story in Sand*.

The main points to appreciate from the blue part (lower part of the figure) of Figure 4.8 relating to *water* transportation are:

- Flowing water picks up grains of a particular size only if the speed of flow exceeds that of the upper curve. The slope of the curve for grain diameters above 500 μm shows that the speed (and thus kinetic energy, Equation 4.4) of the water current must increase to pick up larger grains. The erosion zone above this curve, therefore, describes conditions under which static grains of a particular size can be picked up and moved.

- Grains that have already been picked up can continue to be transported at speeds of flow lower than those required for pick-up (the upper curve). If the flow speed of a particular grain size drops to the lower curve, the flow can no longer transport the grain and it settles. The transportation zone is between these two curves.

- Grains do not move at all at flow speeds below the lower curve. Material of a particular grain size, transported at higher speeds of flow, is deposited when the flow speed drops to the lower curve – this defines the deposition zone.

Figure 4.8 The behaviour of different-sized sediment grains at varying speeds of flow for wind and water. In both cases, the boundaries of the erosion zone, the transportation zone and the deposition zone (see text) were derived experimentally under controlled conditions of flow using sediment grains of uniform density. Note that the scales on the axes are not linear: on the horizontal axis, each division corresponds to a doubling of grain size; on the vertical axis, each major division corresponds to a factor of ten increase in the speed of current. These forms of scaling allow a wide range of flow rates and grain sizes to be shown.

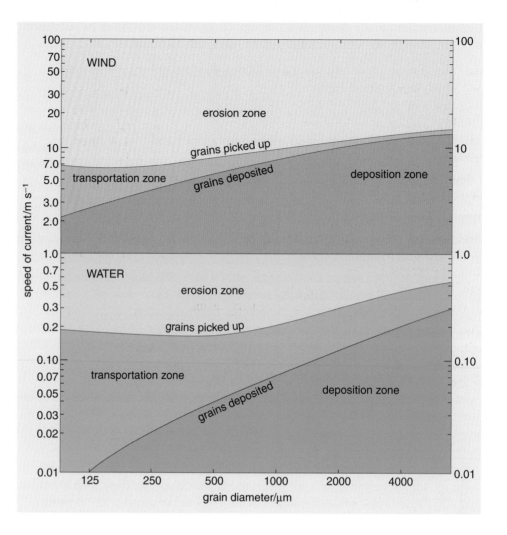

■ From Figure 4.8, at what speed of water current would 1 mm diameter sand grains be picked up and at what speed would they be deposited?

☐ A flow of more than 0.2 m s^{-1} would be required to pick up 1 mm (i.e. 1000 μm) sand grains; but they would not be deposited until the flow speed had dropped to about 0.07 m s^{-1}.

While sedimentary grains are being transported in water they are exposed to both physical abrasion and chemical attack. The chemical decomposition of rock fragments during transport is much the same as in chemical weathering (Section 4.2.1). Reactive minerals (e.g. alkali feldspars) form clay minerals and dissolved ions (Equation 4.3), while resistant quartz remains intact to form individual grains. Inevitably, transported grains collide with each other and the stream bed. The viscosity of water cushions the impacts, so rock fragments tend to become rounded by abrasion, rather than broken by impact. The larger and more massive the grains, the more kinetic energy they have. Consequently, large grains tend to become rounded more readily than smaller ones. You could verify this by examining pebbles and sand in a river bed or on a beach.

4.2.3   Sediment deposition

Figure 4.8 and Activity 4.2 showed you that sedimentary material is deposited when transporting currents slow down sufficiently. Where does this usually occur? In rivers, the downhill movement of water and its sedimentary load involves their gravitational energy being transformed into kinetic energy (Book 3, Section 5.2). On steep slopes, where flow rates are high – a high-energy environment – only coarse material is deposited. As the slope decreases, the flow speed lessens, so that progressively finer grains are deposited in environments which have decreasing energy. Eventually, only very fine grains are left to be deposited in low-energy environments.

Near the source of a river system, the deposits are transient; erosion will eventually remove them. In contrast, thick successions of sediment can accumulate and remain in lowland areas or in the sea. This is because in these areas the crust subsides, because of either tectonic activity, or through the gradual subsidence of the crust beneath the weight of accumulated sediment. These areas of sediment accumulation form sedimentary basins.

The 'degree of sorting' can be used to describe and characterise certain types of sediment, as in the video sequence *A Story in Sand*. It describes the extent to which the grains deposited are of a similar size. Thus a well-sorted deposit (Figure 4.9a) contains a narrow range of grain sizes, whereas a poorly sorted

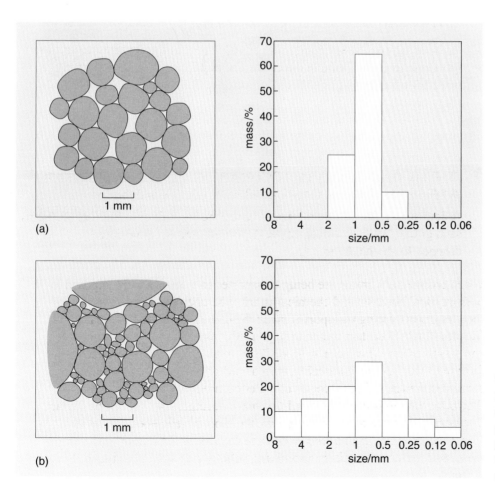

Figure 4.9   Schematic representation of (a) well-sorted and (b) poorly sorted sediment grains with histograms of their grain-size distributions. Note that grain sizes in the histograms decrease from left to right.

deposit contains a wide range of grain sizes (Figure 4.9b); the corresponding, histograms of well- and poorly sorted sediments are also given. Figure 4.8 helps explain why such sorting occurs. The lower curve gives the size of grains deposited at a particular speed of water flow. The curve rises steadily, so there is a direct link between the speed of the current and the size of grains deposited; the result of this is sediment sorting.

What might produce good sorting? According to Figure 4.8, a rapidly flowing current can pick up and carry a range of grain sizes. If the current gradually slows, all the picked-up grains continue to be transported until a speed is reached when the coarsest material is deposited. Finer material is still carried onward. So, when speeds of flow drop slightly – because either slopes flatten or there is a reduction in the volume of flow – a narrow range of grain sizes is deposited. If the speed of flow continues to decrease steadily, grains of successively smaller size are deposited, but grains deposited at one place at a particular time will have a narrow size range and be well-sorted. In contrast, if a rapid flow subsides abruptly, a wide range of grain sizes are deposited all at once, creating a poorly sorted sediment. Thus, the measured degree of sorting of a sediment gives information about the way it formed, especially about the conditions of flow that transported and deposited it.

■ Grains from the Practical Kit sandstone vary in size. Is it a well-sorted or a poorly sorted sandstone? What does that indicate about the conditions of deposition?

☐ In most samples, 0.5–1 mm grains are common, but grain size ranges from <0.1 mm to about 2 mm in diameter. The sandstone is only moderately well-sorted and must have been deposited under somewhat variable flow conditions.

■ A rapidly flowing river carrying a range of sediment grain sizes enters the sea. What happens to the sediment?

☐ The flow speed suddenly slows. As in Activity 4.1, a range of grain sizes begins to settle at once. Coarse grains settle out first and then progressively finer material builds up on top. In still water, all the grains eventually settle.

A rock bed produced in this way will look rather like the sediment that accumulated after you stopped shaking the jar in Activity 4.1. The grain size varied with height but, at any particular level in the jar, the sediment was fairly well-sorted. The gradual decrease in grain size from the bottom to the top of the bed is called **graded bedding** (Figure 4.10). How does this 'grading' of grains happen?

The answer comes from Book 2 (Section 14.1). Two forces affect every grain: one from gravity acting downwards; the other from the resistance of the water (its viscosity) acts upwards. The smaller the grain, the greater this resistance is, and the result is that smaller grains fall more slowly than larger grains. The difference is profound over the natural size range of sedimentary grains. That is why mud-sized sediment remains suspended in stagnant water, even after several days.

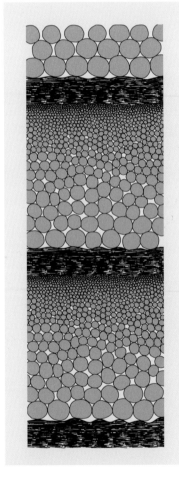

Figure 4.10   Graded beds resulting from deposition as flow speeds repeatedly decline. Successive graded beds are often separated by an eroded surface, reflecting the increase in flow that precedes deposition of the next graded bed.

The upwardly decreasing grain size in graded bedding can help geologists work out the time order in which beds were deposited. In Section 5.2 you will see how such observations reveal that rock strata are sometimes completely overturned by tectonic activity.

Question 4.1

How does weathering in hot, humid climates differ from that in cold, wet climates? What kind of weathering would you expect on the Moon?

Question 4.2

How does weathering affect granite? Explain the effects of physical and chemical weathering on the main minerals of granite (Specimen 6 in the Practical Kit), and write down the main products of weathering.

Breaks down to Quartz, Clay minerals & ions.

4.3   Sedimentary deposits as environmental indicators

As well as the movement of fluids, many other influences, such as climate, biological activity and topography, create a huge diversity of depositional environments. Environments dominated by water, wind and ice each deposit distinct types of sediment, but conditions associated with water are the most diverse. They include rivers and lakes; beaches and deltas; shallow seas and the deep ocean floor. Studying sediments being deposited today plays a crucial part in recognising and making deductions about their ancient equivalents in the rock record – thus providing the keys to understanding past environments.

This section considers three very different sedimentary environments to illustrate the most important concepts used in understanding sedimentary rocks. They involve the transportation of fragmentary material by wind; the crystallisation of salts from water; and the extraction of soluble material from seawater by marine organisms.

4.3.1   Desert sands

By definition, a desert is an environment in which very little lives, because it is a dry, barren wilderness (which could be hot or cold). The most familiar deserts are those where winds create storms of sand and dust, and form sand dunes.

■   What implications does the lack of water have for weathering and for erosion in such a desert?

☐   Lack of water inhibits chemical weathering and the release of soluble ions (nutrients), and the formation of clay minerals (vital components of fertile soils). Physical processes dominate desert weathering. With sparse vegetation there are few roots to bind together fragments of rocks and minerals and little shelter by leaf and branch cover from transporting agencies, so as to resist erosion.

Physical weathering in hot deserts is dominated by extreme temperature changes that cause expansion and contraction of rock surfaces and individual mineral grains. Daytime solar radiation may heat rock surfaces to over 80 °C. Lack of night-time cloud cover allows temperatures to plummet, often to well below 0 °C. Layers of rock flake off, and they break down to particles rich in one mineral or another. There is evidence that dew, which can penetrate grain boundaries, speeds up this physical weathering.

Rock and mineral fragments exposed in deserts are very prone to being eroded and transported by wind, an additional factor being their dryness. Moist material is held together by pore water, as you will have seen in garden soil after rain, or in beach sand when the tide is going out. After heavy rain from rare storms, water runs off the desert land surface rapidly to cause flash floods, which have intense erosive power. Such floods easily erode and transport desert sediment to flat ground, in isolated but spectacular episodes. Strong winds are much more frequent. Although air is 1000 times less dense than water, winds can move large quantities of loose, dry sand grains from the sediments occasionally shifted by flash floods.

Once picked up, dust grains (less than 0.01 mm in diameter) can be carried by a light wind, but it takes a brisk wind to carry sand grains, and pebbles are rarely moved even by very high winds. Dust picked up in suspension may be transported many thousands of kilometres.

Wind transports grains, as water does, in three ways (Figure 4.11): suspended in the air; by rolling surface grains along; and by bouncing so that sand grains, lifted and propelled by the wind, then fall and hit other grains, triggering them to bounce too (you saw this in the video sequence *A Story in Sand*). In windy conditions, the last process may lift sand grains as high as 2 m above the ground, producing a sand blast capable of wearing away both other grains and rock surfaces. It also stings if you walk with bare legs across a dry sandy beach on a very windy day.

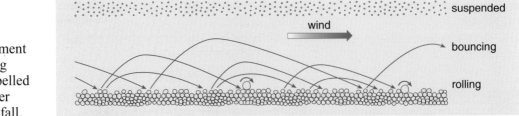

Figure 4.11   The movement of sand by wind. Bouncing often involves grains propelled by the wind knocking other grains into the air as they fall.

Air is far less viscous than water, so does little to cushion impacts between wind-blown grains. Repeated impacts produce well-rounded grains with finely pitted surfaces – often described as a 'frosted' appearance – a particular characteristic of desert sands (as you saw in the video sequence *A Story in Sand*). In contrast, sand grains worn down in water are never so well rounded and they look glassier; they are not pitted because of cushioning by the water around them. Desert sands consist mainly of quartz, the most resistant of the common minerals. Lacking cleavage, quartz fragments resist being smashed by impacts, whereas cleaved minerals easily split into increasingly fine particles. Sand grains in deserts are generally too large to be carried away in suspension but are small enough to be transported by high winds through bouncing or rolling.

■   Would you expect sand from a desert dune to be well or poorly sorted?

☐   It will probably have a fairly narrow range of grain size. Small grains are
carried far away in suspension, while large grains are left behind, even if
they do roll a little. Only the narrow range of grain sizes that can bounce
(Figure 4.8 and 4.11) contribute to a dune, so it will be well-sorted.

Sedimentary rocks in the geological record that contain well-sorted, well-rounded
and frosted grains of quartz sand are most likely to have formed under desert
conditions. However, these characteristics are not sufficient to *prove* deposition
by wind, because desert sand grains could be picked up by flowing water and
redeposited. Consequently, additional indicators are needed to confirm deposition
by wind under arid conditions.

Wherever there is abundant dry sand that wind can move, and if strong winds
blow frequently, the moving sand builds up wave-like features on a range
of scales from small ripples (tens of centimetres) to dunes up to 100 m high
(Figure 4.12a and 4.12b). Figure 4.12c shows how a simple sand wave develops

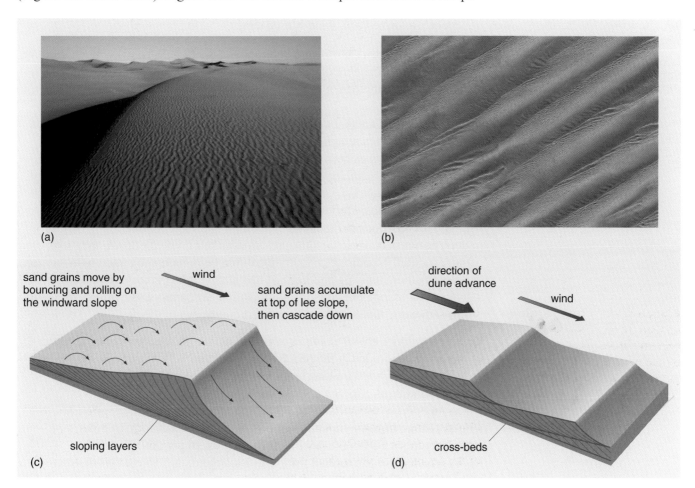

Figure 4.12   Wind-blown sand: (a) ripples on dunes in Death Valley, California, USA. The foreground is about
5 m across; (b) dunes of several scales superimposed on giant linear dunes in the Empty Quarter of Saudi Arabia,
viewed from satellite. The image is 15 km across. (c) Movement of a sand wave and the formation of sloping
layers of sand. (d) Formation of a series of cross-bedded layers when a wave is overridden by another. Note that the
main beds are nearly horizontal. The inclination of the layers between them does not result from tilting but from
deposition on a slope. (Part (b), an image from the *Quickbird* satellite, courtesy of DigitalGlobe.)

on an uneven surface. On the slope facing the wind, grains shift to the wave crest, beyond which they build up in the sheltered conditions of the wave's lee side. Periodically, the accumulation of grains collapses so that sand slides down the lee side of the feature, to form sloping layers. Whenever the wind blows strongly, more sand is shifted from the windward side of the wave and over its crest, to be added layer by layer to the lee side. In this way, the wave itself advances slowly downwind.

Before long, another sand wave advances to ride up the windward side (Figure 4.12b). It may partially erode a previous series of layers. Eventually, a series of beds, each made up of dipping layers, becomes preserved. This creates a sedimentary structure known as **cross-bedding**, whose scale can range from centimetres in migrating ripples, to tens of metres in the case of dunes (Figure 4.12d). Water currents also produce moving sand waves, but the resulting cross-bedding is usually on a smaller scale, with cross-bedding that dips at significantly shallower angles than in desert dunes.

■ Re-examine Figure 4.1, and decide which image is of a sedimentary rock that probably formed as a wind-blown dune.

☐ Figure 4.1b shows horizontal beds about 1 m thick, each made up of dipping layers a few centimetres thick. This cross-bedding is typical of sedimentation in wind-blown dunes.

Another feature of ancient desert deposits is their colour. The lack of vegetation and decaying organic material in deserts, combined with their dryness, results in air filling the spaces between sand grains. As a result, desert sediments experience highly *oxidising* conditions (Book 4, Chapter 8). The iron content of ferromagnesian minerals (i.e. those containing iron and magnesium) is partly in the form of Fe^{2+} ions. During chemical weathering these ions may enter aqueous solution, if conditions are reducing. Although chemical weathering is very slow in deserts, when unstable ferromagnesian minerals do break down, their iron content is rapidly oxidised to highly insoluble Fe^{3+}. Its combination with oxygen to form small amounts of fine-grained hematite (Fe_2O_3) gives desert sand grains a distinct red-orange hue. It is the combination of redness and evidence of wind-blown sediments that truly signifies desert conditions in the past.

Desert sandstones are an example of **red-beds**, which are important indicators of oxidising conditions in the past (Book 2, Section 7.2). Waterlogging in sediments deposited on land (called terrestrial sediments) under humid climatic conditions creates *reducing* conditions. Many such sediments containing preserved, unoxidised organic matter maintain reducing conditions long after their deposition. Oxidised Fe^{3+} minerals do not form in them. Instead, reduced Fe^{2+} commonly forms fine-grained iron sulfide (pyrite, Fe_2S), which gives the rocks a grey to black appearance. (Note that modern weathering of such rocks in humid conditions results in the oxidation of pyrite to form Fe^{3+} hydroxides, giving their exposed *surfaces* a yellow-brown to orange colour.)

As you saw in Section 2.5 vegetation appeared on the land surface only after about 430 Ma ago, and only became prominent during the Lower Carboniferous (350 Ma). Organic matter was rarely, if ever, preserved in earlier terrestrial sediments, irrespective of the climate in which they formed. So, many terrestrial sandstones older than 430 Ma were easily oxidised to form red-beds; thus a red sediment is *not* a universal indicator of desert deposition. The environment under which red-beds formed has to be deduced from the kinds of sedimentary structures in them.

4.3.2 Evaporites – crystalline sediments

The soluble ions released by chemical weathering are predominantly Na^+, K^+, Ca^{2+}, Mg^{2+} and HCO_3^- (Equation 4.1). They are transported at very low concentrations in rivers (freshwater) eventually to reach the sea. In seawater, such dissolved materials amount to about 3.5% by mass, forming a salty solution in which Na^+, Mg^{2+}, SO_4^{2-} and Cl^- ions are the most important (Table 4.2). You might expect that the continuous addition of soluble material to the oceans would lead to a steady increase in the concentrations of salts in seawater over time, but this is not the case. In fact, a more-or-less steady state is maintained, and concentrations are constrained by natural processes.

Table 4.2 Typical concentrations of dissolved ions in natural waters.

Dissolved ion	Concentration in river water/mg l^{-1}	Concentration in seawater/mg l^{-1}
Na^+	7	10 770
K^+	2	380
Ca^{2+}	15	410
Mg^{2+}	4	1290
HCO_3^-	56	140
SO_4^{2-}	11	2650
Cl^-	18	19 500

Note: concentrations in river water are extremely variable.

Rates of evaporation in hot climates are high, especially from bodies of shallow water, which heat up quickly. Evaporation increases the concentration of salts in aqueous solution, until the water becomes *saturated* (Book 4, Chapter 11) and can hold no more dissolved salts in solution. Further evaporation causes dissolved salts to crystallise, forming **evaporite** deposits. These are mined for raw materials used in the chemical industry, and for winter road treatment in the case of common salt. These salts include halite (NaCl or 'rock salt'), and the less soluble salt gypsum ($CaSO_4.2H_2O$), which is used to make plaster, and potassium salts which are vital in fertilisers. (The $.2H_2O$ in its formula signifies that gypsum contains water in its structure.) Such deposits form in several different environments, including the following:

- Enclosed inland basins in arid regions into which rivers flow intermittently, such as the Great Salt Lake, Utah, USA (Figure 4.13a). The trapped water evaporates and the dissolved salts eventually crystallise to form salt flats.

- Shallow coastal lagoons in hot areas, where evaporation is high and salts crystallise (Figure 4.13b). Restricted access to the open sea allows the intermittent inflow of seawater to replenish the supply of salts.

- Coastal mudflats along arid shorelines, such as the Persian Gulf, where water evaporates from tidally exposed mud, in which salts crystallise as it dries out. Seawater replenishes the supply of salty water by seepage into the muds.

(a)

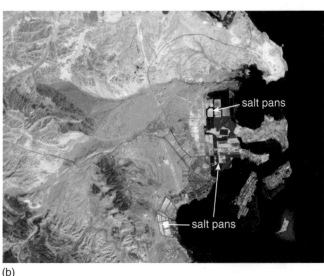
(b)

Figure 4.13   Products of natural evaporation. (a) The salt flats of the Great Salt Lake, Utah, USA. (b) By creating artificial lagoons on arid coasts, seawater can be evaporated to produce a variety of salts commercially. This is a view from space of such salt pans on the Red Sea coast of Eritrea, northeast Africa.

Evaporation forms sedimentary rocks which are not fragmentary but are made of intergrown crystals; an exception to the generalisation that sedimentary textures are fragmental. However, evaporites are usually distinguishable as sedimentary deposits by their layering, and are often associated with red-beds. Rock salt and gypsum deposits are also key indicators of arid climatic conditions in the geological record.

4.3.3   Limestones

Many groups of marine organisms take up calcium (Ca^{2+}) and hydrogen carbonate (HCO_3^-) ions dissolved in seawater to produce shells or skeletons composed of calcium carbonate (calcite). When these organisms die, both whole and broken hard parts accumulate on the sea floor. When sufficiently abundant they form **limestone** deposits containing fragments that are clearly organic in origin (see Practical Kit, Specimen 3). Animal groups such as bivalves, brachiopods, echinoids, corals and foraminifera are often found in limestones.

Even marine phytoplankton produce calcium carbonate; for example, the calcite plates of tiny coccolithophores (Book 1, Figure 7.5a) which form the bulk of the Cretaceous Chalk deposits of western Europe.

Clay and silt suspended in seawater inhibit the growth of many carbonate-producing organisms, so limestones tend to indicate deposition in clear water, away from supplies of land-derived sediment. The most productive marine environments for limestone formation today are shallow, tropical or subtropical seas, between about 30° N and 30° S of the Equator. There, reef-building organisms such as corals are common. By analogy, many ancient limestones were formed in warm, tropical seas that were clear and shallow.

Many animals that secrete hard parts made of calcite are subject to predation, despite their defences. Predators digest the soft parts but excrete calcite as ground-up fragments and mud. This debris also contributes to the formation of limestone, as does fine carbonate material produced by the erosive action of waves and currents on dead remains.

■ Imagine a bed of limestone formed almost completely of fine-grained calcium carbonate, which is now a hard rock. What inference can you make about the strength of currents that were active when the bed was deposited and about the proximity at that time to sources of land-derived sediment?

☐ The limestone must have accumulated in quiet, low-energy conditions where currents were not strong enough to remove the carbonate mud. There was probably no nearby source of land-derived sediment because this would have introduced material such as clay minerals and quartz.

■ Examine Practical Kit Specimen 3, the crinoidal limestone. What evidence is there that currents involved in its deposition were stronger than those depositing the muddy limestone discussed here?

☐ This limestone contains small fragments of broken and haphazardly arranged crinoid stems and plates, some of which exceed 5 mm in size. The currents required to break up and move these sizeable crinoid fragments were certainly far stronger than those that deposited only fine carbonate muds.

Question 4.3

What are the main indicators of arid desert conditions in ancient sandstones?

Question 4.4

Which sedimentary processes are important in maintaining the natural balance of salts in seawater?

4.4 From sediments to sedimentary rocks

If sedimentary deposits form as loose sands or soft muds, how do they become hard rocks, such as the sandstone in the Practical Kit?

Material between the sand grains in Specimen 2 holds it together. The sandstone absorbs water, so this material does not fill spaces inside the rock completely; it merely coats and loosely bonds the grains, so that they can be dislodged (Activity 4.2). The limestone (Specimen 3) holds together much better.

The conversion of loose or soft sediments into sedimentary rocks results from several processes of lithification (Book 1, Section 7.4.3), which can start soon after deposition. Many sediments are deposited by water and, even when desert sandstones are buried, underground water eventually occupies the spaces between the grains.

■ What happens to the water filling the spaces between sediment grains when more and more sediment is loaded on top?

☐ The weight of overlying sediment tends to press the sediment grains closer together, driving the water out from between them.

Muddy sediments may contain up to 60% water when they are deposited, much of which is expelled by **compaction** to form a mudstone. If the mud contains platy clay minerals, compaction and de-watering may align them (Figure 4.14a), making a rock that is easily split into thin layers; a form of mudstone commonly called shale. Coarser sediments, such as sands, do not compact much during burial because their grains pack together tightly when first deposited, whether in air or under water.

Water between the grains in buried sediments may dissolve material, such as calcite, from the surrounding mineral grains themselves. If minerals are

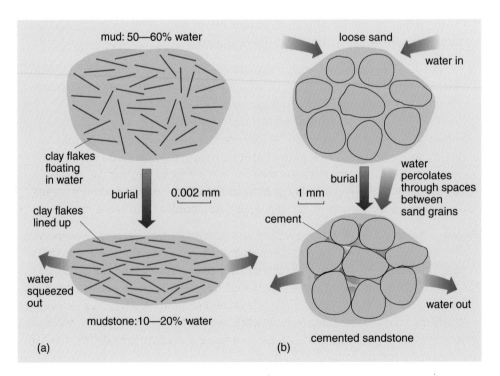

Figure 4.14 Lithification of sediments: (a) burial compacts muds; (b) percolating water precipitates cement between sand grains.

precipitated from the resulting solution in the spaces between the grains (Figure 4.14b), they hold the grains together. This process is called **cementation**. It is the main way in which sandstones and especially limestones are lithified. Interestingly, the weathering of feldspars releases some SiO_2 to solution in natural waters (Equation 4.3). If this precipitates as quartz in the spaces between grains, it forms a particularly strong cement. An analogy for cementation is what happens to damp grains of sugar; on drying out they form a hard lump. The whole process takes much longer in rocks.

Since most sedimentary rocks are lithified after burial, they are normally exposed only when they return to the surface through erosion or earth movements. However, earth movements can also force sedimentary rocks many kilometres deep into the Earth. There they encounter high temperatures and pressures, and may eventually completely recrystallise to become metamorphic rocks (Chapter 5).

Question 4.5

Match the following rock types to an appropriate description from the list below: (i) mudstone; (ii) conglomerate; (iii) limestone; (iv) evaporite; (v) breccia: (*Hint:* each of (a) to (g) may be used once, more than once, or not at all.)

(a) Contains rounded grains of quartz sand

(b) Contains a high proportion of clay minerals

(c) Contains large angular rock fragments

(d) Contains interlocking crystals of water-soluble minerals

(e) Contains layers of sandy and muddy sediment

(f) Contains rounded pebbles cemented by quartz

(g) Contains remains of shelly organisms in fine-grained carbonate mud.

4.5   Summary of Chapter 4

Sedimentary deposits are formed by the processes of weathering, erosion, transportation and deposition at the Earth's surface. Once they are converted to rocks, they are usually distinguished from other rocks by their fragmental texture and by their layering. The size of sedimentary grains provides a means of classifying sediments into muds, sands, pebbles, cobbles and boulders.

Weathering involves the disintegration and decomposition of rocks by exposure to the weather, surface waters and organisms. Physical weathering opens up cracks, breaking down rock into smaller fragments. Chemical weathering involves the breakdown of unstable minerals (e.g. feldspars) by acidic waters to form new, more stable minerals (e.g. clays) and soluble products (e.g. metal ions and silica); resistant minerals (e.g. quartz) are liberated. Erosion is the physical removal of rocks and minerals and the wearing away of rock by debris that can be carried by flowing water, wind and ice.

The size of sedimentary grains picked up and transported by water or wind depends on the energy of the flowing medium (its density and speed of flow). Wind speeds need to be about 50 times greater than water speeds to pick up grains of similar size. Whether or not sediment is eroded, transported or deposited is mainly determined by its grain size and the speed of flow. Materials deposited under a narrow range of flow conditions have a narrow range of grain sizes and are well-sorted. Wind-blown sands are particularly well-sorted. A gradual change in grain size through a bed is known as graded bedding; the upward decrease in grain size reflects a declining speed of flow.

Desert sandstones typically contain well-sorted, well-rounded, finely pitted and reddened grains in quite steeply sloping layers which indicate formation as a result of wind action in an arid environment. Evaporite deposits such as rock salt and gypsum also indicate arid environments where salts have crystallised by evaporation of shallow or enclosed saline waters. The accumulation of calcium carbonate shells or skeletons of organisms produces limestone, which is often indicative of warm, clear marine waters. The observation of depositional processes in modern sedimentary environments provides a means of identifying ancient environments from sedimentary structures in rocks.

During burial, sediments are lithified by compaction and/or by cementation to form sedimentary rocks such as mudstones, shales, sandstones, conglomerates and limestones.

Your study of this chapter involved: comparing information given in diagrams, graphs and computer-based learning resources, including data that you have plotted as histograms; describing and interpreting that information; applying it more widely, and summarising your findings. You have also applied concepts about sedimentary processes to explain variations in sedimentary rocks in terms of various surface environments. By performing a simple experiment using soil, you have developed new insights into your own surroundings.

Chapter 5
Metamorphic rocks and deformation – heat, pressure and force

Large-scale processes in the rock cycle (Figure 5.1) transform the rocks' environment so that they encounter very different conditions. For example, a plutonic igneous rock, having crystallised at depth, reaches the surface after uplift and erosion of overlying rocks. The plutonic rock then begins to contribute to the production of sediments. Conversely, sedimentary burial or compressive tectonic forces may move rocks that were at the surface to deep within the crust. The most extreme cases occur when lithospheric plates converge. This deforms and thickens continental crust to form mountain belts, and oceanic crust in subduction zones descends deep into the mantle (Book 2, Section 8.6). Conditions in the crust may also change without any significant deformation, when hot magmas rise, intrude and heat up older rocks that would otherwise be much cooler. This chapter looks at the processes of metamorphism and deformation that transform rocks when temperature, pressure and tectonic forces rise significantly.

Metamorphic rocks have distinctive textures: interlocking crystals; platy minerals showing clear alignment (Figure 3.1b); other minerals sometimes arranged in bands. Such textures indicate that crystallisation happened in the solid state (Book 2, Section 5.2.3), under the influence of deforming forces. Metamorphic changes occur when mineral structures reorganise themselves in response to temperature and pressure changes in their physical environment. Increased vibration of bonds in mineral structures, caused by rising temperature, encourages elements to leave one structure and enter another that is more stable under the new conditions. This results in the growth of new minerals or recrystallisation of old ones, yet the overall chemical composition of the rock remains unchanged. Metamorphic reactions are very different from familiar chemical reactions in aqueous solutions. In comparison with laboratory experiments, solid-state metamorphic reactions are very slow.

Minerals deep underground encounter far higher temperatures and pressures than at the Earth's surface. If you went down a mine shaft, you would notice that the rocks become hotter the deeper you go. On average, the temperature in the continental crust increases by about 25 °C for every kilometre of depth. This increase is a result of the Earth being heated internally, mainly by the decay of naturally occurring radioactive isotopes, and losing this geothermal heat from the surface. The pressure increases with depth because rocks have to support the weight of those above. The pressure in rock increases by about 1000 times that of the atmosphere at the Earth's surface for every 3.5 km of depth.

South African gold mines penetrate as deep as 4 km below the surface. At such depths temperatures at the rock face may exceed 100 °C. The pressure on the rocks at the bottom of the deepest South African mine is about 1200 times the

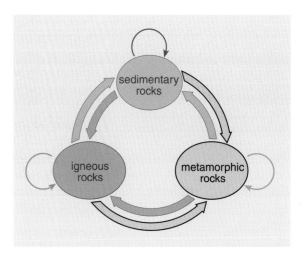

Figure 5.1   Formation of metamorphic rocks in the rock cycle. The three yellow arrows indicate the routes of formation of metamorphic rocks by burial and crystallisation under heat and pressure.

Atmospheric pressure at sea level is 1×10^5 Pa (Book 1, Section 5.1).

atmospheric pressure, or 1.2×10^8 Pa. So, where mining exposes deeply buried rock to atmospheric pressure in the mine workings, huge forces build up in the rock, sometimes sufficient to exceed its strength, when it explodes into the excavation as a 'rock burst'.

Metamorphic conditions can be represented on a graph of pressure versus temperature (Figure 5.2), where the vertical axis shows pressure increasing downwards, as it does beneath the Earth's surface. The rate at which rock temperatures increase with depth is termed the geothermal gradient. The 'typical' **geothermal gradient** of Figure 5.2 (25 °C km^{-1}) is the average beneath tectonically stable continental regions that lack magmatic activity; as beneath much of northern Europe today. In volcanically active areas, the geothermal gradient can reach hundreds of degrees per kilometre. Conversely, where cold oceanic lithosphere is subducted at convergent plate boundaries faster than it can heat up as it descends, the geothermal gradient is lower than normal. So, there is a wide range of pressure and temperature conditions under which metamorphism can occur within the crust.

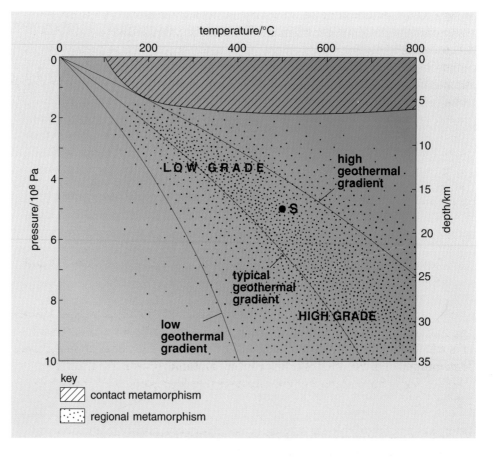

Figure 5.2   Pressure and temperature conditions under which metamorphic rocks may be formed. The two types of metamorphism shown (contact and regional) are discussed in Section 5.1. Regional metamorphic conditions are more commonly developed in the stippled regions close to the line representing a typical geothermal gradient, but vary according to crustal setting. Note that pressure increases *downwards* in this graph. The depth is shown on the right. The point labelled S represents the conditions under which schist might have formed – this is discussed in Section 5.1.2.

The conditions under which metamorphism occurs, and the rocks that form as a result, are generally described in terms of **metamorphic grade**. Thus, both the metamorphic conditions of high temperature and high pressure, *and* the metamorphic rocks produced by them, are called *high grade*. Correspondingly, both the conditions of low temperature and low pressure, and the resulting rocks, are called *low grade* (Figure 5.2).

5.1   New rocks for old

Since drilling is possible down to only about 10 km depth, directly sampling the effects of metamorphism on rocks deep in the crust is impossible. Metamorphism has barely begun 10 km down (Figure 5.2). However, tectonic activity, uplift and erosion may have gradually raised metamorphic rocks from a range of depths (up to 70 km) to the Earth's surface, to reveal minerals that have grown and stabilised under various combinations of temperatures and pressure. Remarkably, the remains of sedimentary structures, such as cross-bedding (Section 4.3.1), show that some metamorphic rocks originally formed as sediments at the Earth's surface. Somehow, they were transported downwards beneath great thicknesses of rock before returning to the surface again.

Earth movements, by uplifting and subsidence, are mainly responsible for moving rocks around the rock cycle (Figure 5.1). Divergent tectonic forces may result in subsidence, to allow thick sequences of sediments and extrusive igneous rocks to build up in depositional basins; the progressive burial of older layers makes them more prone to metamorphism. A more effective process occurs where lithospheric plates converge and squeeze together to form mountain belts, as happened to form the Alps and the Himalaya (Book 2, Section 8.6). Most mountain belts contain large areas of rocks affected by metamorphism. Developed on a regional scale, this is called **regional metamorphism**. The more erosion wears down mountains, the greater the extent of metamorphic rocks exposed at the surface. The stippling on Figure 5.2 shows the more common conditions of regional metamorphism, but there are other environments in which metamorphism may occur.

■ How might rocks near to the Earth's surface get very hot?

☐ They may come into contact with magma at temperatures between 800 and 1300 °C.

Rocks in contact with magma can be heated sufficiently for metamorphic changes to occur on a scale of centimetres to metres at the base of lava flows or around sills and dykes, and on a scale of hundreds of metres to kilometres around plutons. Metamorphism of this kind is called **contact metamorphism**, and usually involves *high* temperatures but *low* pressures (the *high* geothermal gradient in Figure 5.2).

■ Why should contact metamorphism be more extensive around plutons than below lavas or around sills and dykes?

☐ Plutons contain much larger volumes of magma and therefore provide much more heat to be dissipated during cooling. The heat spreads further and the source stays hot for longer.

Sedimentary mudstones containing clay minerals are particularly susceptible to contact metamorphism. Hydrous clay minerals form at the Earth's surface and become unstable when temperature increases. Heating dehydrates them to produce new minerals containing less water. At shallow depths, where plutons cool more rapidly, temperature rises are usually short-lived. Shallow contact metamorphic rocks therefore don't have long to crystallise and are usually finer grained than regional metamorphic rocks. Since contact metamorphism happens under *static* conditions, the resulting metamorphic rocks don't develop aligned crystals; they may *appear* to be igneous but closer examination often reveals signs of the rock's previous 'incarnation'. For instance, preserved sedimentary layering and structures indicate a sedimentary rock that has been changed by contact metamorphism.

Rocks of the oceanic lithosphere at convergent plate margins slide down subduction zones to depths greater than 70 km. Old oceanic lithosphere has a *low* geothermal gradient (Figure 5.2). So, high pressure dominates metamorphic change in subduction zones and it happens at low temperatures. Contact and subduction-zone metamorphic rocks are uncommon, so the rest of this section focuses on products of regional metamorphism.

5.1.1   Metamorphic 'cookery'

In a very crude sense, the ways in which heat and pressure metamorphose rocks are similar to what happens when a cake is baked. A cake comes out of an oven after cooking with a constitution and texture quite different from the mixture that went in. Similarly, metamorphic rocks end up with different textures (and usually different minerals). To continue the analogy, when a cake comes out of the oven, its texture gives clues to the conditions in the oven. A charred lump suggests the temperature was very high for some time; a soggy mass shows it was too low for the ingredients to react.

Metamorphism involves chemical reactions between mineral 'ingredients' in the starting rock. In the case of sedimentary rocks, water also participates in these reactions. The result is a solid mixture of *new* minerals. Just as different ingredients produce different kinds of cake, different metamorphic rocks develop according to the 'blend' of mineral constituents in the starting rocks. For example, the metamorphism of limestone (mainly calcite) produces marble; sandstones (mainly quartz) transform to quartzites; and basalts change to amphibolites (mainly amphibole and plagioclase feldspar), all under similar ranges of temperature and pressure. In the first two cases, the starting rocks contain only a single mineral, so there is no reaction; a single mineral merely recrystallises to form an interlocking mass. In the third case, the anhydrous minerals olivine, pyroxene and feldspar in the basalt react with each another and with water to form the new mineral amphibole (a hydrated chain silicate of mafic composition) plus some recrystallised feldspar.

Textures and new minerals in metamorphic rocks give visible clues to the temperature and pressure of their formation, and to the original rocks before metamorphism, as you will see in the next activity.

Activity 5.1   Comparing metamorphic rocks

We expect this activity will take you approximately 30 minutes.

This activity involves comparing the metamorphic rock sample (schist) in the Practical Kit with photographs of two other metamorphic rocks (slate and gneiss) in Figure 5.3, to see how several characteristic features vary between these three rocks.

Important safety precautions

Take note of the safety precautions given with Activity 4.2.

Equipment required

Kit items

Rock Specimen 4

Hand lens

Non-kit item

Ruler marked in millimetres

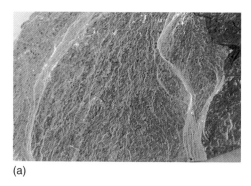
(a)

(b)

Figure 5.3   Examples of metamorphic rocks (with width of field of view): (a) slate (60 mm); (b) gneiss (70 mm).

■   What features could you use to distinguish the three rocks?

☐   Their appearance, in terms of colour, grain size and how the grains are arranged (texture), and their mineral content.

Task 1

Use Table 5.1 to record your descriptions of slate, gneiss and schist. *Note*: wetting the cut surface of Specimen 4 will reveal the mineral grains more clearly. When comparing grain sizes, take into account the scales of the photographs.

You may not be able to recognise all the minerals present in these rocks, especially the slate, but you should recognise some of the minerals in the schist and the gneiss. Compare your completed Table 5.1 with the table in the comments to see whether you missed anything important.

Table 5.1   Comparison of the properties of slate, gneiss and schist.

Property	Slate	Gneiss	Schist
Grain size			
Colour			
Texture			
Minerals			

Task 2

Look at the characteristics you listed in Table 5.1, particularly the grain size and the texture. In what order would you put these three rocks based on a systematic gradation in these two features?

Now look at the comments on this activity at the end of this book.

5.1.2   Changes with metamorphic grade

Activity 5.1 showed that the textures and mineral contents of the typical metamorphic rocks – slate, schist and gneiss – are quite different. However, they are not due to differences between the compositions of the original rocks from which they were formed by metamorphism. Surprisingly perhaps, the slate, schist and gneiss all began as soft mudstones, with essentially the same overall proportions of elements. Their distinctive mineral and textural characteristics developed under different metamorphic conditions; i.e. under different *grades* of metamorphism.

The **slate** is the lowest grade metamorphic rock in the group and would have formed typically at 200–350 °C and 5–10 km depth. The **gneiss** (pronounced 'nice') has the coarsest grain size and formed under high-grade conditions, typically at temperatures of 550–700 °C and a depth of 20–35 km. The **schist** (pronounced 'shist') has an intermediate grain size and might have formed under the conditions represented by point S in Figure 5.2.

Schists typically form at temperatures of 350–550 °C and depths of 10–20 km (3–6×10^8 Pa pressure). The textures of the three rocks differ according to the way their minerals are arranged and their grain size, both of which vary with metamorphic grade.

Slate (Figure 5.3a) can be cleaved into thin parallel flakes with smooth surfaces, hence its use in roofing. Cleavage in rocks originates differently from that in minerals, which is a result of their crystal structure. Slate can be cleaved because of the parallel alignment of very fine-grained metamorphic mica flakes. This aligned growth of platy minerals is a response to compressive tectonic forces (Figure 5.4). Tectonic compression generally operates in a roughly horizontal direction as a result of lithospheric plate movements, distinct from the pressure caused by the weight of overlying rocks.

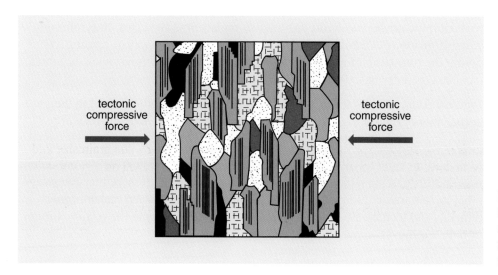

Figure 5.4 Mineral alignment (greatly magnified) developed during metamorphism at right-angles to the direction of tectonic compression.

The schist has shiny, but somewhat crinkly, surfaces made of easily recognised mica flakes. At this coarser grain size, the unevenness is caused by platy crystals that have grown around other, granular, minerals. Individual mineral grains are visible, even without a hand lens; there are flakes of dark and pale mica, grains of glassy quartz and pinkish brown garnet (see the computer-based *Minerals Gallery*).

Gneiss contains even coarser mineral grains, arranged in more or less parallel bands (Figure 5.3b). It contains much less mica than schist. The pale mica (muscovite), breaks down at the high temperatures of gneiss formation, with the loss of water vapour, to form alkali feldspar, in the following, simplified metamorphic reaction:

$$\text{muscovite mica (s)} + \text{quartz (s)} = \text{alkali feldspar (s)} + H_2O \text{ (l)} \qquad (5.1)$$

Along with quartz, alkali feldspar (Activity 4.1) forms blocky crystals, unlike the thin plates of mica it replaces. As a result, gneiss (Figure 5.3b) is a more granular rock, and not as easy to split as schist. Instead, it contains rough bands containing different proportions of quartz, feldspar and the dark mica, biotite.

■ At even higher temperatures, what might happen to gneiss?

□ It might start to melt and form magma.

At very high temperatures (700–1000 °C), rocks such as gneisses may partially melt to produce magmas and hence igneous rocks. This melting of metamorphic rocks, which were once igneous or sedimentary rocks, closes a major loop in the rock cycle (Figure 5.1).

So, at increasing temperatures of metamorphism, minerals that become unstable break down to form new, more stable minerals. Clay minerals, which were stable at low temperatures, are converted into micas at low metamorphic grades and, at high grades, micas are converted into feldspars. Also, with increasing metamorphic grade, less hydrous minerals replace hydrous ones, thus releasing water (Equation 5.1). High pressures also affect mineral stability, tending to favour the formation of minerals with dense, compact structures, such as garnet (see the computer-based resource *Minerals Gallery*).

Figure 5.5 summarises the progressive change, both in grain size and in the arrangement of mineral grains, in rocks formed from mudstone or shale at increasing grades of metamorphism.

Metamorphic mineral alignments form during periods of compression, but do not necessarily coincide with the increases in temperature or pressure that encourage other metamorphic minerals to grow. The relationship between metamorphic minerals and tectonically related alignments provides clues to the relative timing of both. Figure 5.6 shows such an example.

■ Examine the relationship between the pink garnet crystals and the mineral alignment in the schist shown in Figure 5.6b. Which developed first: the garnets or the alignment?

□ The garnets show well-developed crystal faces that cut across the aligned minerals, so the garnets grew *after* the alignment had formed.

The pervasive mineral alignments seen in slate, schist and gneiss are typical of regional metamorphism. They develop in the original rocks as they are moved into crustal environments with different pressure and temperature. This occurs most commonly during the tectonic compression associated with plate collision and mountain building. By contrast, *contact* metamorphic

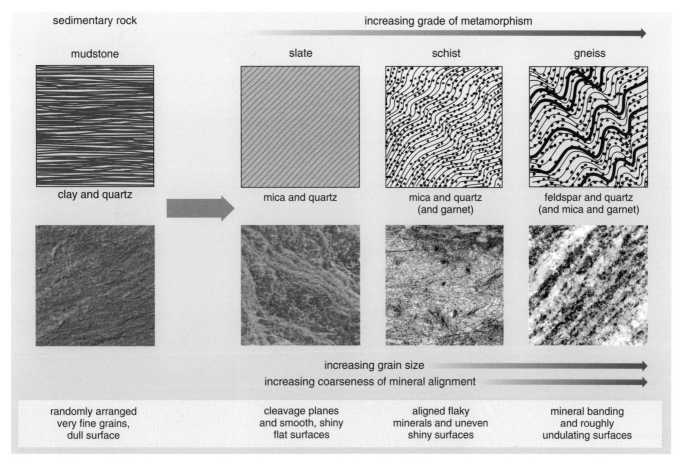

Figure 5.5   Variation in metamorphic rock textures and minerals with increasing grade of metamorphism, as developed from a mudstone or shale. The minerals in brackets occur in small amounts. The images of actual rocks each cover about 5 cm.

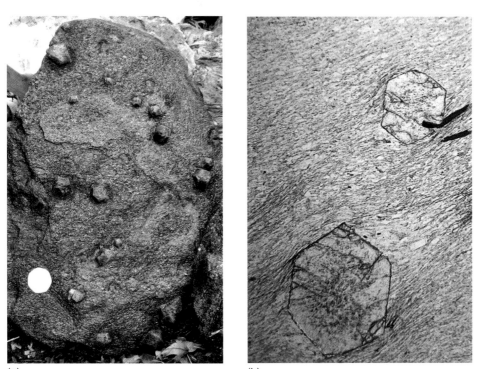

(a)

(b)

Figure 5.6   Garnet crystals set in a mica-rich schist: (a) hand specimen; (b) microscopic view (15 mm wide) of a thin, transparent slice.

rocks are formed by simple, static recrystallisation and normally do not exhibit mineral alignment, although, new minerals sometimes grow over the original textures.

5.2   Rock deformation

Earth movements may buckle once fairly flat-lying sedimentary strata, to form a variety of contorted shapes (Figure 5.7). Metamorphic rocks, formed deep within mountain belts, commonly show these effects of deformation. The scale varies from microscopic, involving mineral banding (Figure 5.7a), to beds in a cliff face (Figure 5.7b), to a vast scale, visible only from the air (Figure 5.7c). Other structures form when movements in the Earth break rocks apart.

(a)

(b)   (c)

Figure 5.7   Deformation features on a variety of scales: (a) microscopic folding of mica flakes in a thin, transparent slice of rock (2 mm across); (b) folded sedimentary beds exposed in a road cutting (5 m across); (c) aerial photograph of large-scale folding of sedimentary rocks of different kinds (5 km across).

Deformation results from any process that causes an object to *change its shape* – by breaking, bending, stretching, or squashing – when a force is applied. A tectonic force directed towards a fixed object produces *compression*; when operating in the opposite sense it produces *tension*.

Materials respond differently to deformation. Grip one end of a French bean, pull the other end and it breaks. Pull on a piece of dough and it stretches and thins before breaking. These are different responses to tension: the bean pod exhibits **brittle deformation**; the dough responds by **plastic deformation**.

Experiments can demonstrate the effects of rock deformation, or geologists can infer the nature of deformation from structures in the rock. Figure 5.8a shows the results from an experiment to compress rock between the jaws of a mechanical press. Figure 5.8b shows how layers of rock in natural exposures have failed under tension.

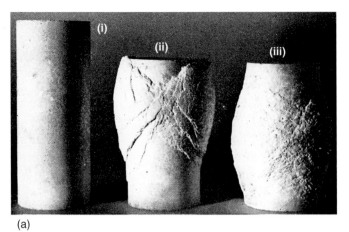

(a)

(b)

(c)

Figure 5.8   Simple deformation. (a) Results of an experiment showing the effect of compression on cylinders of marble under different conditions: (i) undeformed marble; (ii) deformation at low temperature; (iii) deformation at high temperature. (b) and (c) Two different results of tension forces that operated along rock layers: (b) thinning under plastic conditions; (c) fracturing during brittle deformation.

■   Examine the experimental results in Figure 5.8a. How can you tell which of (ii) and (iii) shows the outcome of plastic compression and which shows brittle compression?

☐   The marble cylinder in (iii) has thickened by just bulging, its shape having developed by plastic deformation. Specimen (ii) has thickened by brittle fracturing, which allowed broken parts of the cylinder to move past each other.

It should now be clear how the rock layers in Figure 5.8b and 5.8c responded to tension: those in Figure 5.8b thinned to produce a 'neck' while deforming in a plastic manner; those in Figure 5.8c broke in a brittle fashion and moved past each other.

These two kinds of behaviour seem puzzling; rocks tend to smash when hit with a hammer, and are much stronger than dough or a bean pod. What determines whether they deform in a brittle manner or in a plastic manner? If you try to bend a toffee bar on a hot day, it will almost certainly bend. If you chill it in the freezer and try again, it will be more likely to break. So, the extent to which the deformation is plastic or brittle depends not only on the character of the material itself but also on its temperature; *increasing temperature increases plasticity*.

Here is another experiment that you might try. Place a hard toffee bar in the refrigerator, one end hanging over the edge of a tray, the other held in place with a weight. After a few days you will see that the bar has bent; it behaves plastically.

Remove the bar and hit it sharply with a hammer (take care if you try this yourself); it will easily break in a brittle manner. This demonstrates the way in which something deforms depends on the rate of deformation: *fast-acting forces tend to result in brittle behaviour; slow-acting forces encourage plastic deformation.*

■   Given that temperature increases with depth in the Earth, roughly where in relation to the Earth's surface, would you expect brittle deformation and plastic deformation to occur?

☐   Brittle deformation tends to occur near to the Earth's surface where rocks are cooler; plastic deformation is more likely to occur at considerable depth, where rocks are hotter.

On an even larger scale, the lithosphere behaves in a brittle fashion, whereas the asthenosphere acts as a plastic solid (Book 2, Section 8.1).

5.2.1   Faults

Brittle rocks can fracture because of either compression or tension (Figure 5.8). If a fracture surface shows signs of *dislocation* (that is, where once continuous rock layers no longer line up across the fracture), it is a fault and was probably once the site of earthquakes (Book 2, Section 3.2). Brittle fractures without associated dislocation – joints – are common in all rocks. If you can see a sense of displacement across a fracture surface (Figure 5.9), you can tell whether compression or tension caused the displacement: compression moves rocks closer together; tension moves rocks further apart.

Question 5.1

(a) Which fault in Figure 5.9 formed by tension and which formed by compression? (*Hint*: look at the mudstone bed on either side of each fault.) Draw arrows parallel to the ground surface in Figure 5.9a and 5.9b to show the directions of horizontal movement.

(b) Draw a vertical line downward from point A on Figure 5.9a and 5.9b. Imagine these lines represent boreholes. How would the sequence of rocks in each borehole differ?

(c) The trees in Figure 5.9a and 5.9b were the same horizontal distance apart before the faulting occurred. How has their separation changed in each case as a result of tension and of compression?

Compression faults result in the *repetition* of layers; tension faults locally *omit* layers from the original sequence. This is related to crustal *shortening* and *extension*, respectively.

5.2.2   Folds

The plastic behaviour of rocks under compression results in bending or bulging, to give **folds**, rather than faults (Figure 5.10). Folds (and faults) are most easily

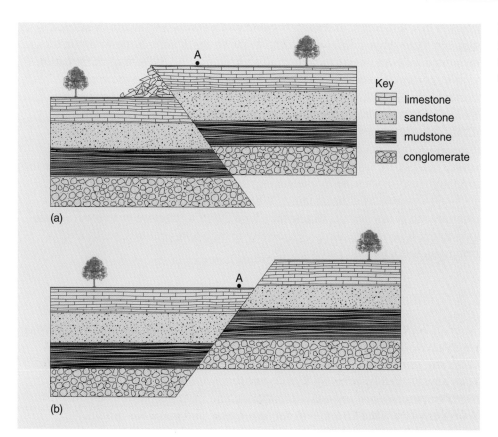

Figure 5.9   Dislocation of rock strata by faulting: examples of faults produced by tension and compression.

Key

limestone
sandstone
mudstone
conglomerate

(a)

(b)

(c)

Figure 5.10   Simple folding of rock layers by compression deformation. (a) An open fold in Cumbria reflects a little shortening. (b) A tight fold in North Devon reflects much greater shortening. (c) An overturned fold in metamorphic rocks near Aberdeen resulted from extreme compression and plastic behaviour sustained over as much as a million years.

detected in sedimentary and metamorphic rocks containing layers or aligned minerals. Fold shapes differ according to the strength and plasticity of the rocks; the amount of compression and overall shortening; and the rate of deformation. A little shortening produces an open fold (Figure 5.10a), whereas greater shortening may produce a tight fold (Figure 5.10b), rather like a concertina. In cases of extreme compression, overturned folds may develop, in which part of the rock sequence is turned upside-down (Figure 5.10c). In such cases, the deformation may have taken as long as a million years, allowing the rocks to behave in a plastic fashion. Faster movements on the same scale may achieve the same immense shortening by the development of brittle thrust faults (Figure 5.9a is a small example of a thrust fault). When rocks are strong but brittle, as they generally are at low temperatures, they tend either to fracture or to form simple open folds. When more plastic, especially at high temperatures, rocks tend to form tight, intricate fold patterns.

5.3   Mountains and metamorphic belts

Crossing large areas of the continents are linear regions of crust containing rocks which have been strongly deformed. They formed as mountain belts, some of which still remain, such as the Alps and the Himalaya. Such belts usually contain rocks transformed by regional metamorphism that deep erosion has exposed. Together, processes of regional deformation and metamorphism constitute an **orogeny** (from the Greek *oros* for 'mountain' and *genic* for 'producing'). Folding and faulting of the rocks within these linear belts indicate large-scale compression.

■ At what kind of plate boundary might this compression have occurred.

☐ At a convergent plate boundary, where subduction of the ocean floor has caused continents to collide (Book 2, Section 8.6).

Mountain belts form during continent–continent collision because the continental crust is too buoyant to be subducted (Book 2, Section 8.6). The collision deforms sediments that were deposited between the converging continents, as well as the continents themselves (Figure 5.11). The compression results in thickening of the crust. Note also from Figure 5.11 that continental crust above the subduction zone thickens as a result of magma intrusion during the formation of a volcanic arc. A good example of crustal thickening is the crust that was deformed when India collided with Asia. The continental crust beneath the Himalaya and the Tibetan Plateau extends down to about 70 km, compared with a thickness of about 35 km for crust beneath most of the continental surface.

The additional mass of mountains raised up by crustal thickening during collision orogenies (e.g. the Tibetan Plateau is an average of 5 km high) depresses the mantle beneath (Figures 5.11c and 5.12a), even though the crust is not as dense as the mantle. Why does this happen and what are its implications?

Over the enormous timescales involved in most geological processes, plastic solids can behave like very viscous liquids. The Earth's lithosphere can be likened to a ship floating on the weaker, but denser *asthenosphere* (Book 2,

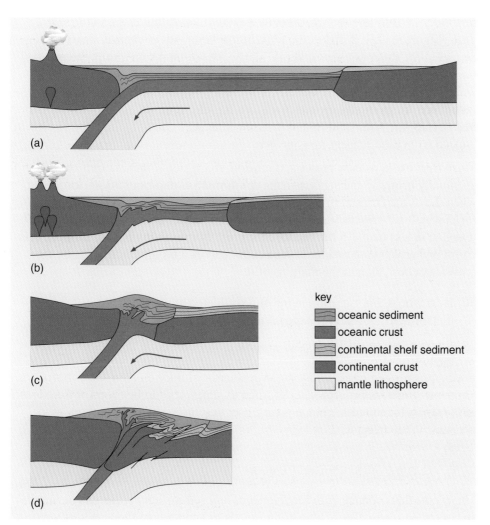

Figure 5.11   Formation of a mountain belt by the collision of continents carried on converging lithospheric plates. (a) and (b) Converging continents, showing magmatic addition beneath a volcanic arc above a subduction zone. (b) and (c) Oceanic sediments deposited between the approaching continents begin to deform close to the subduction zone. (d) Crustal thickening as a result of continental collision. (*Note*: the figures are not to scale.)

key

oceanic sediment

oceanic crust

continental shelf sediment

continental crust

mantle lithosphere

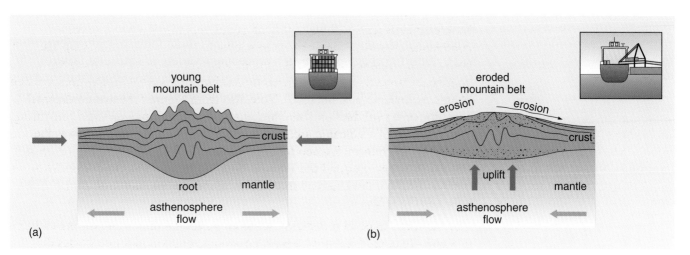

Figure 5.12   Evolution of a mountain belt: (a) compression during mountain building causes crustal thickening which displaces the asthenosphere away from the mountain belt; (b) subsequent erosion and buoyant uplift of the mountain belt brings metamorphic rocks to the surface when the asthenosphere moves back as the load is reduced. The insets show how a ship's hull is analogous to the 'roots' of the mountain belt. Note that the container ship in (b) has offloaded most of its deck cargo.

Section 8.1). Building mountains is then rather like adding cargo to the ship's deck (Figure 5.12a); it makes the hull (lithosphere with thickened crust) sink deeper in the water (asthenosphere). Just as the sea buoys up a ship, the mantle buoys up the thickened lithosphere; the height of the mountains (the cargo) and the depth to the base of the crust (the ship's hull) are in balance. When the mountains are gradually eroded (the cargo is offloaded), the roots of the mountain belt rise up (the hull rises) to maintain the balance (Figure 5.12b) – and to sustain erosion – over immensely long periods.

This effect explains how prolonged erosion of a regional metamorphic belt eventually brings to the surface rocks that formed at depths of 30–40 km, when the overall crustal thickness was as much as 70–80 km. Metamorphic rocks which are presently 10–15 km below the surface of the Himalaya may be revealed in less than 3.5 Ma because the crust there is rising by 4–7 mm per year. Uplift and erosion are greater in the central part of a mountain belt, where the crust is thickest, than at the margins of it.

■ How would this variation in uplift be reflected in the grades of metamorphism observed across the mountain belt?

☐ Rocks of progressively higher grade would be exposed towards the centre of the belt.

Thus low-grade metamorphic rocks, such as slates, tend to be found at the edges of metamorphic mountain belts, giving way to schists, and often to high-grade gneisses, in the interior.

5.4   The rock cycle: review and prospects

The events that produce individual igneous and sedimentary rocks can be simple and occur on timescales of tens of thousands to hundreds of thousands of years. In contrast, mountain building, with which metamorphic rocks are associated, takes millions of years. In many respects it draws together all of the components of the rock cycle; older sedimentary and igneous rocks form the 'ingredients' and tectonic forces act as a 'mixer', producing a variety of structural features. Tectonic forces also transport rocks downwards into elevated temperature and pressure conditions that transform them into metamorphic rocks. Continual uplift, once mountain belts form, drives weathering, erosion and the transportation of eroded debris. In the wake of orogeny, younger sedimentary rocks form and crustal melting may contribute new magmas to complete the rock cycle. Mountain building is undoubtedly complicated, as are its products, and its aftermath is extremely long. However, with what you have learned so far you should be able to recognise events that contribute to orogeny from various lines of evidence.

Piecing together events to discover the geological history of an area affected by mountain building requires a time framework in which to place evidence from the rocks, whether they are sedimentary, igneous or metamorphic. Chapter 2 outlined the approaches used to build such a historical context for past events and the processes involved in them. Chapters 3 to 5 showed how features that you may observe in rocks of different kinds reveal the geological processes of the rock cycle that created those features. In Chapter 6 you will learn how Earth scientists use radioactive decay to determine the ages and duration of geological processes and add the figures to the stratigraphic timescale introduced in Chapter 2.

Question 5.2

Summarise the main differences between the types of metamorphic rock that can be produced from a mudstone at progressively higher grades of metamorphism. (*About 100–150 words*)

Question 5.3

Which two main kinds of evidence suggest that rocks seen in field exposures have been affected by movements in the Earth? (*About 50 words*)

Question 5.4

Briefly outline how metamorphic belts form and how their buried interiors can rise to the surface. (*About 50 words*)

Question 5.5

Annotate the schematic diagram of the rock cycle in Figure 5.13 as follows.

(a) Label the five ellipses using the terms below to show the appropriate processes for each location (you will need to use one label twice): weathering and erosion; deposition of sediments; partial melting; recrystallisation

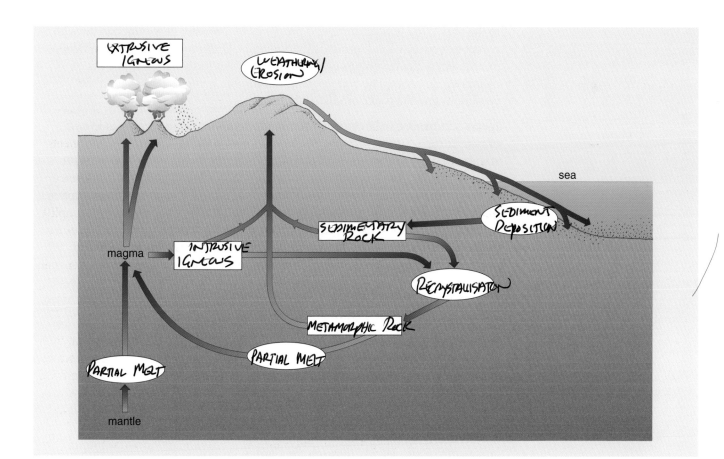

Figure 5.13   Schematic diagram of the rock cycle (for use with Question 5.5).

(b) Label the four boxes with the rock types most likely to be formed there: intrusive igneous rock; extrusive igneous rock; metamorphic rock; sedimentary rock

(c) Rock-forming processes involve some movement of the material from which a new rock is made. Movement is caused by *burial*, *uplift*, agents of *transportation* at the Earth's surface (wind, water and ice), and *eruption* of magma. By labelling arrows, show on Figure 5.13 where these movements occur in the rock cycle.

(d) Label Figure 5.13 with the numbers 1–6 to show where the following processes occur within the rock cycle.

1   A shale is heated and recrystallises to form a gneiss.

2   A gneiss partially melts to form a granitic magma.

3   A granite weathers to form grains of quartz feldspar and mica.

4   Grains of feldspar and mica weather to form clay minerals.

5   Clay minerals and silt accumulate to form shale.

6   Felsic magma cools slowly to form a granite pluton.

5.5   Summary of Chapter 5

Metamorphic rocks form deep in the Earth's crust where older rocks respond to the prevailing temperatures and pressures by growing new minerals through reactions between solid, pre-existing minerals. Different geothermal gradients in different tectonic settings create conditions that form a wide range of metamorphic rocks. The concept of metamorphic grade describes both the conditions and the rocks produced by them.

Igneous intrusions bake the older rocks adjacent to them, generally at low pressure. Such contact metamorphism is a local, static process that produces no alignments of the new minerals. Regional metamorphism affects much larger areas to produce rocks containing aligned crystals or bands of minerals formed by recrystallisation during tectonic compression. During regional metamorphism, mudstone transforms to slate, schist and gneiss, in order of increasing metamorphic grade. With increasing temperature, hydrous minerals break down and less hydrous minerals become stable. With increasing pressure, denser minerals become stable.

Either tension or compression associated with movements in the Earth may deform rocks. Those remaining cool near the surface tend to be brittle and usually deform by fracturing, or by simple folding. Deeper down, higher temperatures make rocks more plastic and folding is more complex. Very long periods of sustained, directed pressure encourage rocks with a brittle response to rapid deformation to deform in a plastic manner.

Tectonic compression and crustal thickening result in linear mountain belts at convergent plate boundaries, especially where continents collide. Uplift and erosion of thickened crust allows belts of regional metamorphic rocks formed by an orogeny to rise slowly to reach the Earth's surface.

Your study of this chapter involved: comparing information given in figures, and by rock hand specimens and the minerals in them; describing and interpreting that information; and summarising your findings. You have also applied concepts about metamorphic and deformation processes to explain features shown by metamorphic and deformed rocks, including their relationships to internal and tectonic processes.

Chapter 6
Geological time

In Chapter 2 you saw how a relative timescale of geological events and biological evolution can be established by applying some simple principles to the study of sedimentary rocks and fossils. In Chapters 3–5 important aspects of minerals and of sedimentary, igneous and metamorphic rocks were described. Together, these different components of the Earth's crust make up the geological record – the detailed history of the outer parts of our planet. Histories, of course, relate to time and the geological record is no exception, but so far you have not explored how the *absolute* ages of rocks, minerals and fossils are determined, as opposed to their *relative* ages. In this chapter you change the focus of your study from materials to time and look at the *quantification* of the geological timescale. This aspect of the development of geology as a science has a fascinating history itself, culminating in the use of natural radioactivity for the radiometric dating of rocks and other geological materials.

6.1   Annual events and cycles

You are probably familiar with the concept of counting tree rings to calculate the age of a fallen tree. Figure 6.1 shows an example of a felled tree that has been prepared to illustrate tree ring development to best effect. Each year a tree grows by laying down new layers of cells below the bark. The annual growth of new cells shows up as a new ring in the trunk.

■ Are all the tree rings in Figure 6.1 the same width?

□ No; on close examination it can be seen that some of the rings are broader than others. In some cases annual rings are little more than thin dark lines.

■ What do you think causes variability in tree-ring width?

□ Ring widths reflect the amount of annual growth; thus broad rings result from favourable growing seasons, whereas narrow rings are produced when conditions are less favourable.

So in addition to acting as a natural clock, a tree is also a recorder of environmental change, although additional evidence is required to interpret fully the meaning of growth ring variations. A narrow growth ring, for example, could mean that the summer was either too hot and dry for much growth, or too cold. More importantly, as all trees respond to annual environmental change in more or less the same way, the pattern of tree rings in different trees from a particular region will be very similar. By comparing ring sequences from different trees that were growing in different but overlapping periods of time, dating by this method – known as dendrochronology – can be extended back thousands of years.

Figure 6.1   A section through a timber from the Barley Barn at Temple Cressing, Essex. The tree used to produce this timber has been quite heavily trimmed on three sides. Eighty annual growth rings have been counted and used to date the timber to the period AD 1108–1187.

■ Can you think of another example of an organism that records rhythmic increments of growth?

☐ You saw in Section 2.2 that the fossil shells of marine organisms may have growth lines, although these do not necessarily record growth at precisely regular intervals such as days, months or years.

Some natural materials therefore have the potential to record details of rhythmic changes or cycles as they grow but we have no means of placing those cycles in a historical context – we do not know how many years ago the organism grew although we may be able to see for how long the organisms lived. Dendrochronology probes back through past millennia to times before recorded human history, but it cannot take us into the realm of dating solid rocks. There is not a long enough unbroken tree ring record stretching back through time and, in any case, many rocks predate the advent of the first trees! Thus while tree rings have enormous value in dating recent changes in climate, they are of no use in dating ancient rocks below the surface. Time measured in thousands of years is barely scratching the surface of *geological* time.

But how do we know that geological time is so vast? How do we know, for example, that the age of the Earth is 4570 Ma and that the dinosaurs became extinct 65 Ma ago? Before showing how such ages can be established, the next section delves into the historical development of ideas concerning the duration of geological time and explores some of the early attempts to quantify its passage.

6.2 Estimating geological time – reason and religion in the 18th and 19th centuries

The problem of the length of geological time was a particular preoccupation of British science during the 19th century. Notions of its duration were based on observing the rates at which geological processes occur today and comparing them with the record of these processes in rocks. One of the early champions of this cause was Charles Lyell (1797–1875) who, together with James Hutton (1726–1797) 50 or so years earlier, laid the foundations of modern geology. In his *Principles of Geology*, published in the 1830s, Lyell argued from a wealth of observation of geological phenomena that geological processes act very slowly and that geological time must therefore be unimaginably long.

Lyell's and Hutton's arguments form the basis of a fundamental principle of geology: the **principle of uniformitarianism**. This is often summed up in the sound-bite 'the present is the key to the past', which states that the processes that produced rocks in the past are the same as those we can observe today or infer from observation. You have already applied this principle in the discussion of tree rings and in Chapter 4 you applied it to sedimentary processes, and to us it seems only common sense. But in the intellectual environment of the 18th and early 19th centuries, dominated by literal interpretations of the Bible, such ideas were, to say the least, controversial.

The alternative to uniformitarianism held that the geological record was one of repeated catastrophes, of which the prime example was Noah's Flood. This was perceived as only the most recent of a series of catastrophic events that had swept the Earth, causing the periodic extinction of life and the episodic construction of rock formations. New species then replaced the old ones, presumably in an act of Divine creation, and populated the newly recreated surface of the Earth. This approach to the geological record, known as **catastrophism**, was more in accord with an Old Testament view of the world and it became the main opponent of uniformitarianism. The debate between their protagonists lasted for many years, but with the publication of Lyell's *Principles* in the 1830s, the basis of modern geology was firmly established.

6.3   Estimating geological time – how old is a volcano?

One of Lyell's many examples in *Principles of Geology* focused on the geology of Etna, an active volcano on the island of Sicily in the Mediterranean, and he outlined a method to estimate its age. He observed from different sections through the main volcanic cone that Etna is made up of many individual lava flows and layers of ash, exactly similar to those seen to form during eruptions at the present day. This, he deduced, was the way in which the volcano grew to its present dimensions. Therefore, by comparing the total volume of the volcano with the rate at which lava is added, it should be possible to calculate an age. Unfortunately, data on the volumes of individual eruptions were not available to Lyell and he could not follow that calculation through to a solution. But, as we now have access to that information, the calculation is now possible.

During its frequent eruptions, lava flows from Etna present a major geological hazard to the local community, periodically destroying buildings, agricultural land and villages (Figure 6.2). As a result of this risk to life and property, and because of the ease of access to it, Etna has been the subject of longer detailed observation than any other volcano and these accumulated observational data can be used to measure the rate at which the volcano grows.

Figure 6.2 Lava flows in the Valle del Bove below the summit of Etna. It was the comparison of new lava flows, such as these, with older flows in the flanks of the Valle that led Lyell to his conclusions regarding the growth of Etna.

One way of illustrating how Etna grows is to plot a graph of eruption volume against the date of the eruption. This is shown in Figure 6.3. The volume of each eruption is simply determined by multiplying the area of a lava flow, calculated from detailed mapping, by its average thickness. Clearly, these volume estimates are subject to uncertainties because of difficulties in measuring flow thickness, but a reasonable estimate can be deduced by taking many different measurements of the thickness over the whole area of each flow.

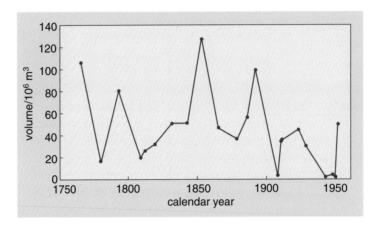

Figure 6.3   The volume of eruptions at Etna, 1766–1951.

■ Do the eruptions appear to be regular in size and frequency? Is there a long period of inactivity before every large eruption?

☐ No. There seems to be no regularity, no pattern to the length of time between each eruption, and no evidence that a large delay is followed by a large flow. Eruptions appear to be random in both size and frequency.

It is quite clear that different eruptions produced different volumes of lava and that we would get very different estimates of the rate of growth from individual flow volumes. Therefore, to calculate a rate of growth we need to take an average over a long period of time.

___

Activity 6.1   Calculating an average growth rate for Etna

We expect this activity will take you approximately 30 minutes.

The purpose of this activity is to calculate the *average* rate at which Etna has grown between 1758 and 1951 by using the dates of historical lava flows and their volumes. The activity will also give you some practice with graphical analysis of data.

In order to calculate the average rate at which the volume of Etna has increased, you will plot a graph of the cumulative volume of the recorded lava flows. The cumulative volume of the erupted lava is simply the sum of the volumes of all lava flows since an arbitrary starting date. The volumes of all the lava flows from 1766 to 1951 are listed in Table 6.1. For the starting year we have used 1758, the year of the eruption prior to the 1766 eruption. The volume of the 1766 lava flow was 106×10^6 m^3, and so at the end of 1766 the cumulative volume since 1758

Table 6.1   Volumes of lava flows from eruptions of Etna, 1766–1951.

Year of eruption	Volume of lava flow/10^6 m^3	Cumulative volume/10^6 m^3
1766	106	106
1780	15	121
1793	80	
1809	19	
1812	25	
1819	31	
1832	50	
1843	50	
1853	128	
1865	46	
1879	36	
1886	56	
1892	100	
1908	3	
1910	34	
1911	36	
1923	45	
1928	30	
1942	2	
1947	4	
1949	3	
1951	50	

was 106×10^6 m^3. (Note that this volume would cover a 10 km $\times$ 10 km square to a depth of just over 1 m.) The next eruption in 1780 added a further 15×10^6 m^3. Adding this to the 106×10^6 m^3 of the 1766 lava flow gives a cumulative volume of 121×10^6 m^3 at the end of 1780. And so on.

Task 1

Complete the cumulative volume column in Table 6.1 by adding the volume of each lava flow to the total of the previous lava flows. *(Note: You can either do this manually on the table or transfer the data to a spreadsheet.)*

Task 2

Now display this information in the form of a graph, either using the blank grid in Figure 6.4, or using a spreadsheet on your computer. Plot a graph of the cumulative volume against the year of eruption. Label the axes clearly, and choose the scales to use as much of the grid as you require to illustrate the information clearly. Then draw a best-fit straight line through the data, and calculate the gradient of this line.

What does the gradient of this line represent?

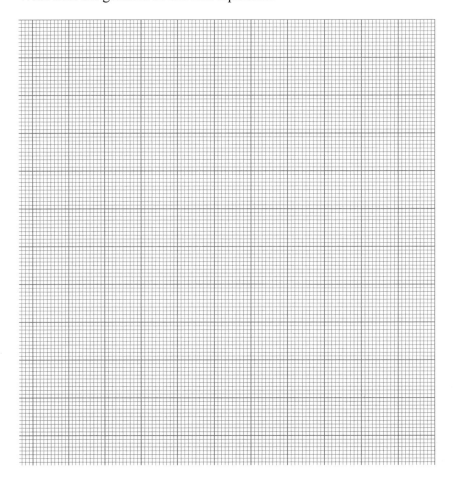

Figure 6.4   A grid for use with Task 2.

■ Now that you know the average growth rate, what extra information do you need to calculate an age for the volcano?

☐ You need to know the total volume of lava in the mountain. An estimate of the age of Etna can then be derived by dividing its volume by the rate of growth.

The shape of Etna is well known because it has been mapped in some detail. It has a roughly circular base, with a summit at 3000 m above sea level. A recent determination of Etna's volume, using modern topographic surveying techniques and seismic profiles to define the detailed shape of the surface on which it is built, gives a volume of close to 350 km³.

Using the volume of 350 km³ and the growth rate calculated in Activity 6.1, calculate the age of Etna. (*Hint:* Make sure that you use consistent units.)

On a human scale the calculated age of Etna is a very long period of time, equivalent to about a thousand average human lifetimes, or three thousand generations. All of written human history represents less than one-tenth of this period. However, Etna is a relatively young geological feature, and is built on a foundation of sedimentary rocks.

■   What does this tell us about the age of these sedimentary rocks?

☐   They must be older than Etna.

The youngest of these sedimentary rocks contain fossils of marine animals that are very similar to, and in some cases indistinguishable from, animals living in the present-day Mediterranean.

■   What does this observation tell us about the rate of evolution of these marine animals, as far as their preservable features are concerned?

☐   It has been very slow or zero over the time taken for Etna to form.

The inescapable conclusion is that even the time required to construct Etna must be insignificant in relation to the time required for the development of the geological sequences in which fossils are preserved. This was one of the major philosophical breakthroughs that Lyell made in his analysis of the geology of Etna, and it contributed to his conclusion that geological time must be measured in terms of many millions of years.

Before leaving Etna, look at the cumulative graph in Figure 6.5. This includes more recent data on volumes of Etna lava flows covering the time period from 1951 to 2004. There is quite clearly a marked change in the eruption rate from 1951.

■   Did the eruption rate increase or decrease in 1951?

☐   The graph steepens, so the eruption rate increased.

After 1951 the eruption rate increased four-fold from about 0.005 km³ y⁻¹ to about 0.02 km³ y⁻¹.

■   Is the change in eruption rate a violation of the principle of uniformitarianism?

☐   No, it is not. Although the rate of growth between 1951 and 1985 was greater than that in the period since 1766, the mechanism of eruption remained the same.

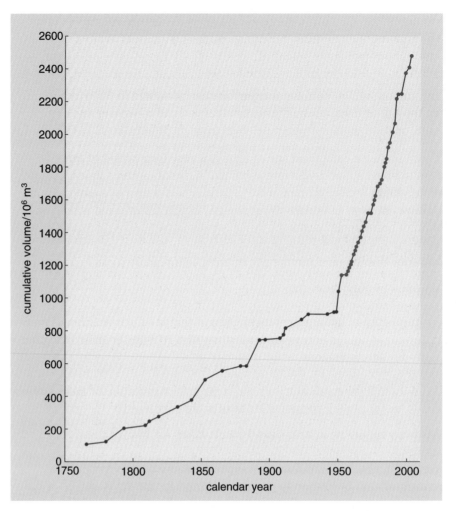

Figure 6.5   The cumulative volume of lava flows from Etna, 1766–2004. The blue dots represent lava flow volumes from 1951 to 2004. Note the marked change in the general slope of the line in 1951.

The term 'uniformitarianism' is often misinterpreted to mean a uniformity in the *rate* of geological processes and a denial of the occurrence of rapid, catastrophic events. What Lyell actually meant when he coined the term was a 'uniformity of natural law', i.e. that all geological events and processes can be understood within the bounds of known physical laws.

■   How would the estimate of the age of Etna change if it was based on the measured eruption rate since 1951?

☐   The volume of Etna remains the same, so the increase in the eruption rate would decrease the calculated age.

Basing our estimate of the age of Etna on the eruption rate between 1951 and 1985, it becomes:

$$\frac{350 \text{ km}^3}{0.02 \text{ km}^3 \text{ y}^{-1}} = 17\,500 \text{ y} \tag{6.1}$$

or 20 000 y to one significant figure, which is only a quarter of our original estimate from Activity 6.1.

This example of Etna illustrates that although it is possible to gain *some* quantitative insight into the duration of geological time, and the timescale of evolution, through the observation of geological processes, such methods cannot form the basis of a reliable method of determining the absolute ages of rocks. The rates of geological processes are simply too variable on long timescales. To determine the absolute age of a rock it is necessary to utilise a natural process that occurs inside rocks at a constant rate and which is independent of external influences.

6.4   Estimating geological time – geology and physics in the late 19th century

Having settled one argument concerning the great duration of geological time in the early 19th century, the new science of geology had to do battle with the scientific establishment in the late 19th century. As you have seen, Lyell argued from observations of the very slow rates of geological processes, and by applying the principle of uniformitarianism, that the Earth must be many millions of years old. His general opinion was that the age of the Earth was indeterminate and that geological time had no bounds. Others, however, thought otherwise and towards the end of the 19th century attempts were made to calculate the age of the Earth.

John Joly, for example, made a quantitative estimate of the age of the Earth in 1898, by calculating the time required for the oceans to attain their present concentration of sodium – an idea initially proposed in 1715 by Sir Edmund Halley. Sodium is readily removed from the rocks of the continents by chemical weathering (Chapter 4), and is washed by rivers down to the oceans where it gradually accumulates – hence the contribution of sodium to the saltiness of the sea. From the volume of the oceans and the concentration of sodium in river water, Joly deduced that the oceans must be 80–90 Ma old. Another attempt that produced a somewhat older age divided an estimate of the total volume of all sedimentary rocks by an estimate of the present rate of deposition.

■   Can you see why this approach would give the wrong answer?

☐   In Chapter 4 you learned that sedimentary rocks are eroded and recycled as part of the rock cycle while the rates of sedimentation vary widely in different environments.

Other estimates of the age of the Earth were also made at around this time and most pointed, albeit rather imprecisely, to ages of 100–1000 Ma.

A counter-argument to these large and variable age estimates was proposed at the end of the 19th century by a leading physicist, William Thompson (later, Lord Kelvin, after whom the SI unit of temperature was named). He recognised that the Earth is losing heat from its interior. As you go down a mine the rocks get hotter – in the deepest gold mines in South Africa, for example, rock temperatures of 100 °C are not uncommon. Therefore, Kelvin argued, the Earth must be cooling from a hotter state which he assumed was initially molten. He also assumed that there was no additional source of energy within the Earth and that the Earth was cooling by conduction of heat from its centre to the surface. The time taken for the Earth to cool to its present, rather solid, condition could then be calculated from the present temperature gradient within the Earth, as measured in mines.

Kelvin's results demonstrated that the Earth could only be at most 20–40 Ma old. Herein lay the source of the controversy: a scientific estimate of the age of the Earth based on fundamental physical principles – and a few well-reasoned assumptions – pitted against an array of qualitative and semi-quantitative estimates based on geological observation. And all of the geological estimates were substantially greater than the 20–40 Ma which the physical arguments demanded.

Early in the 20th century, shortly after Lord Kelvin's death, severe doubts were raised about his conclusion when it was recognised that at least one of his assumptions was incorrect – there *is* a long-lived internal source of energy within the Earth: natural radioactivity.

All radioactive decay processes liberate energy and the low-level but ubiquitous occurrence of radioactive isotopes in rocks provides a long-lived source of energy within the Earth. Although radioactivity was discovered in 1896, a decade before Kelvin's death, it was only with the later recognition that natural rocks contain small but measurable amounts of radioactive isotopes that the possible implications for the thermal history of the Earth were realised (see Box 6.1).

Box 6.1   The real reason why Kelvin got the age of the Earth wrong

A popular version of the development of geochronology, and one loaded with false irony, is that Kelvin arrived at his erroneously low estimate of the age of the Earth because he ignored heat production by radioactive decay. When radioactivity was discovered and estimates of radiogenic heat production within the Earth were added into Kelvin's calculations, they increased the calculated age of the Earth, bringing it more in line with geological estimates. This is because the Earth would need more time to get rid of the excess radiogenic heat in order to cool to its present state. However, we now know that early assumptions about the distribution and concentrations of potassium, uranium and thorium, the most important radioactive elements in the Earth, were inaccurate and too high. When modern estimates are used, the effect on the age of the Earth calculated by taking into account the contribution of radiogenic heat is much less significant.

The real reason for Kelvin's low estimate of the age of the Earth was that his other major assumption that the Earth cools by conduction alone, was also wrong. We now know from plate tectonics that the Earth's mantle moves and this movement is driven by thermal *convection* – hot material rises and cold material sinks. This process 'evens out' the temperature within the deeper Earth but maintains a higher temperature gradient near the surface than is generated by purely conductive cooling. In other words, the Earth cools by conduction near the surface but by mainly convection in the deeper layers. By using the surface gradient in a model which assumed that conduction is the only way of transporting heat throughout the whole Earth, Kelvin arrived at his erroneously young age; and he would have done so even if he had included the correct estimates of radiogenic heat production. The failure to account for radioactivity was cited at the time as the main reason why he was wrong but it was not until the advent of plate tectonics, in the latter half of the 20th century, that the real reason for the discrepancy between Kelvin and the geologists was finally resolved.

6.5   Absolute ages from radioactive decay

Many elements consist of several stable isotopes (Book 4, Section 3.2). For example, hydrogen has two stable isotopes; hydrogen with an atomic nucleus of one proton and deuterium with a nucleus of one proton and one neutron. Both hydrogen and deuterium have the same chemical properties, it is simply that their mass differs by the addition of the extra neutron. A few elements have isotopes that naturally contain excessive numbers of neutrons relative to protons in their nuclei, making them inherently unstable. The more unstable the neutron–proton balance, the greater the chance that the atom will break down at any instant by radioactive decay, to form a stable isotope of another element. Thus hydrogen has a third isotope, tritium, with a nucleus with one proton and two neutrons, which is radioactive. Book 7 (mainly Chapter 6) discusses radioactive decay in more detail. For now, you just need to know that the end product of radioactivity is a stable isotope called a **daughter isotope**, which has formed by the decay of the original, radioactive **parent isotope**.

By decaying, the abundance of a radioactive parent isotope decreases with time, while its daughter isotope becomes more abundant. Since every nucleus of a particular radioactive isotope has a particular chance of decaying or staying intact, this decay averages out among billions of atoms to a constant, measurable rate. The proper expression for this rate is known as the decay constant which is an expression of the probability that a nucleus will decay in a particular period of time. A more useful expression, however, is the time taken for half the radioactive nuclei in an isotope sample to decay – the isotope's **half-life**. Half-lives range from fractions of a second for some rare, artificially produced isotopes, to over a hundred billion years for a few naturally occurring isotopes. Tritium, for example has a half-life of 12.32 years. Every isotope has a particular half-life that enables the age of a sample to be deduced and Figure 6.6 illustrates some of the naturally occurring isotope systems more commonly used for **radiometric dating**. Activity 6.2 takes you through a simplified case to illustrate how an isotope's half-life bears on absolute or radiometric dating. A reminder that isotopes of each atomic element may be represented by a symbol as shown in Figure 6.6. Letters are used to indicate the name of the element itself, and two numbers are used to indicate the mass number (upper) and atomic number (lower), though the atomic number may not always be shown when referring to isotopes of an element, e.g. ^{235}U.

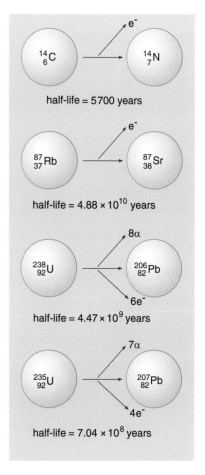

Figure 6.6   Some radioactive decay schemes commonly used in radiometric dating. The decay of ^{235}U to ^{207}Pb and of ^{238}U to ^{206}Pb occurs via a number of intermediate, short-lived isotopes. (Alpha (α)-decay involves the loss of a $^{4}_{2}$He nucleus, e$^-$ decay (also known as beta (β)-decay) involves the loss of an electron and the conversion of a neutron into a proton in the daughter nucleus.)

Activity 6.2   Radioactive decay: the key to absolute time

We expect this activity will take you approximately 30 minutes.

Task 1

Suppose a mineral sample contains, in addition to the elements that make up its bulk, 1024 atoms of a radioactive isotope whose half-life is 3 days.

(a) Starting with 1024, calculate the number of atoms of the parent isotope that remain after 3, 6, 9, 12 days and so on; for example, after 3 days 512 atoms remain. Record the number of half-lives that have elapsed and the remaining number of atoms (P) of the parent isotope in Table 6.2, in the appropriate rows.

(b) Now calculate the number of atoms (*D*) of the daughter isotope after each half-life, and record them in Table 6.2.

Table 6.2   For Tasks 1 and 2 of Activity 6.2.

Time/days	0	3	6	9	12	15	18	21	24	27	30
Half-lives (*n*)	0	1	2	3	4						
Atoms of parent isotope (*P*)	1024	512	256	128	64						
Atoms of daughter isotope (*D*)	0										
***D/P* ratio by division**											
***D/P* ratio by Eqn. 6.7**											

(c) Plot on Figure 6.7 (or using a computer programme if you prefer) the numbers of parent (*P*) and daughter (*D*) isotope atoms (vertical axis) against

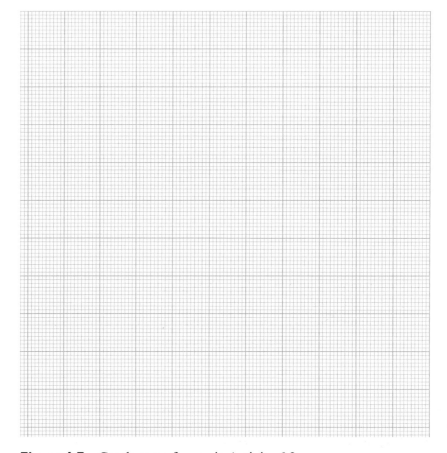

Figure 6.7   Graph paper for use in Activity 6.2.

time (horizontal axis), expressed as the elapsed number of half-lives (n). Draw a smooth curve through each set of data points, using different colours or line styles for each, and briefly describe the shape of the two graphs.

Two algebraic expressions can be derived from your results in Task 1:

- At any time the sum of the atoms of parent and daughter isotopes ($P + D$) is equal to the original number of atoms of the radioactive parent (P_0), expressed mathematically as:

$$P + D = P_0 \qquad (6.2)$$

- The number of atoms of the parent isotope (P) after n half-lives is the original number (P_0) divided n times by 2 (i.e. divided by 2^n), or:

$$P = \frac{P_0}{2^n} \qquad (6.3)$$

So, how do these relationships help in calculating an age from radioactive decay? Both P and D can be measured in a sample of a mineral known to contain an element that includes a radioactive isotope as well as stable isotopes. For instance, natural rubidium includes some ^{87}Rb, which is radioactive and very slowly decays to a stable isotope of strontium, ^{87}Sr. So a mineral that contains rubidium will also contain some of this daughter isotope that has accumulated since the time the mineral formed. If that mineral occurs in an igneous rock, it will have accumulated ^{87}Sr produced by ^{87}Rb decay from the time the mineral had crystallised from magma and cooled down. The next step is to use Equations 6.2 and 6.3 to get an expression for the value of D/P.

Rearranging Equation 6.2 gives:

$$D = P_0 - P \qquad (6.4)$$

which is how you worked out D in Task 1 for each half-life.

Rearranging Equation 6.3 gives:

$$P_0 = 2^n P \qquad (6.5)$$

So the proportion of daughter to parent isotopes is given by combining Equation 6.5 with Equation 6.4 (see Book 3, Section 5.6):

$$D = 2^n P - P = P \left(2^n - 1 \right) \qquad (6.6)$$

and so:

$$D/P = 2^n - 1 \qquad (6.7)$$

The value of this **daughter to parent ratio** (D/P) depends on how many half-lives (n) have elapsed since the parent isotope entered the mineral being dated. It is this relationship that allows a mineral to be dated. The elegance lies in not having to know how much of the parent isotope (P_0) was originally present when the mineral formed.

Task 2

From the values for P and D in Table 6.2 that you calculated at half-lives 1 to 10, calculate D/P firstly by dividing D by P, and then secondly, by using Equation 6.7. Record these values of the daughter to parent ratio (D/P) in Table 6.2, and plot them on Figure 6.7 in a different colour or line style. You will need to make another axis on the right-hand edge of Figure 6.7, using 1 cm for $D/P = 100$, etc. Read the comments on this activity at the end of this book before continuing.

Activity 6.2 demonstrates two ways in which the daughter to parent ratio (D/P) produced by the decay of a radioactive isotope in a sample gives a time since the sample formed. One is mathematical, the other graphical, and both show an age in multiples of the isotope's half-life. That seems simple enough but, in practice, there are two important conditions.

- Atoms of both parent and daughter isotopes must remain locked in the sample; if either is added from outside or lost, the calculated age is not the true age.

- This simple approach only works if there were no daughter atoms in the sample when it formed.

For many isotope systems, corrections have to be made to overcome both these challenges, but these are beyond the scope of this book. However, one widely used and extremely precise method of radiometric dating avoids them.

The mineral zircon (zirconium silicate, $ZrSiO_4$) is sometimes used as a cheap substitute for diamond in jewellery. It forms in small amounts (less than 1%) when magmas crystallise. Zircon concentrates uranium to much higher levels than those in the magma from which it crystallises, which is why it is commonly used in radiometric dating. Crystals of zircon can be dated using two schemes for the decay of the two naturally radioactive uranium (U) isotopes to stable isotopes of lead (Pb): ^{235}U to ^{207}Pb and ^{238}U to ^{206}Pb. Both these U–Pb decay schemes involve a sequence of intermediary radioactive isotopes, but end in a stable, but different daughter isotope of lead. Zircon is very handy because, although its structure can incorporate uranium atoms, it contains very little lead other than that produced by uranium decay. It is also extremely stable with a 'tight' molecular structure, into and from which atoms rarely move. Zircon avoids both of the practical constraints described above and hosts both uranium decay schemes. This means that $^{207}Pb/^{235}U$ and $^{206}Pb/^{238}U$ are two *independent D/P* ratios; they involve half-lives of 704 Ma and 4470 Ma, respectively.

Question 6.2

The value of $^{207}Pb/^{235}U$ (the D/P value) in a zircon sample from a granite intrusion is 3.0. What is the age of the zircon and hence the granite to two significant figures? (*Hint*: you will need to use your completed Table 6.2.)

Not every rock or mineral is suitable for radiometric dating. Some sedimentary rocks contain minerals that grew while sediment was being deposited. Of these minerals, a few contain traces of radioactive ^{87}Rb and can be dated, but they are rare. Many sediments contain organic carbon compounds. Since ^{14}C is a naturally produced radioactive isotope, it might seem that radiocarbon dating can give an absolute age to most sediments, back to the very earliest ones. However, ^{14}C has a half life of only 5700 years which is too short to date rocks that are millions of years old. You can see from the Figure 6.11 that after a number of half-lives, the amount of parent isotope will decay away to a vanishingly small amount. A general rule is that a system is of use up to 10 half-lives, so ^{14}C can only be used to date samples that are up to about 60 000 years old – far too young to date all but the very youngest of rocks. Had all ^{14}C formed, like most other natural isotopes, long ago in exploding stars (more of which in Book 7), it would now be undetectable. The reason why ^{14}C is available for dating very young geological events is because of its continual formation from nitrogen (^{14}N) in the upper atmosphere by the effects of cosmic rays.

6.6   Calibrating the stratigraphic column

So far in this book you have learnt how sedimentary rocks can be dated relatively using fossils and the principle of superposition (Section 2.8), and how igneous rocks are dated absolutely using radiometric methods. In this section you will combine these two approaches to demonstrate how sedimentary rocks are dated *absolutely* to reveal the true timescale of biological evolution.

Igneous rocks crystallise at high temperatures and their constituent minerals become closed to external influences before they cool to surface conditions: in other words, once the composition of an igneous mineral has been set by crystallisation it is resistant to further changes in its composition. The same cannot be said for sedimentary rocks. Sediments form at low temperatures on the Earth's surface by a combination of physical and chemical processes (Chapter 4). After deposition, they are subjected to further processes, such as compaction and cementation, heating and interactions with fluids, that turn sediments into sedimentary rocks. All of these processes have an effect on the ability of a sedimentary rock to retain the parent and daughter isotopes of the radioactive decay schemes. Hence the closed system condition that is typical of igneous minerals is rarely met in sedimentary rocks, and this prevents the successful application of radiometric dating in all but a few specific cases. How then can the age of deposition of sedimentary rocks be dated absolutely? To do this it is necessary to apply some other geological principles that allow us to determine the relative ages of rocks in slightly more complex situations than those explored earlier.

Although igneous rocks are not always present in association with sedimentary sequences, when they are found in place they provide critical markers that can be dated absolutely using radiometric methods. The best examples are lavas because, like sedimentary rocks they obey the law of superposition (Section 2.8), being younger than the rocks below them and older than those above. However, as you saw in Section 3.2.1, not all magma reaches the surface; sometimes it is trapped in fissures, to form dykes and sills, or it forms larger bodies (plutons). In these cases the principle of superposition does not apply, but it is obvious that the rocks surrounding the pluton or smaller intrusion must have existed for the magma to intrude into them! The surrounding rocks must be older than the intrusion, whatever its size.

■   What is the boundary in Figure 6.8b between strata D and the older strata A and the granite intrusion called?

☐   An unconformity (Chapter 2).

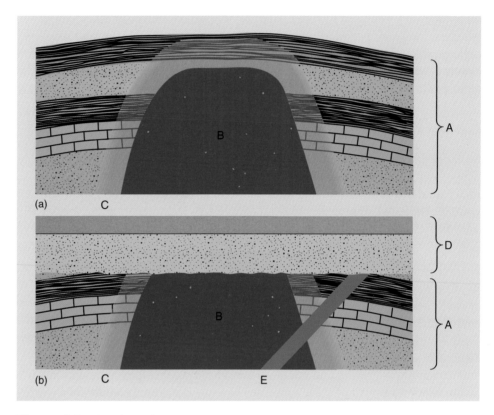

Figure 6.8   Sections through two granite intrusions showing different relationships with the surrounding sedimentary rocks. See text for discussion.

Unconformities indicate periods of erosion and often represent long intervals of geological time for which there are no sediments preserved in that particular area.

■   What is the relative age of the dyke (E) in Figure 6.8b? Explain your answer.

☐   The dyke cuts across the older strata (A), the granite (B) and the zone of contact metamorphism (C), but is truncated by the unconformity between A and D. It is therefore younger than the granite but older than the younger group of strata (D).

Question 6.3

Figure 6.9 is a sketch of a cross-section summarising several relationships observed in an area of well-exposed rocks. The main features are labelled A to G. From the relationships shown write a short account (up to 175 words) of the geological history of the area as a sequence of events in relative time. Write your account starting with the oldest event, and work progressively through younger ones. (*Hint*: before you start writing, find the youngest and simplest feature and work backwards to discover progressively earlier ones.)

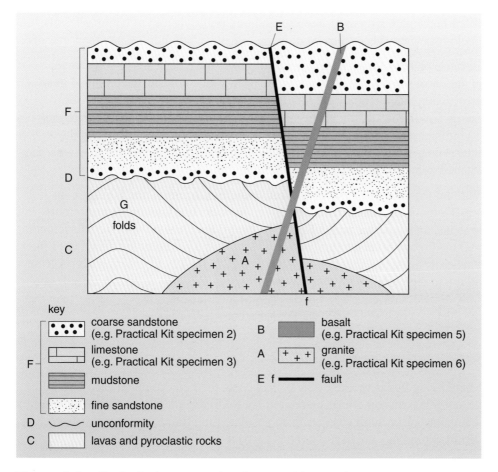

Figure 6.9   Geological cross-section for use with Question 6.3.

Having established the relative order of geological events in the section in Figure 6.9, what information would you need to give an absolute age to the rock formations? The two igneous intrusions, A and B, offer the best opportunity for absolute ages, being igneous rocks with minerals that may be dateable using natural radioactive isotopes.

■   If rock A has a radiometric age of 650 Ma, and rock B a radiometric age of 250 Ma, what can you say about the ages of the sedimentary strata above the unconformity D?

☐   They are older than B and so older than 250 Ma.

Similarly the age of 650 Ma for the granite gives a minimum age for the tectonic event that produced the folds G and a maximum age for the fault E. Using these principles it is possible to date the ages of sedimentary rocks and other geological events by **bracketing** them between igneous rocks of known absolute ages.

The stratigraphic column of the Phanerozoic, so finely divided by fossils before radiometric dating was invented, now has a global, real-time framework. Using Smith's principles, palaeontologists in the 19th and 20th centuries were able to match stratigraphic sequences on every continent. Where the stratigraphic column in one place was missing some sedimentary strata, another location filled in the gap. Except for the Precambrian rocks, devoid of tangible fossils, geologists knew where they were in the sequence, but didn't know their true age.

Because plate tectonics never stops, volcanoes have been active somewhere at the Earth's surface at all times in the past. While volcanism continued in an area, sedimentary strata were interlayered with lavas and pyroclastic rocks. So, on a global scale, the Phanerozoic stratigraphic column can be calibrated by radiometrically dating the volcanic layers and bracketing the age of the intervening sedimentary layers. Instead of a well-known sequence of events, the Phanerozoic became a quantitative history.

Without fossils as time markers in sedimentary sequences, the Precambrian was far more difficult to date. Moreover, its rocks had undergone many more igneous, metamorphic and deformation events than had those of the Phanerozoic, making Precambrian geology on every continent more complex than that of the Phanerozoic. Again, the igneous rocks provided the key to ordering events from region to region in a time frame, but details of the global sequence are still not fully agreed. Consequently, the division of the Precambrian is 'coarser' than that of 'the times of visible life', the Phanerozoic.

6.7   Summary of Chapter 6

Many living things record cyclical changes in their environment each year and these cycles can sometimes be seen in the fossil record. However, it is usually difficult to place these changes in an absolute time frame, and techniques such as dendrochronology are useful only as far back as 5000–10 000 years.

The principle of uniformitarianism states that the processes that produced the Earth's rocks in the past are the same as those we can observe acting on the Earth today, or infer from observation. Uniformitarianism developed as the successful alternative to catastrophism in the early 19th century.

The geological timescale cannot be quantified accurately by extrapolating from observed rates of active geological processes because these rates are too variable over long periods of time.

The only way in which geological time can be measured absolutely is through the use of naturally occurring radioactive isotopes with very long half-lives. Examples of radioactive decay schemes used in radiometric dating are the decay of uranium to lead and rubidium to strontium. The ratios of daughter to parent isotope atoms in rocks and minerals can be used to calculate their ages, but care must be taken to ensure that the sample has remained a closed system since the rock or mineral formed. Ages determined by this method are always subject to experimental uncertainty. Although the uncertainty can be as low as ±0.1%, even this small value translates to an absolute uncertainty of ±2 Ma for a determined age of 2000 Ma, and the uncertainties associated with radiometric ages are often greater than this.

Sediments can only rarely be dated using radiometric techniques. The stratigraphic column is calibrated by bracketing sedimentary formations with intrusive or extrusive igneous rocks that can be dated radiometrically.

Your study of this chapter has developed your knowledge of geological time and how it is determined. You have also developed your skills in the manipulation of numerical information, displaying and interpreting numerical information on graphs, including drawing a best-fit line through scattered data and calculating the gradient of the line to determine the rate of a process.

Chapter 7
Geology of the British Isles: perpetual change

Study note

Several place names in the British Isles are referred to in the text. If you are unfamiliar with them, an annotated map is supplied as a computer-based resource.

The geological evolution of the British Isles has a special place in the development of the science of geology, being one of the areas that was the first to be mapped in detail. This historical importance is reflected in some of the names of the major stratigraphic periods, most notably Devonian, named after the county in south-west England, Cambrian, after the Latin name for Wales and Ordovician and Silurian, named after Iron Age Welsh tribes. The British Isles also display a great variety of geological formations, including rocks from all of the major stratigraphic divisions established in Chapter 2, evidence of orogenic and tectonic activity ranging in age from the earliest Precambrian through to the Cenozoic, and igneous rocks spanning a similar age range.

In this chapter you will use some of the skills and knowledge that you gained earlier in this book to assess some key geoscientific observations that helped to unveil the remarkable history that shaped the crust beneath the British Isles. Four approaches are involved:

- establishing a sequence of events in relative time
- interpreting maps showing where rocks occur at the surface and extend beneath it
- assessing the conditions which produced rocks and the structures in them
- reconstructing past environments.

The aim is to give you a 'feel' for how history on the grand scale is pieced together in the context of local, regional and global geography and plate tectonics of the past. At several points in this chapter you will need access to computer-based resources.

7.1   Geological observations in time and space

Geologists have developed broad ideas about the relative timing of major events in the Earth's history from observations at unconformities (Section 2.8). An unconformity represents a gap in time, when weathering and erosion stripped the surface down, often after an orogeny (Section 5.3 and Figure 5.12). A surface of unconformity was once the landscape or seabed upon which sediments began to accumulate once uplift and erosion stopped, and often that surface was almost flat. Observations of the rocks below and above an unconformity provide a 'before and after' record of geological events that affected an area. Three profoundly significant unconformities break up the geological history of the British Isles.

7.1.1   The vestige of a beginning

The oldest unconformity in the British Isles is limited to a small area of the Highlands of northwest Scotland, where several isolated, steep-sided mountains rise above a low-lying but irregular surface spangled with lakes (Figure 7.1).

Figure 7.1   Aerial view of the distinctive mountain Suilven in Sutherland, Scotland, looking towards the northeast.

■ Which kind of rock makes up Suilven (Figure 7.1): igneous, sedimentary or metamorphic?

☐ The prominent horizontal layering suggests that the rocks are probably sedimentary in origin. The mountain in the background, Canisp, shows similar layering.

The topography surrounding Suilven is rough and uneven and its few exposures of rock show no clear layering. From an aerial view it is not possible to suggest the kind of rock that lies beneath this lower part of the landscape. An abrupt change in slope marks the base of the mountain, and tracing the slope change suggests that the base is roughly horizontal. The base of Suilven is a major geological boundary. A few kilometres to the north a roadside cutting exposes that boundary. Figure 7.2a shows a very sharp, horizontal contact between layered upper rocks and apparently featureless but hard ones below.

■ Briefly describe the upper rocks in Figure 7.2a, from the more detailed view in Figure 7.2b.

☐ Apart from the white patches of lichen, the rocks are reddish brown. There are coarse fragments in some of the layers and cross-bedding is present.

(a)

(b)

Figure 7.2   Exposures near Suilven. (a) A major geological boundary exposed by blasting in a nearby road cutting. (b) Close-up of the upper rocks in (a). Note that the pale patches in both photographs are lichens growing on the rock surface.

These observations confirm that the upper rocks, which form the mountain Suilven, are sedimentary. They are beds of sandstone and conglomerate, laid down by a moving fluid, hence the cross-bedding. Locally, they are known as the Torridonian Sandstones. Were they deposited by water or by wind? If by water, was it on land or are these marine sediments? A closer look at a hand specimen and through a microscope (Figure 7.3) helps answer these questions.

Question 7.1

After looking at the hand specimen and thin, transparent slice in Figure 7.3, answer the following questions.

(a) (i) Is the upper rock well or poorly sorted? (ii) Are the grains well or poorly rounded? (iii) Were these sedimentary rocks deposited in a high- or low-energy environment?

(a)

(b)

Figure 7.3   The rocks in Figure 7.2b: (a) hand specimen; (b) microscopic view, about 7 mm across, of a thin, transparent slice of (a). The cloudy, pale yellowish grains are alkali feldspar; the clear ones are quartz.

(b) In what kind of environment was the rock deposited: by wind in a desert; by water on land; on a beach? (If you need a reminder of transport and sorting, refer back to Activity 4.2.)

(c) Were the grains in the upper rock exposed for long to chemical weathering?

The Torridonian Sandstones were deposited by flowing water and are red-beds (Section 4.3.1), indicating oxygen-rich conditions when they formed. The cross-bedding (Figure 7.2b) is typical of the many-channelled streams which today flood across flat ground at the foot of most large mountain ranges. Yet Torridonian Sandstones contain neither animal nor plant fossils, and therefore probably pre-date the colonisation of the land surface. Radiometric dating of rare minerals that grew while fine-grained Torridonian sediments were being lithified dates them between 1200 and 1000 Ma.

The rocks beneath the unconformity, which form the low-lying, rough and uneven ground in Figure 7.1, are generally coated with lichens and often hidden by vegetation and peat as their terrain is poorly drained. As so often in the British Isles, these rocks show best when exposed on the seashore (Figure 7.4).

(a)   (b)

Figure 7.4　The lower rocks in Figure 7.2a. (a) A fresh shoreline exposure of the lower rocks in Figure 7.2a, about 2 m across. (b) A microscopic view, about 5 mm across, of a thin, transparent slice of (a). It contains clear quartz; white and cloudy feldspar; green amphibole; and the grey mineral slightly below centre is garnet.

These lower rocks are texturally very different from those above the unconformity.

■ Are the lower rocks in Figure 7.2a (shown in Figure 7.4) igneous, sedimentary or metamorphic? Once you have decided, suggest a name for the rock type.

☐ They are banded and coarsely crystalline, i.e. metamorphic. They are an excellent example of a gneiss (see Activity 5.1).

■ From Figure 7.4 and the information in its caption, suggest the chemical composition of these gneisses in terms of what you learned in Section 5.1.2.

☐ They contain roughly equal numbers of mafic and felsic bands. The felsic bands are quartz and feldspar, i.e. roughly granitic, whereas the mafic bands contain a lot of amphibole, i.e. roughly basaltic. So, overall, they are of intermediate or roughly andesitic composition.

These Lewisian gneisses – so-called because they make up most of the Hebridean island of Lewis – form the continental crust beneath northern Britain. Dating of zircons (Section 6.5) shows that the Lewisian formed originally as andesitic igneous rocks between 2800 and 3000 Ma ago – they are Europe's oldest rock formation – and were metamorphosed at around 2600 Ma. The last major deformation to affect them occurred around 1800 Ma ago. So, the unconformity beneath the Torridonian Sandstone records a period of between 600 and 800 Ma during which there is no sign that sediments were deposited or that magmas formed in what is now northern Britain. Instead a mountain range made of thickened continental crust was slowly eroded down.

The later geological record of the British Isles is much more complete. The next step in its division involves a second unconformity, where the immensity of geological time first dawned on one of the founders of the geosciences.

7.1.2 Witness to orogeny

Lawyer and physician James Hutton (1726–1797), who lived in Edinburgh during the late 18th century, was a keen observer of his surroundings. On one excursion along the coast of southeast Scotland he was confronted by the rock exposures shown in Figure 7.5, now known widely as Hutton's Unconformity. In Figure 7.5a, the geologists are sitting just above the unconformity on the upper rocks which dip gently northwards (to the left). The lower rocks, beneath the unconformity are different, and you may be able to trace the unconformity from right to left as a fairly sharp line on the picture.

(a)

(b)

(c)

Figure 7.5   Siccar Point on the Berwickshire coast of Scotland: (a) Hutton's Unconformity, looking eastwards; (b) the upper rocks in close-up; (c) the lower rocks in close up – the coin is 30 mm across.

Activity 7.1   The Siccar Point unconformity

We expect this activity will take you between 15 and 30 minutes.

The aim here is to deduce the steps in the geological evolution of southeastern Scotland from the relationships and other features at Siccar Point by studying Figure 7.5 and referring, if necessary, to earlier chapters.

Task 1

The upper rocks in Figure 7.5a are about 380 Ma old (Upper Devonian). They are shown in close-up in Figure 7.5b. Describe them and suggest an environment in which they may have formed (*50–100 words*).

Task 2

The lower rocks in Figure 7.5a contain fossil trilobites (which you looked at in Activity 2.1) and are about 420 Ma old (Upper Silurian). They are shown in close-up in Figure 7.5c. Describe them and suggest an environment in which they may have formed (*50–80 words*).

Task 3

Suggest a sequence of tectonic and surface processes that would account for the unconformity (*50–100 words*).

Now read the comments on this activity at the end of this book.

The unconformity at Siccar Point signifies that between 420 and 380 Ma, southern Scotland experienced an orogeny and then erosion of the resulting mountain belt. By the time the surface of southern Scotland had been reduced to an almost flat plain, erosion had not penetrated to a depth in this area where regional metamorphism had occurred during the orogeny. James Hutton was the first to realise the implications of unconformities, and for this reason is numbered among the 'fathers' of geology.

Through the rest of the Devonian and the succeeding Carboniferous Period, most of southern Scotland, England and Wales experienced almost unbroken sedimentation. In northern Scotland, there are no Carboniferous sedimentary rocks. That absence can be explained by the continued rise of the mountain belt in northern Scotland where erosion unloaded the lower crust and asthenosphere (Figure 6.12). This 'passive' behaviour was interrupted at the end of the Carboniferous Period (300 Ma) by orogenic events that are recorded in the rocks of much of central and western Europe, southern Ireland, South Wales and southwestern England, to produce a third fundamental unconformity.

7.1.3   The Permian Desert

The third unconformity which helps to divide the geological history of the British Isles is best exposed in Southwest England, close to the South Devon coastal resort of Torquay (Figure 7.6).

(a)   (b)

Figure 7.6   (a) Permian rocks resting unconformably above more steeply dipping Devonian rocks near to Torquay in southwest England. The unconformity is about two-thirds of the way up the cliff, beneath the conglomerate, and marked by its angular discordance with the tilted beds below it. Although it is not obvious, the lower rocks dip at about 50° away from the viewpoint. (b) Modern boulder beds laid down by a torrent in Death Valley , California, USA.

In this case, the upper rocks in Figure 7.6a are of Permian age, about 270 Ma old. They are red conglomerates containing large, rounded boulders; this is clear evidence of very high-energy transportation by water and deposition on land under the oxidising influence of the atmosphere. Crude bedding in the conglomerates dips gently towards the right. Figure 7.6b shows a modern analogy for their probable environment of deposition: boulder beds deposited on the floor of Death Valley by torrents that drain occasional heavy rainfall from the surrounding mountains.

The rocks beneath the unconformity are layered on a scale of tens of centimetres and are fine-grained mudstones and siltstones. Their layering dips more steeply than that above the unconformity. They are Devonian, roughly the same age (~380 Ma) as the upper rocks at Siccar Point (Figure 7.5a). Despite their red coloration by Fe^{3+} oxide, these are not terrestrial sediments. They contain fossil brachiopods and other marine animals, and were deposited on a deep sea floor to the south of the Devonian land surface that covered the rest of Britain. They are red because they were exposed at the land surface and weathered before being covered by the Permian conglomerates. The unconformity at the base of the Permian elsewhere in southwest England rests on similar deep-water marine mudstones and siltstones that are Carboniferous in age, and also on the granites shown in Figure 3.4.

Although slightly disturbed occasionally by far-off orogenies, much of the record of the British Isles for the following 270 Ma is one of more or less continual sediment deposition, with one dramatic episode of volcanic activity (Section 7.2.5). The rocks take the general form of a simple 'layer cake' in

147

which the principle of superposition shows the upwards passage of time and events. Activity 7.2 reveals changing environments in southwest England through the first 50 Ma of this relatively quiet period, during the Permian and Triassic Periods.

Activity 7.2   A geological field trip

We expect this activity will take you approximately 60 minutes.

You will need to view and work through the computer-based activity, *A Geological Field Trip*.

This interactive activity simulates three field visits to Permian, Triassic and lower Jurassic rocks that are exposed in southwest England. While using it you will learn how to record observations in note form and as geological sketches. You may find it useful to refer back to Chapter 4, especially Activity 4.2 and Section 4.3.1.

The field techniques covered by this activity are used widely by geologists. The first step is to get a general, broad view of an exposure from around 10–50 m, to see how the various parts are related. Then you can move in to examine specific features of interest in more detail, and to look at hand specimens of the rocks. Hand specimens help to identify particular rock characteristics (such as texture and the minerals present), which in turn will help you to identify the rock type and the conditions under which it formed. A final look at the exposure from a greater distance again often enables you to see additional features which you missed at first. In practice, field studies involve repetition; a lot of prowling around rocks.

Field notebook pages recording observations at each site provide an essential summary of the main features exposed there and their interpretation. Typically, a notebook will also include annotated sketches illustrating particular features. Of course, photographs will show detail that is impossible to draw, but a simple sketch is a vital reminder of your main geological observations.

Task 1

Visit the sites in order of decreasing age of the exposed rocks, starting at Dawlish with Permian rocks that occur just above the conglomerates in Figure 7.6a. Then go on to Budleigh Salterton, and finally visit Aust Cliff.

At each locality you should make notes on what you see in the notebook pages that follow; the headings on the left will give you an indication of what to look for. (You should look at the Main view, the Close view and then the Rock specimen screens.) When you have completed each locality, check your notes against the information that is given by working through the Notebook section. *Don't worry if you miss some of the details* – it takes time to understand which features are important and to be able to recognise them in a new situation. You will probably see more if you repeat each visit; then you can add any details that you missed.

Notebook pages

Locality: Dawlish, Devon	Description
Rock age: Upper Permian (255 Ma) Rock characteristics Colour: Texture: Grain shape: Grain size: Grain composition: Features: Rock identification:	

Locality: Budleigh Salterton, Devon	Description
Rock age: Middle Triassic (240 Ma) Rock characteristics Colour: Texture: Grain shape: Grain size:	

contd overleaf

Sorting: Features: Rock identification:	

Locality: Aust Cliff, Avon (focus on upper part of cliff) Rock age: Upper Triassic to Lower Jurassic (220–200 Ma) Rock characteristics Colour: Texture: Grain size: Grain composition: Sorting: Features: Rock identification:	**Description**

Task 2 Producing a geological sketch from a photograph

After studying the 'sketches' sections at each locality, and noting the guidance on drawing sketches, try sketching part of the cliff at Dawlish, shown in Figure 7.7a. (The top and bottom of the sketch have been started for you in Figure 7.7b.) You might be wondering 'Why make a sketch, when I have a photograph of the cliff?' The point is that nature is 'messy', mixing geological features with vegetation (the many plants on the cliff), manufactured objects (the fence), and products of recent sediment deposition (beach sediments). A sketch should *emphasise* and *simplify* the features in the rocks by omitting non-geological detail in order to bring out geological relationships.

(a)

(b)

Figure 7.7 (a) View of the cliff face at Dawlish. (b) Space for a sketch of the cliff face shown in part (a).

Now look at the comments on this activity at the end of this book.

Figure 7.6a and Activity 7.2 illustrated isolated exposures of sedimentary rocks whose short periods of deposition are separated from each other by tens of millions of years. However, they reveal that each short interval witnessed very different environments in the Lower Permian to Upper Triassic as follows.

- At the start of the Permian, what is now the Torquay area (Figure 7.6a) experienced torrential floods that deposited conglomerates immediately above the unconformity. It probably lay at the foot of rapidly eroding mountains made of deformed Devonian and Carboniferous marine sedimentary rocks. Erosion of the mountains also exposed undeformed granite plutons that had intruded those earlier sedimentary rocks (Figure 4.4). Fragments of these granites occur in the Permian conglomerates, so the granites are older than Permian but younger than the Carboniferous rocks of the area, and the deformation. Radiometric dating shows that granite intrusion took place between 293–273 Ma.

- At Dawlish, red desert dune sandstones of Permian age overlie the same conglomerates as seen at Torquay, showing that the area was dry, highly oxidising and windy during the Permian.

- The Middle Triassic conglomerates of Budleigh Salterton show a return to torrential transport of debris being eroded from the remaining mountains of southwest England. Their red coloration indicates continued hot, oxidising conditions.

- Aust Cliff exposes lower red mudstones deposited under low-energy conditions on land, which probably had become quite flat by Upper Triassic times. The red-beds are abruptly succeeded in the upper part of the cliff by fine-grained, green-grey mudstones and limestones, which contain abundant marine fossils of Lower Jurassic age. Either the crust had subsided locally or sea level had risen globally, to inundate what had been land for at least 60 Ma.

Other Permian and Triassic exposures in southwest England fill in the time gaps, to show a continuous history of changing environments from 270 to 200 Ma. However, in the same way as human history records different sequences of events in different areas, so geological history has a geographic dimension. Because modern environments of many kinds (e.g. deserts, rain forests and bare mountains; coral reefs, deep sea floor and tidal coasts) make up the global picture, a similar environmental diversity probably characterised the geological past, whatever the overall global climate. One aim of studying geological history is to reconstruct the **palaeogeography**, to see how that relates to evidence for plate tectonic influences and how it changed through time. Section 7.3 introduces this wider dimension, including the arid Permian Period in the British Isles, and then how local palaeogeography can be seen in a global context.

Generally, observations of the kind you made in Activities 7.1 and 7.2 are recorded in a field notebook, each visited locality warranting its own record. Many records spread over wider geographical areas provide information that can be expressed on a map, but one that is different in many respects from those you may be familiar with. A geological map expresses the kinds of rock, and rocks of different ages, lying immediately below the land surface, sometimes to be exposed where soil and vegetation have been stripped away by erosion, as in Activity 7.1. Published geological maps contain a vast amount of information, simply because even the small area represented by a standard 1:50 000 topographic map may contain rocks of many different kinds that span tens or even hundreds of millions of years. Yet, given a few basic observations, it is not difficult to begin working out events in Earth history from the features that geological maps show.

7.2   Geological maps: charts of Earth history

Study note

To study this section fully you need to view detailed digital images (supplied as a computer-based resource) of some of the figures.

As well as observations of rocks and their relationships on the ground, much more familiar observations of the environment help in constructing geological maps. Rocks vary greatly in the way they respond to erosion. Some are more resistant than others and tend to form higher, more rugged ground. As a general rule, sedimentary rocks are much less resistant than crystalline igneous and metamorphic rocks. Among sedimentary rocks, beds of sandstone and limestone tend to form escarpments and ridges, whereas finer-grained siltstones and mudstones are picked out by erosion to form low ground between upstanding, tougher sedimentary rocks (Figure 7.8). The older a sedimentary rock is, the more likely it is to have become strongly lithified (Section 4.4) through cementation by carbonates and quartz precipitated from waters that have percolated through when it was buried by younger sediments. Older sequences of sedimentary rocks, subject to deeper burial, also have a greater chance of being deformed by folding and faulting during orogenies.

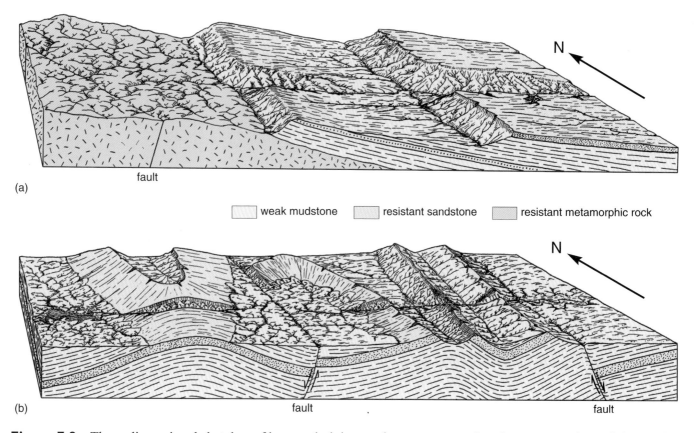

Figure 7.8   Three-dimensional sketches of how underlying geology may control surface topography and the trends and patterns of streams flowing across it. (a) Simply dipping sequence of sedimentary rocks overlying crystalline rocks. (b) A folded and faulted sequence of sedimentary rocks.

Figure 7.8a shows in 3D how beds of sedimentary rocks that are simply dipping beneath the surface are picked out according to their resistance: more resistant beds form escarpments, while less resistant ones are etched out to form valleys. Also shown are the minor streams that tend to flow on such a landscape. On the left there are older crystalline rocks that the sedimentary rocks had once buried beneath an unconformity. By resisting erosion uniformly, the crystalline rocks control landforms that have no particular orientation, except where faults occur. Being products of repeated earthquakes, faults shatter the rocks they cut through and become weak zones which erosion may etch out (Book 2, Figure 3.3) to create clear linear elements in the landscape.

Figure 7.8b shows more complicated landforms which may form when erosion has cut through a folded sequence of sedimentary rocks. Steeply dipping resistant beds tend to form linear ridges rather than the more irregular escarpments that develop on horizontal or gently dipping strata. Alternating resistant and softer strata pick out the effects of folds on the topography as broad curved features.

Topographic features controlled by the underlying geology are best identified from far away, using images and other data captured by Earth-orbiting satellites.

Figure 7.9 shows topographic elevation across the British Isles given a 3D appearance by computer-generated 'illumination' from the west. Study it for a few minutes, looking for evidence of escarpments formed by gently dipping sedimentary strata, sharp straight lines that may be major faults or ridges controlled by steeply dipping sedimentary strata, and curved linear features that may outline large folds. The areas to focus on are outlined. The features will be clearer if you view the enlargeable digital images of those areas of Figure 7.9.

Some of the clearest linear features are in Scotland (area 1). One stretches NE–SW between Inverness and Fort William and marks the line of the Great Glen Fault – a transform fault (Book 2, Section 8.2) which was active between 400 and 300 Ma. Another is the straight southern edge to the Scottish Highlands, running ENE–WSW from Stonehaven to just north of Glasgow. This is the Highland Boundary Fault which was formed by tensional tectonic forces. To the south of it, the crust beneath the Scottish Midland Valley has dropped by more than one kilometre. It too began forming around 400 Ma ago, and is still occasionally active. About 80 km SSE, a series of thin, sharp lines mark the northern limit of the hills in southern Scotland. This is the Southern Uplands Fault, against which the crust dropped down to the north.

Southernmost Ireland (area 2) shows other linear features in 'batches' of short, roughly parallel ridges and valleys that trend WSW–ENE. These features are controlled by sedimentary strata that dip steeply into the Earth. Some resist erosion and form ridges, while others that are less resistant define valleys.

The east of England (area 3) is very different. There are no sharp linear features and the topography is quite gentle and at low elevations. However, it is possible to trace a series of broad tracts of slightly higher land that trend roughly N–S and have west-facing escarpments. Each is underlain by a resistant sedimentary stratum that dips gently eastwards (similar to Figure 7.8a). Some of the escarpments can be traced to the southwest of area 3, where they swing around to trend NE–SW.

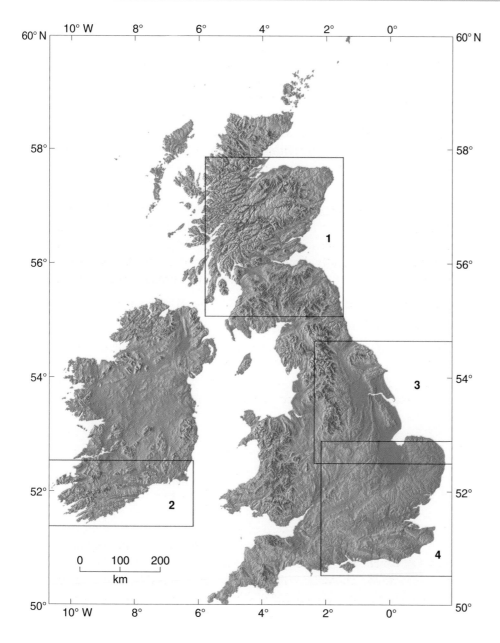

Figure 7.9 The topography of the British Isles measured by radar from a satellite and shaded by 'illumination' from the west – the topography is exaggerated so that features are easier to see. The colour coding ranges from greens for low elevations through browns to grey at elevations greater than 500 m. Concentrate on areas 1–4 which are shown by black outlines. You are encouraged to use the enlargeable digital images – see the module website for details.

Now shift your focus to southeast England (area 4). There are features in the topography that outline a strange, crudely elliptical shape, cut through by the English Channel in the east. The features seem to have been bent and, as you will see in Section 7.2.1, this is the case.

Despite the possibilities presented by space technology, such as that used to make Figure 7.9, mapping rocks still involves field observations and data recording. In a small, densely populated area, such as the British Isles, geologists have examined nearly every surface rock occurrence, and then plotted on a map the boundaries between occurrences of different types and ages of rock, helped by rock-related topographic features. The resulting geological maps have a striking appearance because of the colour scheme needed to signify where rocks of different types and ages occur at the Earth's surface.

Figure 7.10 is a highly simplified geological map of the British Isles. The top eleven coloured divisions in its key correspond to sedimentary rocks that were laid down during the Periods of the Phanerozoic, and to older (542–1000 Ma), non-fossiliferous sedimentary rocks of Precambrian age. Four enlargeable digital versions of Figure 7.10 are available which superimpose the geology on the topographic image in Figure 7.9 (see the module website for details of where to find them). They cover the four study areas shown in Figure 7.9 and will help you to appreciate how geology controls landforms.

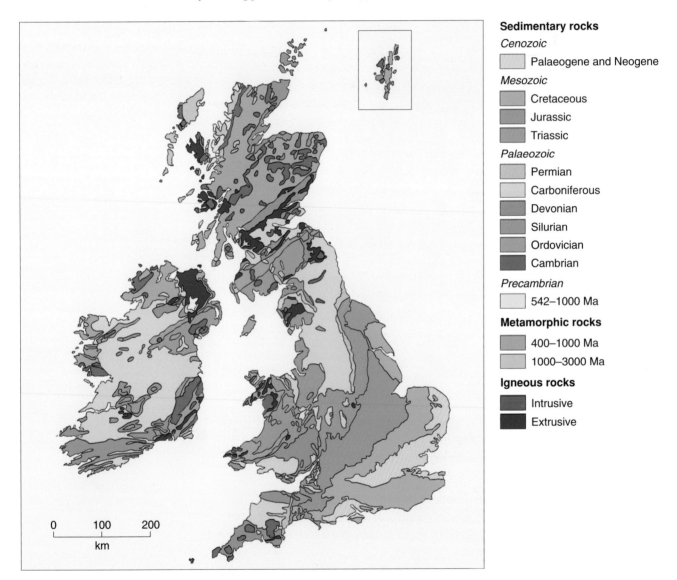

Sedimentary rocks

Cenozoic

Palaeogene and Neogene

Mesozoic

Cretaceous

Jurassic

Triassic

Palaeozoic

Permian

Carboniferous

Devonian

Silurian

Ordovician

Cambrian

Precambrian

542–1000 Ma

Metamorphic rocks

400–1000 Ma

1000–3000 Ma

Igneous rocks

Intrusive

Extrusive

0   100   200
km

Figure 7.10   Simplified geological map of the British Isles. Each division includes a very wide range of different kinds of sedimentary, metamorphic and igneous rocks. Digital versions combining geology with the topography of Figure 7.9 are available for the four study areas in Figure 7.9.

■ Which parts of the British Isles are dominated by sedimentary rocks?

☐ They are most abundant at the surface in the southern two-thirds of the landmass.

Below the sedimentary divisions there are two rock groups signifying that they were greatly transformed by regional metamorphism. One group of metamorphic rocks formed during orogenies between 400 and 1000 Ma (Section 7.1.2); the other group formed at various times between about 1000 and 3000 Ma (Section 7.1.1).

■ Where do each of these metamorphic divisions occur at the surface?

☐ That between 400 and 1000 Ma dominates northern Scotland and northwestern Ireland, whereas the older group occurs in northwestern Scotland and the Hebrides, and in small patches in the west and southeast of Ireland.

Regionally metamorphosed rocks of the younger division also occur in the southern two-thirds of the British Isles, but only in small areas. Their key colour shows as a narrow belt in the promontory of southeastern Ireland. Follow its trend to the northeast across the Irish Sea, and you will discover it again in the island of Anglesey and the Lleyn Peninsula of North Wales.

The final division is into intrusive and extrusive igneous rocks. The two distinctive key colours reveal that the British Isles is dotted with evidence for the intrusion and extrusion of magmas. Note, however, that sedimentary rocks of Carboniferous and younger ages are barely, if at all, interrupted by igneous materials. The igneous rocks are not divided by age to keep this map simple (that detail will appear in Figure 7.16).

The geological map of the British Isles confirms the immense timespan represented by rocks in this small area, and that they were assembled by processes operating in all three fundamental parts of the rock cycle. This section uses two fundamental unconformities (Section 7.1) in the British Isles to introduce you to understanding and 'reading' geological maps. An unconformity separates younger and structurally simpler rocks above it from the more complicated geology formed by older events. The later of these unconformities (Section 7.1.3) is a useful and easily understood starting point.

7.2.1 Above and below the Permian unconformity

Permian and Triassic sedimentary rocks extend continuously from southwest England to the Midlands, where they split into two belts that extend to North

West and North East England (Figure 7.11a). There are isolated exposures elsewhere. Permian and Triassic terrestrial red-beds lie above a major unconformity, and they are important markers representing arid tropical conditions, which deposited sediment on top of eroded mountains.

Figure 7.11a shows only the main occurrences of sedimentary rocks of Permian and Triassic age, including the area in southwestern England which you studied in Activity 7.2. To simplify matters, it groups all older rocks beneath the Permian unconformity as a single unit and younger rocks on top of the Permian and Triassic red-beds as another. The more rugged landscapes of northwestern Britain are mainly underlain by rocks which are older than Permian. The line separating the older (brown) rocks from the Permian and Triassic, is where the Permian unconformity occurs at the surface (more about that in Section 7.2.2).

The younger (Mesozoic and Cenozoic) rocks occur mainly in the dominantly lowland areas of eastern and southeastern England; the exceptions are three large patches of Cenozoic igneous rocks in Northern Ireland and the Inner Hebrides. Figure 7.11b adds the younger Mesozoic and Cenozoic sedimentary rock divisions. The roughly parallel swathes of colour show where each division – Permian, Triassic, Jurassic, Cretaceous and Cenozoic – occurs at the surface.

Display the enlargeable, digital version of Figure 7.10 (area 3) to examine eastern England at full resolution. Bands of colour superimposed on the topography correspond to Mesozoic and Cenozoic rocks. (Refer to Figure 7.11b for the Permian, Mesozoic and Cenozoic colour divisions.)

■ Are there any topographic features that seem to be related to the geological divisions younger than, and to the east of, the Permian?

☐ Several long escarpments trend roughly parallel to the geological boundaries whose steep 'well-lit' slopes face towards the west to northwest.

These escarpments are controlled by resistant Jurassic and Cretaceous limestones, including the Cretaceous Chalk that underlies the downlands and wolds of southeastern and eastern England. Resistant Jurassic sandstones underlie the hills in Cleveland. The roughly coincident patterns of land forms and geological Periods show that the underlying geology has a major influence on the landscape. Travelling eastwards from Triassic rocks progressively give way to younger Jurassic, then Cretaceous and finally Cenozoic sedimentary rocks.

All the prominent sedimentary strata of Permian and younger ages in this area slope or *dip* at a few degrees to the southeast, from the Midlands towards London – Figure 7.8a can help you visualise this. This dip is imposed by regional tilting of the crust, after deposition of the youngest Cenozoic rocks, and results in strata of each Period descending eastward beneath the surface, to be hidden

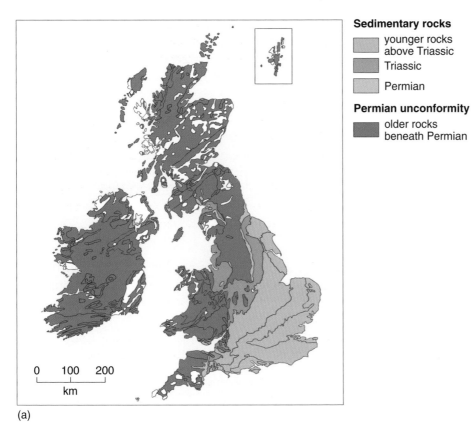

Sedimentary rocks

younger rocks above Triassic

Triassic

Permian

Permian unconformity

older rocks beneath Permian

(a)

Figure 7.11 (a) Map showing the occurrence of Permian and Triassic sedimentary rocks, and younger and older rocks. (b) Map of sedimentary rocks that are Permian and younger. Note that the blank areas in both maps are igneous rocks of various ages (see Figure 7.16).

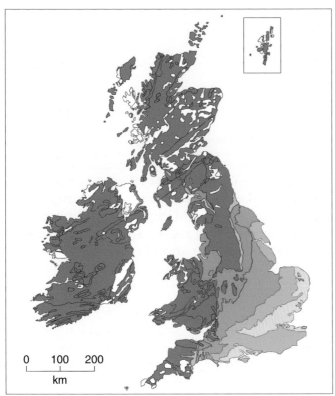

Sedimentary rocks

Cenozoic

Palaeogene and Neogene

Mesozoic

Cretaceous

Jurassic

Triassic

Palaeozoic

Permian

Permian unconformity

older rocks beneath Permian

(b)

by those of the next younger Period (Figure 7.12a). Their dip also suggests that Mesozoic and Cenozoic sedimentary rocks once extended over areas further to the west of their present exposures. The erosion which followed the tilting has removed them from the former western extents.

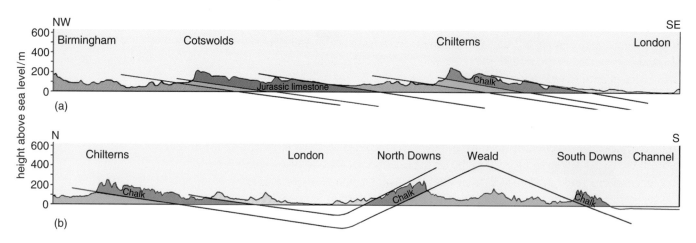

Figure 7.12   (a) Simplified NW–SE topographic and geological cross-section from Birmingham to London. (b) Simplified N–S topographic and geological cross-section from the Chilterns to Brighton. (*Note*: the vertical scales of both sections are greatly exaggerated, so the angles appear much larger than they are in reality.)

■   If a borehole was drilled vertically below Norwich what is the downward order of rocks that you would encounter?

☐   Cenozoic rocks occur at the surface and because the older rocks dip eastwards beneath Norwich, the next rocks down would be Cretaceous in age, then Jurassic, Triassic and Permian. If the borehole penetrated deep enough, eventually it would pass through the Permian unconformity.

Conversely, a borehole in Birmingham would pass through only the Triassic and perhaps the Permian, before hitting the Permian unconformity, because younger rocks were long ago eroded from their former extent.

Further south, beyond the Chilterns (area 4), the Cretaceous and Cenozoic divisions form more complex patterns in Figure 7.10. Cenozoic rocks around London define a 'V' shape pointing westwards, and an 'eye' shape surrounding Southampton. A broad area of Cretaceous rocks separates the two shapes. Once again, clues come from topographic features in the digital version of Figure 7.10, area 4. Figure 7.8b should help you understand the topography. Landforms on Cretaceous rocks define a prominent 'eye' shape in Sussex and Kent. Bearing in mind that the topography is 'illuminated' from the northwest, you should be able to see that the shape is outlined by two escarpments, running E–W to the north and south of the shape, and 'bending' around to meet in the west. The northern escarpment (the North Downs) faces steeply towards the south – in shadow – whereas the southern escarpment (the South Downs) faces north – well lit. An elongated topographic dome separates them. The thick Cretaceous Chalk forms both escarpments. In the South Downs the chalk dips gently southwards, whereas in the North Downs it dips to the north. The 'eye-shaped' topographic feature is controlled by an open, eroded upfold trending E–W.

A cross-section running NW–SE from the Chilterns to London and then N–S to Brighton (Figure 7.12b) shows this upfold and a related downfold beneath London. Cenozoic sediments have been preserved in the downfold, but eroded away from the crest of the upfold, across which they would once have extended (see Figure 7.8b). The downfold is responsible for the westward 'V' shape of the Cretaceous rocks in Figure 7.11b.

Returning briefly to the distribution of Permian and Triassic sedimentary rocks (Figure 7.11a), the Triassic rocks are more widely distributed than the Permian ones. This is partly because the younger Triassic rocks may be hiding buried Permian strata. However, note how, around the Severn Estuary, in the West Midlands and the plains extending to west Lancashire, the Triassic sits directly on pre-Permian rocks. The simplest explanation is that no Permian deposition occurred in these areas. They were uplands during the Permian, and only when erosion had worn them flat did Triassic deposition begin there above an unconformity. Such inferences from geological observations help the visualisation of long-vanished landscapes and geography, a subject to which you will return in Section 7.3.

7.2.2   Devonian and Carboniferous sedimentary rocks

The Devonian and Carboniferous sedimentary rocks in Figure 7.13 occur above the Devonian unconformity (Section 7.1.2) but are below and partly hidden by rocks above the Permian unconformity. Orogenic events folded and faulted both Devonian and Carboniferous rocks, accounting for their more irregular patterns than those of Permian and younger rocks. By reference to Figure 7.11, you can see in southwest England how E–W strips of Carboniferous and Devonian rocks become hidden beneath the Permian unconformity.

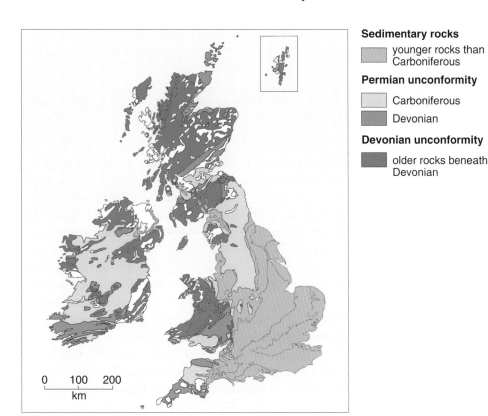

Sedimentary rocks

younger rocks than Carboniferous

Permian unconformity

Carboniferous

Devonian

Devonian unconformity

older rocks beneath Devonian

0   100   200
km

Figure 7.13   Map showing the occurrence of Devonian and Carboniferous sedimentary rocks, and younger and older rocks. Note that the blank areas are igneous rocks of various ages (see Figure 7.16).

■ Look at southern Ireland and southwestern England on Figure 7.13. How might the repetition of E–W strips of Devonian and Carboniferous rocks have come about, bearing in mind the patterns you saw in the Cenozoic of southeastern England (Figure 7.11b)?

□ They might be caused by tight upfolds and downfolds affecting rocks of the two Periods. This impression is stronger if you examine the digital image of area 2 in southern Ireland (Figure 7.9).

The Devonian and Carboniferous rocks of both areas, and those in South Wales, are indeed strongly folded (Figure 7.14a). They were deformed during mountain building that affected Belgium, France, Portugal and Spain at the end of the Carboniferous in the **Variscan Orogeny**. Southern Ireland, South Wales and South West England were then at the northern limit of the Variscan mountain belt. Elsewhere in the British Isles, both Devonian and Carboniferous rocks were much less deformed by those tectonic forces (Figure 7.14b). They were, however, broadly folded, as shown in northern England by the distribution of Carboniferous strata (Figure 7.13).

(a)

(b)

Figure 7.14   (a) Large folds in Carboniferous muddy marine sediments in North Devon, England. (b) Undeformed horizontal beds of Carboniferous limestones resting unconformably on vertical Silurian mudstones at Horton, North Yorkshire, England.

Question 7.2

From what you learned about regional fold structures in Section 7.2.1, suggest an explanation for the distribution in Figure 7.13 of Carboniferous rocks in northern England (ignore the small occurrences in the south).

Much of central Ireland comprises almost horizontal Carboniferous and Devonian rocks. In Scotland, the Midland Valley has Carboniferous rocks flanked to the north and the south by older Devonian rocks; a pattern that suggests a broad ENE–WSW-trending downfold. Further north, in Scotland, the Devonian occurs alone to form an eastern fringe around the Scottish Highlands. Interestingly, from Birmingham to the border of Scotland there are no Devonian rocks beneath the Carboniferous. During that Period, northern England was probably an upland area.

7.2.3   Getting to the roots: beneath the Devonian unconformity

In general, the older that rocks are, the more likely it is that an orogeny has affected them. Except for its southernmost parts, the crust beneath the British Isles was extensively deformed before the Devonian during the **Caledonian Orogeny**. The 100 Ma preceding the Devonian unconformity saw the creation of the crustal mass that now forms the basement of the whole British Isles. Evidence for that bold conclusion comes from rocks in the more rugged west and northwest.

Figure 7.15a highlights rocks that are older than the Devonian. The colour scheme shows a clear division between a northern block dominated by regionally metamorphosed rocks, and one exposed patchily to the south that consists mainly of sedimentary rocks ranging from Cambrian to Silurian in age (542 to 416 Ma). The Devonian unconformity at Siccar Point (Section 7.1.2), and throughout England, Wales and southern Ireland, signifies mountain building to the *south* of the Scottish Midland Valley which occurred between 420 and 380 Ma ago, during a southern phase of the Caledonian Orogeny, followed by intense erosion.

Devonian terrestrial sedimentary rocks in the north of Scotland and in Northern Ireland cover and partly hide older rocks that are very different from the lower rocks at Siccar Point. Most were once sediments but they are Cambrian or older (510–1000 Ma). These northern, pre-Devonian rocks are immensely deformed, and have been regionally metamorphosed to such a high grade that some of the sediments partially melted. That northern phase of the Caledonian Orogeny reached a climax around 470 Ma ago, during the Ordovician. At that time, marine deposition continued over much of the rest of the British Isles.

How could a mountain-building event as extreme as those which much later created the Himalaya and the Alps, in the north of such a small region, leave the south unscathed, until it too was deformed, but far less intensely, at least 50 Ma years later? Major tectonic structures in the British Isles, which formed before the Devonian unconformity, provide clues that help resolve this paradox in space and time (Figure 7.15b).

7.2.4   Faults and fold trends

The three largest faults in Figure 7.15b are the Great Glen, Highland Boundary and Southern Uplands Faults (Section 7.2). To the northwest of the Great Glen Fault there is another huge fault, the Moine Thrust that dips eastwards, on top of which the high-grade metamorphic rocks of the Scottish Highlands were pushed sideways and westwards. All four faults began to form during the Caledonian Orogeny. The big faults were crustal responses to forces that also intensely folded both the high-grade northern Caledonian mountain belt and its low-grade southern part. The main fold trends are shown in Figure 7.15b. The boundary between the northern and southern parts of the Caledonian Orogeny seems to coincide with the Southern Uplands Fault. Structures formed by the Variscan Orogeny cut across those of the Caledonian orogenic belt in South Wales and southern Ireland.

The relatively simple, younger geology of the southern and eastern British Isles is just a thin veneer that now hides a deeper complexity, which stemmed from two great orogenies, Caledonian and Variscan. Some idea of this complex 'basement'

Figure 7.15   (a) Map showing the distribution of pre-Devonian rocks from 415 to 3000 Ma old, and the area of younger rocks resting on top. The blank areas are igneous rock of various ages (see Figure 7.16).
(b) Map showing the major faults and alignments of folds in the orogenic belts of the British Isles. The grey areas are where almost undeformed rocks occur at the surface.

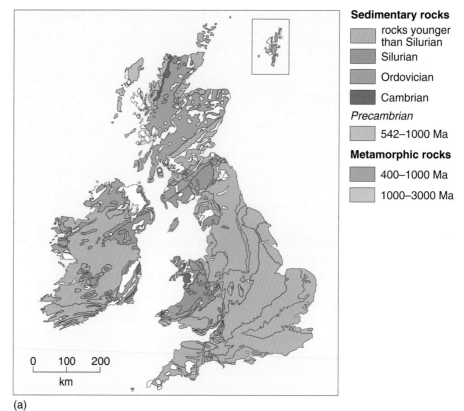

Sedimentary rocks
- rocks younger than Silurian
- Silurian
- Ordovician
- Cambrian

Precambrian
- 542–1000 Ma

Metamorphic rocks
- 400–1000 Ma
- 1000–3000 Ma

(a)

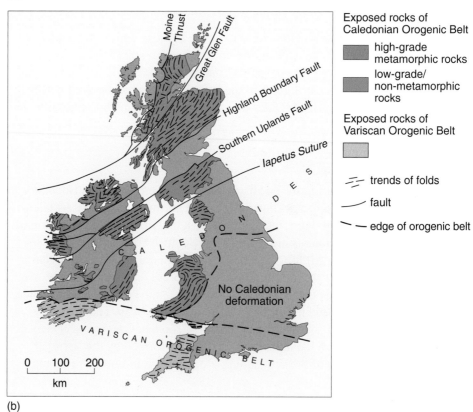

Exposed rocks of Caledonian Orogenic Belt
- high-grade metamorphic rocks
- low-grade/ non-metamorphic rocks

Exposed rocks of Variscan Orogenic Belt

- trends of folds
- fault
- edge of orogenic belt

(b)

comes from a few small surface occurrences of the older rocks, from deep boreholes and from geophysical measurements of the magnetic and gravitational fields over the region. Deep boreholes through the younger rock cover in the English Midlands found no evidence for Caledonian deformation in the deep, pre-Devonian rocks, and the irregular dashed line in Figure 7.15b seems to be its southeastern limit. Were future erosion to remove all the Permian and younger sedimentary rocks, it would reveal a crustal 'architecture' made of a series of narrow slivers of complex older rocks. Each sliver came into being at different times and probably as a result of different tectonic processes and settings, which are most clearly revealed by evidence from igneous rocks of the British Isles.

7.2.5   Volcanic episodes and plate tectonics

The British Isles are now far from active plate margins or hot spots, and not noted for their active volcanoes. So the information in Figure 7.16 might be a surprise; rocks of the northern and western parts record a lot of ancient igneous activity.

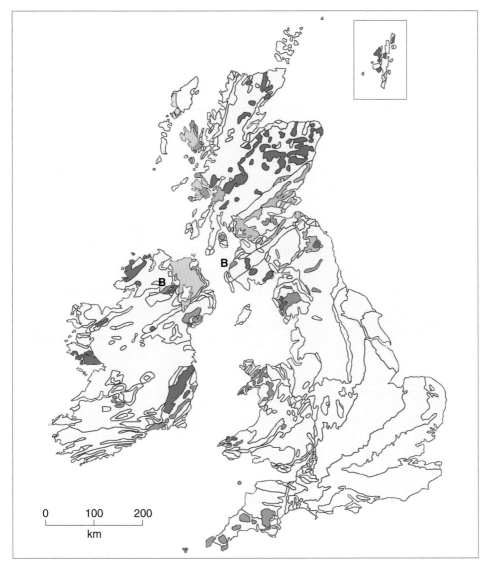

E	I	Cenozoic
E	I	Carboniferous
E	I	Devonian
E		Ordovician
	I	Precambrian

Figure 7.16   Occurrences of igneous rocks in the British Isles, colour by age; N.B. those of SW England are Permian. In the key, E signifies mainly extrusive igneous rocks and I intrusive. Lines through the non-igneous rocks are the geological boundaries shown on Figures 7.10, 7.11, 7.13 and 7.15a. (See text for explanation of labels 'B'.)

Apart from Precambrian occurrences (which are not considered here), during pre-Devonian times only the Ordovician Period witnessed major volcanic activity. Lavas and pyroclastic rocks occur in North Wales, the English Lake District and southern Ireland. Ordovician sedimentation in all three areas was marine, and magmas of intermediate, andesitic composition dominated the volcanic rocks, some submarine and others erupted on a land surface.

■ Suggest a likely tectonic setting for these three areas of Ordovician volcanism.

□ They experienced processes at a convergent plate margin associated today with *oceanic* volcanic arcs. (Divergent plate margins and hot spots would be basaltic.)

One other kind of Ordovician igneous activity, in southwest Scotland and Northern Ireland, is noteworthy despite its small extent (Bs in Figure 7.16). It produced basaltic pillow lavas and serpentinised peridotites at the very base of the Ordovician sequence. These occurrences provide clear evidence that the rocks along a line B–B were originally oceanic crust (Book 2, Section 8.5). The significance of this and of the Ordovician oceanic volcanic arc will become clear in Section 7.3.

The Devonian volcanic rocks extending from northern England through Scotland to the Orkney Isles, like those of the Ordovician, are dominantly andesitic. However, they formed on continental crust composed of products of the Caledonian Orogeny – the metamorphic complex of the Scottish Highlands, and the folded Ordovician and Silurian sediments of the Southern Uplands (Figure 7.15a). The Devonian sediments accompanying the volcanic rocks were deposited from mountain-front torrents, rivers and lakes. The Devonian igneous activity was that of a *continental* volcanic arc. Magmas rising from the mantle over a subduction zone accumulate beneath continental crust, undergo fractional crystallisation (Section 3.4) and sometimes partially melt older crust, so granite magmas may form. The Lower Devonian was a period of massive intrusion of granites into both parts of the Caledonian orogenic belt (Figure 7.16).

Magmatic events during the Carboniferous and Lower Permian were of two fundamentally different kinds: again, northern and southern varieties. In the Scottish Midland Valley and northern England, basaltic magma poured out from chains of volcanoes along fissures and was injected between beds of Carboniferous sedimentary rocks to form sills (Figure 3.3).

■ In what tectonic setting would the northern Carboniferous basaltic igneous rocks have formed?

□ That area had been tectonically inactive since the time of the Devonian unconformity, and would have been within a plate. The basaltic magmas may well have been derived from a mantle plume below a hot spot (Book 2, Section 9.2).

Carboniferous igneous rocks in southwestern England are very different. They are dominated by granites that intrude Devonian and Carboniferous sediments that had been deformed during the Variscan Orogeny, but the granites (293–273 Ma old) are not deformed. The granite magma probably formed by the melting of deep crust once it had been thickened by orogenic events. Like the Devonian igneous rocks in the north, they formed at a convergent plate margin.

No extrusive or intrusive igneous rocks are associated with the Permian to Cenozoic sedimentary veneer of the eastern British Isles. However, from 60 to 55 Ma ago floods of basaltic lava inundated parts of Northern Ireland (Figure 3.2b) and the Hebridean islands (Skye and Mull in particular). Later erosion has removed most of the flood basalts, to reveal the cores of several sizeable volcanoes marked by occurrences of intrusive gabbro and granite. The southernmost example is the granite forming the tiny island of Lundy in the Bristol Channel. These volcanic centres define a N–S line about 700 km long.

7.3   Ancient geography

The disposition of different kinds of rock of various ages in different parts of the British Isles, which the geological map reveals, forms the basis for reconstructing the geography of the ancient past, and how that changed through time. Before the Devonian Period, the continuous slab of continental crust beneath what is now called the British Isles was a series of independent fragments. To understand how they came together to form part of the supercontinent Pangaea (Book 2, Figure 7.1) by the end of the Variscan Orogeny requires a global scope (Section 7.3.1). Pangaea did not exist throughout all of previous geological time but was assembled by plate tectonics during the Palaeozoic, which drove isolated continents and oceanic volcanic arcs into a clump. Rocks of the British Isles played a seminal role in allowing geoscientists to understand how tectonic processes assembled Pangaea.

Once the crust of the British Isles became a united whole, the various kinds of sedimentary rocks deposited at different places (or the absence of sedimentary strata) reveal the character of various environments on land and beneath the sea at different times in the past. Beginning with the Permian Period, Section 7.3.2 shows how the geography of the British Isles evolved during a long lull in local tectonic activity.

Vast as it once was, Pangaea ultimately began to break up about 200 Ma ago. Sea-floor spreading then began to drive its fragments around to the present positions of continents. Some of that sea-floor spreading began near the British Isles and almost split the crust beneath them apart (Section 7.3.3).

Geological information analogous to that accumulated for the British Isles is available for much of the Earth's continental surface. Bringing together that global wealth of data about geological processes results in a series of 'time-lapse frames' of global geography which go back almost a billion years. In Activities 7.3 and 7.4 you will follow the evolution of Earth's continents and oceans, specifically charting how the British Isles behaved during that long global evolution.

7.3.1   Uniting the British Isles

The pre-Devonian crust exposed in the British Isles formed in several fragments:

*   the Caledonian Orogeny occurred at different times to the north and south of the Scottish Midland Valley, around 470 Ma (Lower Ordovician) and between 420 and 380 Ma (Upper Silurian to Lower Devonian) respectively

- the northern orogeny created a hugely deformed, high-grade metamorphic complex, whereas that in the south merely folded Lower Palaeozoic rocks at low metamorphic grades

- in the southern part, Ordovician events involved igneous activity characteristic of an oceanic volcanic arc

- between these two parts, the oldest rocks on which the Ordovician sedimentary rocks were deposited are typical of oceanic crust.

Three geologically quite different blocks of pre-Devonian crust underpin the region (Figure 7.15).

1   The Caledonian metamorphic complex of northern Scotland is made predominantly of highly metamorphosed, 1000–1500 Ma sedimentary rocks. They are underlain by even older (1800–3000 Ma) high-grade metamorphic rocks exposed in northwestern Scotland (Figure 7.15a). This block is made of very old continental materials.

2   The Scottish Southern Uplands are made of marine Ordovician and Silurian sedimentary rocks resting on oceanic crust no older than the Lower Ordovician (~490 Ma).

3   England, Wales and southernmost Ireland formed partly as a volcanic arc, but in places the pre-Devonian Palaeozoic rocks rest on Precambrian sedimentary, igneous and metamorphic rocks (you need to look closely at Figure 7.15a, as the number of occurrences is small), so some older continental crust is present there too.

Some evidence points to a fourth block, an oceanic volcanic arc – now deep beneath the Scottish Midland Valley – separating blocks 1 and 2. Huge faults mark the main boundaries (Figure 7.15b), except that separating 2 and 3, which is hidden by younger rocks. As you will discover, that is the most important of the boundaries.

So many different tectonic settings with similar ages are unlikely to have developed near to each other. Resolving this seemingly strange 'alliance' involved using a simple technique – roughly equivalent to a compass needle frozen during those times.

A compass needle lines up with the Earth's magnetic field to show the direction to the north magnetic pole. What is less obvious is that if you turn a compass on its side, so that the magnetised needle can swing about in a vertical plane, the angle at which it settles is different depending on the latitude. At the magnetic poles it hangs vertically, but at the Equator it settles in a horizontal position. At latitudes in between, the angle is approximately equal to the latitude.

The Earth's field magnetises iron oxide minerals formed when igneous rocks crystallise and cool. That locks into the rock both the direction to the magnetic poles and the rough latitude *at the time of their crystallisation* (Book 2, Section 7.3.1). Tiny fragments of magnetised minerals also line up in this way as they settle with other grains to form sediments. Assuming that the Earth's axis of magnetism has always been as it is now, the place of formation of igneous and sedimentary rocks can be located from measurements of their ancient magnetisation.

The results for pre-Devonian Palaeozoic rocks in the blocks that now make up the British Isles, and for those on other continents, are surprising. Figure 7.17 shows the positions of blocks in the Lower Ordovician and at the end of the Silurian. About 480 Ma ago (Figure 7.17a) the blocks that now constitute the British Isles were

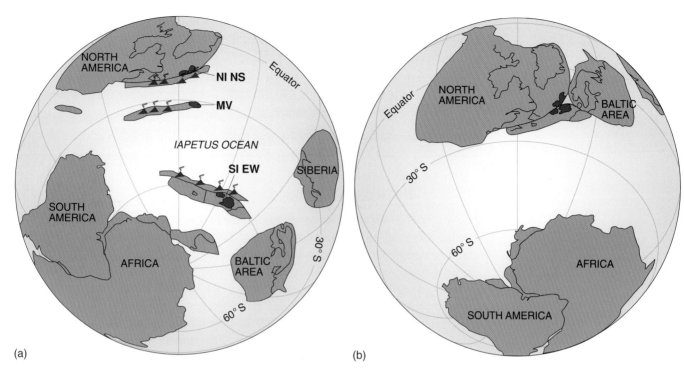

Figure 7.17   Reconstructions of the possible distribution of continental masses at two stages in the Palaeozoic Era. Both show the Southern Hemisphere of the time. (a) In the Lower Ordovician (480 Ma), continental crust now beneath the British Isles (shown in red) was in two pieces on either side of the Iapetus Ocean. Subduction zones are marked by volcano symbols (blue triangles). (b) By the end of the Silurian (410 Ma), the Iapetus Ocean had closed to drive the Caledonian Orogeny and unite the crust under the British Isles. NI = Northern Ireland; NS = northern Scotland; MV = Scottish Midland Valley; SI = southern Ireland; EW = England and Wales.

scattered far and wide across the **Iapetus Ocean** (Iapetus was the father of the Greek god Atlas, from whom the name of the Atlantic Ocean is derived). By about 410 Ma (Figure 7.17b) all the blocks constituting the British Isles, the Baltic area and North America had collided to form a large continent – eventually part of northern Pangaea. This was achieved by sea-floor spreading, together with subduction of oceanic lithosphere beneath oceanic volcanic arcs.

The addition of ancient magnetic measurements to the evidence used in Book 2, Section 7.2 to reconstruct Pangaea and chart the opening of the oceans that split it apart after 200 Ma reveals global geography back to almost a billion years ago. You can see the results in the computer-based resource *Plate Motions Through Time*, which forms part of Activity 7.3.

Activity 7.3   How Pangaea was made – plate motions through time

We expect this activity will take you about 30 minutes.

View the animation of global palaeogeographic evolution in *Plate Motions Through Time* frame by frame from 600 to 240 Ma. At this scale it is not possible to show all the details of the crustal slivers that make up the British Isles (Figure 7.15b). Instead, the northern and southern parts are shown in blue and red, respectively.

Describe in about 500–600 words the changes in the global distribution of continental crust during this time. Note in particular the changing positions of the two main parts of the British Isles crust, relative to one another and to latitude.

Note: the terms Early and Late are used in the animation with reference to Periods; these terms are interchangeable with Lower and Upper. The Proterozoic Eon is the last part of the Precambrian.

Now read the comments on this activity at the end of this book.

7.3.2   Removing the wrinkles

The line of the Variscan Orogeny in Figure 7.15b extends into Europe, and a similar zone runs all the way down the eastern side of North America. That line marks where two massive continents collided to create Pangaea at the end of the Carboniferous. The British Isles then lay well within the supercontinent: a landlocked region extending roughly from 15 to 25° N of the Equator, similar to the present range of the Sahara desert. So the results of your brief exploration of Permian and Triassic rocks (Activity 7.2) are not surprising; the area was arid desert affected by occasional flash floods and the development of wind-blown sand dunes. However, it was not a monotonous surface of continuous desert sedimentation. Large tracts are devoid of Permian rocks (Figure 7.11) having been uplands subject to continual erosion. Surface occurrences of Permian sedimentary rocks (Figure 7.11), together with cores from boreholes where they are hidden beneath younger rocks, provide evidence for different environments.

Permian rocks throughout southwest England and the Midlands are essentially the same: sheets of debris eroded from the Variscan mountains and the remaining Caledonian mountains, together with dune fields of sand winnowed out by the wind. In northwest England and southwest Scotland the same association prevails, but with the addition of a thin bed of limestone and evaporites; a sign of a short-lived inundation by a shallow sea prone to evaporation.

The Permian in northeastern England is different (Figure 7.18). Just above the unconformity there are sands with dune cross-bedding (Figure 7.18A), but their top surface is full of burrows. The burrowing organisms were tiny brachiopods which signify marine inundation of the desert. The next bed (Figure 7.18B) is finely laminated shale containing exquisitely preserved fossil fishes. That a shallow sea covered northeastern England for most of the Permian is clear from the succeeding thick fossiliferous limestones (Figure 7.18C). That sea extended across northern Europe to the foot of the Ural Mountains in Russia. It was neither deep nor always connected to true oceans, for across that vast area the limestones are interlayered with thick beds of evaporite salts. Figure 7.19 is an artist's impression of how the British Isles region might have appeared from space during the Permian.

Much the same desert conditions dominated the Triassic, but relentless erosion gradually wore down the Variscan and Caledonian mountains, to deposit terrestrial Triassic sediments more widely than Permian ones (Figure 7.11a). Triassic sedimentation gradually filled the shallow sea, which retreated

Figure 7.18   Signs of the Permian desert and tropical sea in northeastern England. Working quarry exposing three Permian sedimentary rocks – A, B and C. The arrows point to the base and top of the central unit (B). A – cross-bedded dune sands, overlain by B – finely layered mudstones (containing fossil fishes) and C – rubbly reef limestones.

Figure 7.19   Reconstruction of landscape in the area of the British Isles during the Upper Permian, as would be seen from a satellite.

eastwards. As the surface became flatter, the energy of transportation decreased so that soft mudstones dominate the Triassic of the British Isles. Beds of evaporites in the mudstones indicate that much deposition was in ephemeral lakes (the lower part of Aust Cliff in Activity 7.2). Northern Europe at the end of the Triassic had become almost flat as a result of erosion and sediment deposition. A global rise in sea level easily inundated huge tracts (as recorded by the top of Aust Cliff in Activity 7.2). However, those parts of the crust most affected by the Caledonian and Variscan Orogenies were still not completely flat.

■ Suggest a reason why mountain belts linger for immense timespans.

☐ Thickened crust beneath mountain belts 'bobs up' as erosion unloads their low-density roots (Figure 5.12).

For the next 140 Ma sea level rose globally, eventually standing 200 m above present levels during the Cretaceous, to flood vast areas of continental crust. Shallow marine sediments or those of estuaries and deltas covered most of the southern British Isles during the Jurassic and Cretaceous Periods. These seas extended continental shelves, in many cases right into continental interiors. Jurassic and Cretaceous sediments are characterised by limestones and shales, many of which are rich in organic carbon (Figure 7.20a) and record the high biological productivity of the oceans during this period.

During the Cretaceous, calcium carbonate plates of phytoplankton (coccolithophores, Book 1, Figure 7.5a) accumulated in unimaginable numbers on the floors of shallow seas. This formed the thick chalk limestones, now in the white cliffs either side of the Channel (Figure 7.20b). In other areas, calcite-secreting corals, brachiopods, molluscs and echinoids thrived, to produce reefs or accumulated as ground-up debris to form other kinds of limestone (Figure 7.20c). Free-swimming animals benefited too, the most common being ammonites, whose rapid evolution and widespread distribution allow the intricate relative time division of the Jurassic and Cretaceous.

Activity 7.4   The break-up of Pangaea – plate motions through time

We expect this activity will take you about 30 minutes.

Look at the computer-based animation of global palaeogeographic evolution in *Plate Motions Through Time* frame by frame from 240 Ma to the present. This activity covers the period during which modern ocean floors formed, and you may want to refer to the ocean floor age map in Book 2 (Figure 9.7) to check the evidence for initiation of break-up in different places.

(a) Describe the timing of separation of each of the modern continents from one another, and times when there were major continent–continent collisions (*about 300–400 words*).

(b) Describe the evidence for sea-level change during the Mesozoic and Cenozoic (*about 200–300 words*).

Now read the comments on this activity at the end of this book.

(a)

(b)

(c)

Figure 7.20   (a) Hydrocarbon-rich Jurassic mudstones in Dorset. (b) Chalk cliffs of the Kent coast. (c) Cretaceous limestone from Croatia crammed with fossils of large, colonial molluscs.

7.3.3   Great tension in the early Cenozoic

The lull in tectonic and magmatic activity in northern Europe throughout the Mesozoic was rudely interrupted in the British Isles during the early Cenozoic (53–63 Ma). Volcanic and plutonic igneous rocks of this age define a narrow zone that runs from the Hebrides southwards to the island of Lundy in the Bristol Channel (Figure 7.16). Sea-floor spreading had been driving North America away from Africa to form the Central Atlantic since 200 Ma (Activity 7.4). Yet the North Atlantic did not develop in the Mesozoic, except as a shallow seaway to the early Arctic Ocean. Around 63 Ma, a massive linear burst of volcanism almost cut the British Isles in two. It involved the effusion of lava to cover the Inner Hebrides and Northern Ireland with kilometre-thick flood basalts. As well as the volcanoes in the northwest, a swarm of basaltic dykes running NNW–SSE cut through much of the region as magma followed cracks opening in the crust. The crust beneath the British Isles was being pulled apart. Then, as suddenly as it began, the rifting and volcanism stopped.

This 10 Ma pulse of within-plate igneous activity extended well beyond the British Isles. The then-adjacent region of East Greenland was covered by even more flood basalts. Together, the two centres represent the influence of a hot spot (Book 2, Section 9.2) which developed beneath the still-united northern Europe and Greenland. The hot spot eventually formed Iceland, where it is still active today, as part of the Mid-Atlantic Ridge.

Question 7.3

Cretaceous and Cenozoic sedimentary rocks in southeastern England (Figures 7.10 and 7.12b) are affected by folds trending roughly E–W. Was there an episode of mountain building elsewhere in Europe which might explain the tectonic forces that buckled these rocks? If so, where did it happen, what was the tectonic event to which it probably related, and roughly when did it take place? You will need to review the later parts of the animation in Activities 7.3 and 7.4, concentrating on Europe.

The Cenozoic record for the rest of Britain is mainly restricted to sedimentary deposits in the south. The retreat of the seas that covered much of Britain during the Cretaceous continued and the merging land surface and shallowing marine environment produced sequences of Cenozoic clays and sands that are exposed in several areas of southern England. Then, at about 30 Ma the distant collision of Africa with Europe produced the Alps and the effect on Britain is seen in the large scale folds of the North and South Downs, as described in Figure 7.9, Area 4.

7.4   Summary of Chapter 7

Evidence from the earliest continental crust beneath the British Isles indicates that the northern part of the region began to form about 3 billion years ago. For the last billion years the region's evolution involved a uniquely diverse range of processes. Rocks of all kinds accumulated almost continuously for the first half of that time, but on what were widely separated continents.

At 500 Ma, the region's southern part was a small continental mass about 60° south of the Equator. The northern part was at a latitude of about 15° S, at the edge of a large continent dominated by modern North America. Between them lay the Iapetus Ocean, whose closure involved subduction and andesitic volcanism in several arcs. Progressive collision of the two continental masses caught up the volcanic arcs and created the Caledonian mountain belt. By 400 Ma (Lower Devonian), the British Isles' crust had become a unified whole, as part of a large North American continent.

The Devonian erosion of Caledonian mountains deposited thick red sandstones, which everywhere lie with profound unconformity on the older, more complex rocks. The large continent drifted northwards, to straddle the Equator during the Carboniferous. Tropical conditions supported huge rainforests, whose debris accumulated to form coal seams between the muds and sandstones of Upper Carboniferous coastal swamps in northern Europe. At the end of the Carboniferous, closure of another ocean in the south united nearly all continental crust during the Variscan Orogeny.

Erosion of the Variscan mountain belt and sediment deposition produced another great unconformity, at the base of Permian strata. Permian and Triassic dune sands indicate arid desert conditions over part of the region. A shallow sea inundated low-lying areas to deposit limestones similar to modern barrier reefs. Periodically the sea dried up to produce thick evaporite deposits. The rise in sea level in the Jurassic covered much of the region, to deposit limestones, shales and sandstones. The Upper Cretaceous sea level was so high that few areas of land remained in northern Europe. Chalk deposits, composed mainly of the tiny calcite plates of phytoplankton, blanketed much of the British Isles.

The last volcanism to affect the British Isles was in western Scotland and Northern Ireland from 63 to 53 Ma. The region then lay above a mantle plume – now located beneath Iceland – which flooded either side of the North Atlantic with basaltic lavas. The linear trend of the igneous rocks suggests that the crust almost separated to initiate sea-floor spreading. However, the British Isles drifted away from the mantle plume and volcanism stopped. The North Atlantic then opened to the west of Ireland to develop into the ocean of today.

In this chapter you have brought the skills that you developed in earlier chapters to bear on understanding the geological evolution of a large segment of continental crust – that beneath the British Isles. In doing so you have developed skills needed to interpret geological maps and the information that they contain about the 3D distribution of different kinds of rock, and the relative timing of tectonic, sedimentary, igneous and mountain-building events. It has involved you with many highly informative maps, observing, recording and interpreting field evidence. Through use of computer-based learning resources, you have addressed the geological evolution of a region in terms of global processes, and written substantial accounts of your deductions.

Chapter 8
Physical resources and the Earth system

8.1   Introduction

Physical resources refer to the materials and energy that are obtainable from the inorganic world, either at or beneath the Earth's surface. In essence they involve rocks, water and energy. Throughout the history of humanity, humans have exploited the physical resources found in the natural environment. Whether those resources are flint – a rock rich in silicon dioxide – for stone axes or silicon for computer chips, society is reliant on the solid Earth to provide the materials and energy on which a technological society is dependent.

■   Which of the following materials are classified as physical resources: milk, water, wood, salt, cotton?

☐   Water and salt. Both are derived from the inorganic environment around us: in other words they would be present on Earth even if it were lifeless. All the other materials are organic: they are products of the biosphere.

The products of some ancient biological systems are, however, immensely important physical resources today. Oil, coal and gas are called fossil fuels because they are the products of the burial and decay of living things from the geological past. Similarly, limestone is a largely organic deposit, being composed of the hard parts of ancient organisms, and although not a source of energy it is used in the manufacture of concrete and other building materials.

The extraction of physical resources invariably has an **environmental impact**. Despite the commonly held belief that in a pre-industrial era, society had a minimal impact on the environment, even the extraction of flint for the manufacture of stone implements almost 5000 years ago had an impact on the landscape that is still visible today (Figure 8.1).

Figure 8.1   Photograph of the traces of Neolithic flint mining at Grimes Graves, Norfolk, UK.

Today, environmental impacts resulting from the exploitation of physical resources are all around us and many are damaging the environment in such a way that recovery may take many thousands or even millions of years. Land and groundwater become contaminated with metals such as copper and lead from mining activities, radioactive leaks from nuclear plants allow dangerous materials into the atmosphere and hydrosphere, greenhouse gases emitted from burning increasing amounts of fossil fuels drive climate change. All of these effects and many more are a consequence of humanity's exploitation of physical resources. You have already explored some of these implications, most notably global warming in Book 1. In this final chapter of Book 6 you will see how the Earth's physical resources are intimately entwined with the various natural cycles – the rock, water and carbon cycles – that you have been exploring at various stages throughout S104 and discover how human activity is becoming a major agent for change in the Earth system.

8.2   Metals

You may be surprised to discover that almost any rock that you pick up contains just about every naturally occurring element in the periodic table. Many, however, may be present in only vanishingly small amounts, perhaps only a few parts in a million, or a few atoms per billion. Such dispersed elements are often referred to as minor or **trace elements**. Extraction of elements at such low concentrations would be impractical and very costly. To extract any metal from the Earth requires the assistance of geological processes that have concentrated metals in particular minerals known as **ores**.

Some of the metals in everyday use are abundant in the Earth's crust, whereas others are not. Take, for example aluminium (Al). Aluminium comprises ~8.5% of the Earth's crust, being an essential chemical element for many common rock-forming minerals especially feldspars. Yet aluminium mines are located in relatively few places in the world.

■ Can you suggest a reason why this might be the case?

□ It is difficult to extract aluminium from feldspars in which it is strongly bound to oxygen and silicon. Mines are located where aluminium is in a form from which the metal can be easily extracted using the minimum amount of energy.

That form is the mineral gibbsite, a hydrated aluminium oxide, $Al(OH)_3$, that is found in bauxite, a product of extreme weathering under tropical conditions. There are relatively few places in the world where bauxite is found in large quantities.

Another element in common everyday use is copper, Cu. Unlike aluminium, copper only occurs in small quantities in the Earth's crust, which has an average copper content of about 30 ppm (parts per million) or 30 g per metric tonne. Extracting copper from ordinary rocks is clearly not feasible, yet it played a significant role in the development of Bronze Age technologies. This only happened because copper occurs in the mineral chalcopyrite, $CuFeS_2$, from which the copper can be easily extracted, and chalcopyrite occurs in distinctive veins in many rocks, having a brassy appearance, somewhat like pyrites, FeS_2 (fools gold).

Thus 'normal' rocks, such as granite and basalt seldom provide exploitable sources of metals. For metals to be exploitable they have to be present in the form of an ore in which the metal is bound in a chemically simple form in high enough concentration to make extraction economically viable. Most ores are relatively simple minerals such as oxides, sulfides and carbonates, all of which can yield their metals by simple chemical reactions involving reduction or oxidation (Book 4, Chapter 8).

But how do ores form? How does aluminium become concentrated in bauxite and copper in copper ores? All ores are rocks and therefore part of the rock cycle and the evolution of ore bodies is the result of extreme examples of rock cycle processes. The presence of ore deposits depends on the concentration of metals by geological processes that involve the separation and accumulation of minerals. These include, quartz sands, clays, evaporites, limestones and coal, all of which result from weathering, erosion and sedimentary processes (Chapter 4). Similar processes are responsible for the formation of some ore deposits at the Earth's surface and bauxite is one of these. In addition concentration of metals can also result from igneous processes and the extraction and mobilisation of metals by hot, watery fluids (**hydrothermal** processes).

8.2.1 Ore-forming processes in sedimentary rocks

All ore-forming processes have a number of common features (Figure 8.2).

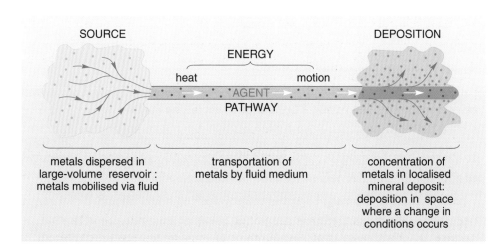

Figure 8.2 A schematic relationship between the source, pathway, agent, deposition and energy involved in the formation of an ore deposit.

Firstly, a fluid agent acts on a source rock in which the metal is dispersed in a large reservoir. The fluid extracts and transports the metal to a new environment. Physical changes in the new environment, either a drop in temperature or pressure, or both, encourage the deposition of the element in concentrated form.

■ Thinking back to earlier chapters, where are fluids most active in the rock cycle?

☐ In the formation of sedimentary rocks.

Sedimentary rocks have their origins in the weathering and erosion of pre-existing rocks and weathering is often mediated by water – you should recall from Section 4.2.1 that rocks in a warm wet tropical environment weather more rapidly than those in a cold dry climate. Many sediments are also transported and deposited by water, which is also capable of sorting grains by size as a consequence of variations in current speeds (Figure 4.8, Section 4.2.2). As explained in the caption to Figure 4.8 the data were derived from experiments using grains of uniform density. Most rock-forming minerals have a density that lies within a narrow range of between 2.5 and 3.0×10^3 kg m^{-3}. By contrast, metal-rich grains are in general much denser than silicate minerals and so their transport properties will be different from silicates.

■ Magnetite, Fe_3O_4, an important ore of iron, has a density of 5.2×10^3 kg m^{-3}. How will this affect the range of current speeds that are capable of transporting magnetite as opposed to silicate grains of the same size?

☐ For a given grain size, magnetite grains will be almost twice as heavy as silicate grains. Therefore they will require more energy to be kept in suspension and so will be deposited at higher current speeds than silicate grains.

Sedimentary environments facilitate the separation and deposition of heavy minerals known as **placer** deposits. A contemporary example of a beach placer deposit is the black sands of eastern Australia which are rich in magnetite and provide a rich source of titanium, whereas the enormous gold deposits of South Africa were formed as placers more than 2000 Ma ago.

The dense minerals found in these placer deposits – minerals such as chromite (iron chromium oxide), cassiterite (tin oxide) and rutile (titanium oxide) – were derived from igneous rocks and are concentrated in sedimentary regimes because they are dense and chemically resistant.

In addition to placer deposits, there is a class of sedimentary mineral deposit that is produced by the chemical deposition of metals by surface waters. These include evaporites, as already covered in Section 4.3.2, ironstones, especially banded iron formations, and deep sea, manganese nodules found on the sea floor (Figure 8.3c). The latter are scattered across large areas of the deep ocean floor and although rich in a variety of metals that have precipitated out of seawater, they have yet to be exploited commercially because of their inaccessibility.

Banded iron formations comprise alternating bands of iron oxide and chert (Figure 8.3a). They cover large areas of the major continents and are almost all exclusively older than 2000 Ma. At this time during Earth evolution there was no free oxygen in the atmosphere and large parts of the ocean were anoxic. As a result the oceans were capable of dissolving large quantities of iron in the form of reduced Fe^{2+}. Moreover, the dominant life forms were stromatolites and blue-green algae living in shallow water environments and depending on sunlight for photosynthesis.

■ What is the important by-product of photosynthesis?

☐ Oxygen.

(a)

1 cm

(b)

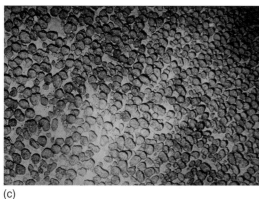

(c)

Figure 8.3   (a) Sedimentary iron ore: alternating bands of chert, a fine-grained rock rich in silica, and brown iron oxide in a polished specimen of banded iron formation. (b) Banded iron formation exposed as a rusty weathering outcrop in the Hamersley range of Western Australia. (c) A view of manganese nodules lying on the ocean floor (nodules are ~10 cm in diameter).

In these shallow seas, the oxygen liberated by blue-green algae oxidised the iron in seawater which was rapidly precipitated in the form of ferric oxide, Fe_2O_3 to form the banded ironstones. This is the dominant form of iron mined today in places such as Hamersley, Western Australia (Figure 8.3b). Banded iron formations thus could be said to have a biological origin and are related to the early carbon cycle. They serve to illustrate how life has had a dramatic effect on the geology of the planet as well as on the atmosphere and ocean.

8.3.2   Igneous and related ore-forming processes

In addition to the silicate minerals (Section 3.1), igneous rocks also include small amounts (usually less than 1%) of other minerals. These can contain large concentrations of minor and trace elements that are not included in the structures of the more abundant rock-forming minerals. They usually occur in small amounts (often <1%) and are not an essential component of any given rock type. However, certain accessory minerals tend to occur in particular rocks so that, for example, gabbros and basalts contain oxides of iron (mostly magnetite), chromium and titanium while granites include a whole spectrum of minerals including zircon (zirconium silicate) and monazite (cerium phosphate).

When magma intrudes into the crust, in the form of, for example, a granite batholith, the magma cools and crystallises. The final portions of the magma that remain after most of the batholith has solidified become enriched in all of those elements that will not fit easily in the major rock-forming minerals. Additionally, any water dissolved in the magma is released and forms a separate fluid phase that is extremely reactive. This potent mixture of residual silicate melt and hot water is a very effective medium for concentrating, moving and depositing metals such as tin, tantalum, niobium, uranium, beryllium and caesium within the solidified rock.

The mineral rich water can also percolate into the rocks surrounding the batholith and many granite batholiths are surrounded by zones of mineralisation that are related to the temperature of the fluid as it moves away from the solidifying magma. Metals such as tin and tungsten are deposited close to the granite, copper further away and lead–zinc at the furthest distance.

Such hydrothermal activity is also characteristic of mid-ocean ridges (Book 2, Section 7.3). Here, seawater penetrates newly formed crust to depths of 1–3 km and is heated to temperatures in excess of 300 °C. Under these conditions, hot saline water is highly reactive and it extracts sulfur and metals such as iron, copper and zinc, amongst many others from the surrounding basaltic rocks. On contact with the sea, the fluid cools rapidly and the metal sulfides are precipitated, producing a so-called black smoker (Book 2, Figure 7.4).

Eventually, ores formed at depth are exposed at the surface as a consequence of uplift and erosion, while those formed on the seabed may be emplaced into the crust as a result of tectonic activity.

■ Whereabouts on Earth would you expect to find igneous-related mineral deposits forming today?

☐ In Chapter 3 you learned that much igneous activity occurs at plate boundaries and so plate boundaries should be where mineral deposits are forming today.

A good example of the association of mineralisation with igneous and tectonic activity is in the Andes of South America and the North American Rockies where large reserves of copper and molybdenum, known as porphyry copper deposits, are associated with igneous intrusions of Cretaceous or Palaeogene age (Figure 8.4), exposed as a consequence of the uplift and erosion of the orogenic belts.

8.3   Energy

Any modern technological society requires energy – lots of energy. In 2008, for example, the UK primary energy use was equivalent to 9.85 EJ ($1 \text{ EJ} = 10^{18}$ J) about 5.6 kW per person averaged over a population of 60 million. Of that energy over 90% came from fossil fuels, with the remainder from nuclear and renewable sources. Fossil fuels – coal, oil and natural gas – are so-called because they are the product of living organisms that existed during the Phanerozoic and are closely linked into the biosphere and the carbon cycle.

Figure 8.4   Bingham Canyon open pit porphyry copper mine, Utah. The pit is about 1.2 km deep and 4 km wide with a total area of 7.7 km² and is allegedly the world's largest excavation.

Some countries place a heavier reliance on nuclear energy for which the raw material is uranium. As uranium is a metal, it can be considered in the same way as other metal resources, economic ore deposits being found in both igneous and sedimentary environments.

8.3.1   Coal

Coal is a type of sediment (Figure 8.5) made up of lithified plant remains that were originally deposited in a fresh or brackish water environment – a swamp

Figure 8.5   An open cast coal mine in Staffordshire, England. Nine individual seams, or beds of coal, ranging in thickness from 0.1 to 1.35 m, were worked in this mine.

183

such as the Everglades in Florida is a modern analogue. Its occurrence is therefore restricted to rocks that formed after land plants first evolved.

■   What is the oldest age a coal deposit could be?

□   Land plants first emerged in the Devonian (Chapter 2) and so coal deposits must be younger than the Devonian.

During coal formation the dead plant material rots under anoxic conditions to form peat. With time the swamp subsides and the peat becomes covered with further layers of sediment and as yet more layers of sediment and peat build up at the surface, the older layers are compressed, slowly squeezing out water and gas from the pore spaces. This progressive process of compaction eventually compresses the peat to the density of coal.

The second phase in the evolution of coal converts the dense peat, or brown coal to proper coal, by increasing the carbon content. The organic components in peat contain hydrogen and oxygen, in addition to carbon. These compounds gradually break down in response to increasing heat and pressure, releasing methane, water and carbon dioxide and increasing the carbon content of the coal. The end product of this process in extreme cases is pure carbon or graphite, but more usually the product is a bituminous coal or anthracite. Thus the generation of coal relies in the first instance on the carbon cycle and subsequently on that part of the rock cycle in which sedimentary rocks are buried and lithified.

8.3.2   Petroleum

Petroleum is a complex mixture of hydrocarbons and lesser quantities of other organic molecules containing sulfur, oxygen and nitrogen and has a more protracted history than that of coal. Compounds in petroleum range from the simplest organic molecule, methane (CH_4), through ethane (C_2H_6), propane (C_3H_8) and butane (C_4H_{10}). These all have boiling points below 0 °C and so are gases under ambient conditions. Larger compounds, ranging from pentane (C_5H_{12}) to hexadecane ($C_{16}H_{34}$) are liquids under ambient conditions, whereas even larger compounds with even greater molecular weights form waxy solids. Petroleum therefore includes such resources as natural gas, crude oil and bitumen.

The formation of petroleum requires a number of conditions.

•   Firstly there is the need for a source rock – a sedimentary rock rich in organic remains that could potentially generate hydrocarbons.

•   Changes in temperature and pressure through time induce the organic remains to undergo chemical reactions that produce hydrocarbons.

•   A pathway along which the hydrocarbons can migrate. As they are less dense than rocks and water they tend to migrate upwards towards the Earth's surface and can even emerge at the surface to form tar pits and oil seeps.

•   An impermeable rock somewhere along the migration pathway, beneath which the hydrocarbons can become trapped.

The raw material for petroleum is once again organic material although in the case of petroleum the organic material is most frequently of marine origin. The most productive source rocks are shales that are rich in organic material. These are produced in off-shore marine environments during times of unusually high biological productivity. As organisms die, their remains sink to the bottom of the sea where under normal conditions they are oxidised to form carbon dioxide and water. However, during periods of high biological productivity, the process of decay uses all the available oxygen in the water column and the organic material simply accumulates, along with detrital sediments on the sea floor. Eventually the organic material is buried producing an organic-rich shale or mudrock. The action of time and temperature then converts the organic material into hydrocarbons that migrate towards the surface.

■ At what period in the geological past will most source rocks have formed?

☐ During the Phanerozoic – the period of abundant life.

Although one of the first commercially exploited petroleum deposits, in the Scottish Midland Valley in 1850, was from black 'oil shales' of Carboniferous age, most source rocks are of Carboniferous age or younger. The most important in the North Sea is the Kimmeridge Clay formation which is of Jurassic age.

■ What is the ultimate source of the energy stored in fossil fuels?

☐ The Sun.

The organic material that constitutes fossil fuels was originally derived from the biosphere and the biosphere ultimately relies on the sun as the primary source of energy via photosynthesis. Thus when we are driving our cars along the motorway or luxuriating in a hot bath we are enjoying the benefits of solar energy radiated from the sun many millions of years ago, albeit trapped by a complex combination of organic and geological processes. The carbon buried in geological deposits, either as organic carbon, fossil fuels or as carbonate in limestones, was all taken out of the atmosphere as a result of biological activity. As you learned in Book 2, Section 10.1, the Earth is constantly supplying fresh CO_2 to the atmosphere from volcanic activity and it is the processes of life that keep the atmospheric levels of CO_2 tolerable.

The present concentration of carbon dioxide in the atmosphere is about 380 ppm and society is currently concerned about an increase to possibly 450 or 500 ppm. Try to imagine if all of the carbon locked up in the form of limestone, coal and oil was in the atmosphere. Calculations suggest that if that were the case the atmospheric pressure would be almost 100 times greater than today and the runaway greenhouse effect would raise the surface temperature to hundreds of degrees Celsius. Surface conditions would be similar to those prevailing on Venus – intolerable for life and certainly not an environment that any would wish to see reproduced on Earth.

8.4   The economics and availability of physical resources

The previous brief descriptions of metal and energy resources reveal how they were formed over geological times and at geologically slow rates. By contrast, humanity is now exploiting those reserves over much shorter periods of time and with a global population predicted to increase to over 9 billion by 2050, the problem of exhausting the Earth's physical resources is becoming a reality. Figure 8.6 uses the example of aluminium to show how the rapid growth in production and consumption have gone hand-in-hand over the past century. This is just one example of how modern technology and growing global population places ever-increasing demands on our planet's limited resources.

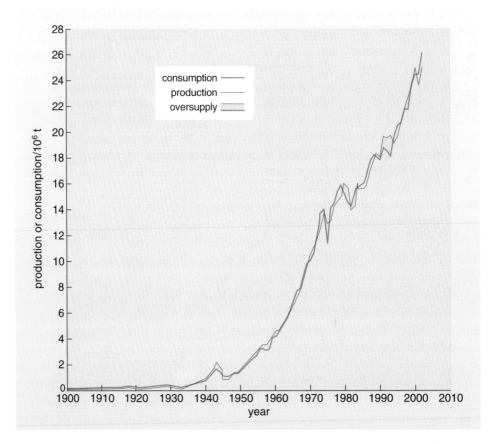

Figure 8.6 Global production and consumption of aluminium since 1900. Periods of over-supply, when production exceeded consumption are shaded yellow.

How can we determine how long a particular physical resource will continue to supply our needs? One method is to compare current consumption rates with estimates of the global reserves of a particular commodity. Some resources, such as coal have accumulated in considerable quantities over geological time and reserves allow continued consumption at current rates.

■ Global coal consumption is of the order of 5.10×10^9 tonnes y^{-1} and global reserves are estimated to be 990×10^9 tonnes. How long will the global reserves last?

☐ The answer to this can be determined by dividing the total amount of the reserves by the rate of consumption:

$$\text{Lifetime of coal resources} = \frac{\left(990 \times 10^9\right)}{\left(5.10 \times 10^9\right)}\,y = 194\ y$$

There is therefore little danger of coal supplies being exhausted in the foreseeable future. A different picture emerges when considering petroleum. At current rates of production, a similar calculation suggests that oil reserves will last for about 40 years. However, when the same calculation was done in 1989, over 20 years ago, petroleum reserves were found to be good for 44 years.

■   Why has the estimated lifetime of oil reserves only fallen by four years in the past 20?

☐   New reserves have been discovered.

As demand for oil has increased so the price of the raw material has increased and the search for new reserves intensified. In addition, some resources that were uneconomical in 1989, either because they were too expensive to extract or the estimated size of the reserve was too small, are now economically viable because of the increase in demand and hence price.

Box 8.1   Indium and the electronic industry

Recently, there has been concern that global reserves of the metal indium were limited. Indium is a rare metal, similar to aluminium with a low melting point and a lustrous silver appearance. However, unlike aluminium which is a major constituent of the continental crust, the average crustal abundance of indium is only 0.25 ppm and it has no common ores – indeed it only has about 20 known distinct minerals. It occurs mainly as an impurity in zinc ores. Until the 1990s indium had few uses, but then it was discovered that indium–tin oxide has specific properties that are critical for the electronic industry. Indium tin oxide is an electrical conductor and transparent when produced as a thin film. It is used extensively for flat and touch screen displays and at the time of writing there is no substitute. As a consequence of these unique properties the demand for indium rose sharply to about 450 tonnes per year. At that time global reserves were estimated at 6000 tonnes.

■   Using the figures above, how long would the global reserves of indium last?

☐   The reserve lifetime is given by dividing the total reserves by the rate of consumption:

$$\frac{6000 \text{ t}}{450 \text{ t y}^{-1}} = {\sim}13 \text{ y}$$

Needless to say this raised concerns over the ability of the Earth to sustain a growing electronics industry that was reliant on such a rare resource for some of its critical components. Subsequently, however, concern about the supply of indium has reduced.

■   Why do you think this is the case?

☐   The demand for indium encouraged the discovery of more reserves.

As it happens, the new reserves were found in the waste heaps of old mine workings – the waste of a previous generation became the raw material of this one.

These examples serve to show that there is a complexity in calculating the lifetime of global reserves. There is a play-off between supply and demand, the cost of extraction and the price of the raw commodity. Nothing drives a renewed search for natural resources more than an increase in the price. Demand often encourages the search for new resources and as they become exploited and the price rises, so it becomes economically feasible to look for less accessible or lower concentration reserves. The calculations shown above are very approximate but lie behind any newspaper headlines that authoritatively state, for example, that oil reserves will only last another 40 years. Notwithstanding the economics of supply and demand, the reserves of any natural physical resource are finite and therefore have a finite lifetime – and that lifetime is invariably shorter than the time it takes to replenish those reserves over geological time.

8.5   Living in the Earth system

Having explored aspects of the evolution of the Earth, its relationship to biological evolution and how physical resources have often resulted from interactions between the two, it is perhaps appropriate to end with a view on how humanity is currently modifying the Earth system. At times throughout the history of the Earth, changes in biological evolution have triggered changes in the environment. Thus the evolution of cyanobacteria and photosynthesis 3500 Ma ago started a process that eventually led to the presence of oxygen in the atmosphere. Today, humanity is also forcing changes in the environment by using the atmosphere and oceans as 'dumps' for the waste products of technology, thereby driving environmental change that may be equally irreversible. However, as you have seen, environmental change is not restricted to the recent past but has been ongoing for thousands of years.

In the hands of a small group of hunter-gatherers, stone tools and less durable artefacts of wood and bone might not seem environmentally threatening. But even these modest technological advances may have had effects on natural ecosystems prior to historic times. The rise of modern humans during the last few million years coincides with extinctions of a number of large mammals that were potential prey to human hunters. Prior to 2 Ma ago, the genus extinction rate amongst large mammals was 10–20 Ma^{-1}; after 2 Ma that rate rose tenfold to more than 100 Ma^{-1}. Controversy rages whether extinctions had a human cause or were the result of climate change – 2 Ma is about the same time as major Northern Hemisphere glaciations – but coincidence does not necessarily imply cause and effect.

The clearest support for a human cause comes from the Americas and Australia, where extinctions rose dramatically in the last 100 ka. In Australia significant numbers of large marsupial species became extinct shortly after human occupation around 60 ka. By contrast, in the Americas the bulk of large mammal extinctions followed the first signs of human occupation at about the same time as the last glacial maximum, at ~18 ka. It is more difficult to relate extinctions to human migration in Africa and Eurasia because of the paucity of archaeological remains – there is ample evidence in both Australia and the Americas to track the progress of human migration – but the possibility remains that the earlier extinction patterns in those continents were related to the development of stone-age technologies. Today extinction rates are such that many biologists are talking of a sixth mass extinction (Chapter 2), but this time induced by human activity.

Starting with the Bronze Age (roughly between 5.5 and 3.2 ka) the last 5000 years of human culture has become increasingly one of metal use, and the concomitant need for ever more powerful sources of energy. The social and political advantage offered by metal tools of ever increasing sophistication has driven society to become a significant geological force. The amount of rock and soil that needs to be moved to extract energy and mineral resources is quite mind-boggling, and Figure 8.7a gives an idea of the extent to which society now intervenes in the Earth system to extract physical resources. Both archaeological and modern civil engineering structure show up clearly on satellite images of the Earth's surface (Figures 8.7b and c) and involve shifting large amounts of soil and rock.

(a)

(b)

(c)

(d)

Figure 8.7   Human movement of material. (a) The world's largest earth mover, used to mine coal from the surface. (b) The 4 ka old pyramids of Giza, Egypt. (c) Beach development on an artificial island on the Persian Gulf shore of Dubai. (d) Soil erosion in South Dakota, USA.

What is less obvious is the effect of technological agriculture on the Earth system. Continual cultivation of fertile regions without replenishing the nutrients that agriculture requires removes the natural materials that protect soils from erosion. The consequence is soil degradation on a large scale. Perhaps the most notorious example of such soil degradation occurred in the plains of the United States in the 1920s and 1930s, which resulted in the dust bowl. Millions of tons of soil were literally blown away by strong winds during drought conditions, never to be replaced, transforming fertile plains into desert. In upland regions removal of natural vegetation renders the soil equally vulnerable to erosion by rainfall (Figure 8.7d) and whereas some cultures have developed terracing systems to reduce the effects of such erosion, many parts of the developing world are being degraded as a consequence of the removal of natural vegetation.

The natural rate of erosion estimated from the mass of sediment deposited over the last few thousand years is about 2×10^{13} kg y^{-1}. Human induced erosion at the beginning of the 21st century is estimated to be about 8×10^{13} kg y^{-1} – quite clearly human society has become a significant agent in shaping the Earth system.

Energy to drive what has become an industrial economy is now a major requirement of all developed and developing countries. Industry first turned to coal and then rapidly to oil and natural gas as convenient forms of high energy-content fuels. Burning fossil fuels reverses the ancient reduction of water and carbon dioxide to organic hydrocarbons by oxidation back to CO_2 and H_2O. The annual output of CO_2 from human activity is currently estimated to be equivalent to more than 7 Gt of carbon per year, compared with ~0.08 Gt C y^{-1} from volcanic emissions – about 100 times as great. As you saw in Book 1, this is now recognised as a major contributor to the greenhouse effect and global warming. Moreover, estimates of carbon emissions to the atmosphere at times of climate change in the geological past suggest that the rate at which CO_2 is being introduced into the atmosphere today is as great or greater than natural processes have achieved at any time in the last 500 Ma.

These examples illustrate that human society is now a significant agent for change in the Earth system and that some human activities rival natural processes in magnitude and scale. Currently our greatest concern is our effect on the global carbon cycle but our effect on soil and other resources should also be cause for deep concern. Ultimately, the Earth renews these resources. Erosion will produce more soil, carbon dioxide will dissolve in the sea and be precipitated as carbonate and tectonic processes will generate and reveal more mineral deposits ready for exploitation. But the problem for society is that these processes operate only on very long timescales. The few centuries that have passed since the Industrial Revolution are trifling in comparison with the tens and hundreds of millions of years taken to produce the coal and oil on which it relied for its energy source.

Equally important is that the effects of industrial modification to the environment may be irreversible on the timescale of civilisation. If we continue to burn fossil fuels at the rate we are currently doing for the next century or more, global mean temperatures will continue to rise, the polar ice caps, first Greenland, and then Antarctica, will melt and sea levels will rise. It has been estimated that the

Greenland ice cap alone contains enough water to raise sea level by 7 metres, while all the ice on Antarctica could raise sea level by another 60 metres! Sea levels of this magnitude have probably not occurred since the Cretaceous.

8.6   Summary of Chapter 8

In this chapter you have been introduced to the concept of physical resources, in particular those that supply the material and energy needs of a modern technological society. The exploitation of physical resources has an effect on the natural environment and these effects can last for millennia. Mineral, metal and fossil fuel resources are products of the rock cycle and the carbon cycle. Many metal deposits result from extreme processes in the rock cycle that fractionate and concentrate elements from a dispersed source and transport them to a new environment where they are deposited as ore minerals. Metal ores can form as a result of igneous, sedimentary and hydrothermal processes and are frequently in the form of sulfides, oxides and carbonates. For an ore deposit to be economical it has to be present in a high enough concentration in a mineral form from which the metal can be easily extracted.

Energy released when fossil fuels are burned was originally derived from solar radiation trapped by photosynthesis and the carbon buried to form coal or petroleum was originally trapped from the atmosphere. Burning fossil fuels is reversing the processes that produced them but at a rate that is much faster than would happen naturally.

The reserves of physical resources are as dependent on economic pressures and demand as they are on their natural availability. As demand increases so does the value of the natural resource. As a consequence, resources with lower concentrations in less accessible forms become economically viable. The drive to extract materials from the Earth to sustain an ever-increasing population is having a marked effect on the environment and in shaping the Earth. Human activity is now physically removing more material from the Earth than erosion and river transport and is supplying carbon dioxide to the atmosphere at a greater rate than volcanic emissions. There is also the distinct possibility that this activity is driving a sixth mass extinction. It is clear that the Earth system cannot sustain this level of activity indefinitely.

Answers to questions

Question 2.1

(i) The garden slug is extremely unlikely to find its way into the fossil record because it has only soft parts, and these will be eaten or rapidly decay after death. In any case, living on land, it is in an environment with little chance of long-term burial by sediment. (ii) The garden snail at least has a shell, but this too is readily destroyed, and overall the snail also has a low preservation potential because it lives on land. (iii) The whale has huge bones, and being marine should stand a fair chance of fossilisation. (iv) The jellyfish, although living in the sea, has no hard parts, and, not surprisingly, fossil jellyfish are very rare.

Question 2.2

(i) As we saw in Question 2.1, any *individual* whale has, on average, a high preservation potential, but there are very few blue whales so the species is likely to be very rare in the fossil record. (ii) The garden earthworm occurs in huge numbers, and is widespread, but, because it is soft-bodied and lives on land, both its body and its burrows are unlikely candidates for inclusion in the fossil record. (iii) Despite having hard bones and teeth, the low numbers of individuals, the non-marine setting, and the fact that organic material on land in the tropics tends to rot away very quickly, largely explain why early human fossils are so rare. (iv) The oyster species is abundant, thick-shelled and marine, all of which give it by far the best preservation potential of these four species.

Question 2.3

(ii), (iii) and (v). (ii) The trace fossils record its activities; (iii) the other groups could provide independent evidence of the environment; (v) the more complex the hard parts, the more clues to go on. Conversely, having few living relatives (i) tends to make fossils difficult to reconstruct as living organisms, and, (iv), the more separated the hard parts, the more difficult to see where they fitted together, or whether they came from the same individual.

Question 2.4

$$\frac{4570\,\text{Ma} - 542\,\text{Ma}}{4570\,\text{Ma}} \times 100\% = 88\%$$

The Precambrian therefore represents about 88% of geological time. Another way of expressing this is about seven-eighths of geological time: $(7/8) \times 100\% = 87.5\%$.

Question 2.5

The events in order, starting with the oldest, are as follows:
- origin of the Earth: 4570 Ma
- first evidence of life (chemical fossils) in oldest sedimentary rocks: 3850 Ma
- first fossil structures (including stromatolites): 3500 Ma
- permanent accumulation of free atmospheric oxygen: 2200 Ma

- first eukaryotic cells in the fossil record: 2100 Ma
- first multicellular organisms (algae): 1200 Ma
- first animals (Ediacaran fauna): 580 Ma
- Cambrian explosion: 542 Ma
- Burgess Shale fossils: 510 Ma

Question 2.6

(a) Massive objects travelling at high speed have high kinetic energy (Book 3, Section 3.1). Impacts happen quickly, so the power (rate of energy conversion; Book 3, Section 4.3) involved is enormous. The transformation of kinetic energy to other forms of energy can do a lot of work (Book 3, Section 4.1). The impact would have excavated rock, involving immense heat, to spray molten rock into the atmosphere. [You might also have considered tsunamis had the strike been in the ocean, and gases released by vaporisation of seawater, freshwater or water contained in rocks on land.]

(b) In comparison, even the greatest volcanic upheavals represented by flood basalts are slow, low-power events. They more than make up for that by the sheer mass of material released, including gases, especially CO_2 and SO_2. Each basalt flood would involve a renewed pulse of gas that convection could transfer to the stratosphere.

Question 2.7

Fossils are absent from virtually all igneous rocks (formed from molten magma) and metamorphic rocks (recrystallised at high temperatures and pressures). There are a few interesting exceptions, such as lava flows and volcanic ashes that have trapped living creatures, and metamorphic rocks such as marbles that retain ghostly vestiges of fossils which were in the original (unmetamorphosed) rock.

Question 2.8

The events in order, starting with the oldest, are as follows. The *approximate* absolute dates are also given only if they are mentioned in the text:

- first fishes: Cambrian
- start of main diversification of fishes: late Ordovician
- main invasion of the land by plants and invertebrates begins: middle Silurian (430 Ma ago)
- first amphibians: late Devonian
- first reptiles: early Carboniferous (350 Ma ago)
- first dinosaurs: middle Triassic
- first mammals: late Triassic (210 Ma ago)
- first birds: late Jurassic
- first flowering plants: early Cretaceous
- radiation of mammals: early Cenozoic
- first *Homo sapiens* (125 000–200 000 years ago)

Question 3.1

(a) Both quartz and feldspar are light-coloured, often colourless or white to pale grey (sometimes feldspars are pale pink – the green variety shown is rare). Both are quite hard and may have a glassy lustre and form prismatic crystals; it is not easy to tell them apart using any of these properties. However, cleavage should give the answer; quartz shows none, whereas feldspar shows two. A mineral's cleavage controls the way in which it fractures. Consequently, broken feldspar crystals will show flat surfaces that reflect light almost like a mirror. Quartz will break irregularly, usually along curved surfaces in a similar fashion to glass (note that this often gives small broken quartz crystals a somewhat 'greasy' lustre).

(b) Both dark mica and pyroxene can be black. They also show cleavage, but the two cleavages in pyroxene are poor compared with the single perfect cleavage in micas. In fact, mica's cleavage is so good that it reflects light extremely well, which is something of a give-away! Apart from being similar in colour, pyroxene and dark mica are different in all their other physical properties; for instance, mica is soft enough to scratch with your fingernail.

Question 3.2

(a) Granite is composed of large crystals, arranged randomly. It crystallised slowly from magma, deep in the crust.

(b) Feldspar porphyry consists of large feldspar crystals, formed first during slow cooling at depth, and set in a fine-grained groundmass. The groundmass solidified rapidly after the magma was erupted or intruded as a sill or dyke, when cooling speeded up.

(c) Rhyolite is fine-grained throughout. It is difficult to distinguish individual crystals. It crystallised quite rapidly on eruption at the Earth's surface.

(d) Pumice is a rough-textured rock but few, if any, individual grains are visible. In fact, the solid material is a glass and the roughness is caused by innumerable bubbles. On eruption, the magma released gases while the magma chilled to form glass; pumice is solidified magma froth.

(e) Obsidian looks like glass, and so it is. Very rapid cooling solidified the magma faster than silicate minerals could crystallise. All parts of the rock are the same composition as the original magma.

Question 3.3

(a) (i) Granite and rhyolite contain the highest proportion of quartz. (ii) Gabbro and basalt contain the highest proportion of mafic minerals. (iii) Gabbro and basalt do not contain alkali feldspar.

(b) Diorite may contain pyroxene; granite does not. Diorite contains more plagioclase feldspar and amphibole than granite; granite contains more alkali feldspar and quartz than diorite.

(c) Diorite contains more silicon, sodium and potassium, but less magnesium, iron and calcium than gabbro.

Question 3.4

Quartz, alkali feldspars and pale mica (all felsic minerals) are rich in Si and have complex framework or sheet structures made of connected SiO_4 tetrahedra. Magnesium- and iron-rich silicate minerals (mafic minerals) contain less Si, so have quite different, and somewhat simpler, structures: olivine is based on separate SiO_4 groups; pyroxene's is based on SiO_4 chains.

Question 4.1

In hot, humid regions, chemical weathering is rapid, whereas in cold, wet regions it is very slow, but physical weathering, through repeated freezing and thawing (frost shattering), is much more important. Water is essential for chemical weathering – without it, rocks are not decomposed – and it plays a major role in physical weathering. Although there are extremes of temperature on the Moon that can cause some physical shattering, in the absence of water there is no chemical weathering of lunar rocks.

Question 4.2

Granite is a coarse-grained rock, composed mainly of feldspar, mica and quartz crystals. Physical weathering breaks down the rock into smaller fragments and may release individual mineral grains. Chemical weathering decomposes unstable minerals such as feldspar and mica, forming stable clay minerals and soluble metal ions (e.g. Equation 4.3); it also liberates resistant quartz grains.

Question 4.3

Arid desert conditions are indicated in ancient sandstones by the presence of well-rounded, well-sorted quartz grains, with pitted (or 'frosted') surfaces, as a result of wind transportation, and a red surface coating of iron oxide, resulting from oxidising conditions.

Question 4.4

Chemical weathering provides a steady supply of soluble ions, especially Na^+, K^+, Ca^{2+}, Mg^{2+} and HCO_3^-. These ions are removed from seawater by: (i) the crystallisation of salts, extracting Na^+ and Ca^{2+}, especially during the formation of evaporites; and (ii) the growth of marine organisms responsible for many limestones, which 'lock away' Ca^{2+} and CO_3^{2-} ions in calcium carbonate.

Question 4.5

(i) Mudstone = (b); (ii) conglomerate = (f) and also (a); (iii) limestone = (g); (iv) evaporite = (d); (v) breccia = (c).

[*Note*: the descriptions are appropriate to the rocks given, but do not represent definitions of those rocks. For example, not all conglomerates contain pebbles in a quartz cement.]

Question 5.1

(a) Figure 5.9a represents compression; the mudstone to the right of the fault has moved leftwards to override the mudstone on the left. Figure 5.9b represents tension; the mudstone on the right has moved to the right, away from the mudstone on the left. In the case of the compressional fault, horizontal movements were towards one another, and away from one another for the tensional fault. Directions of movement are shown in Figure 5.14.

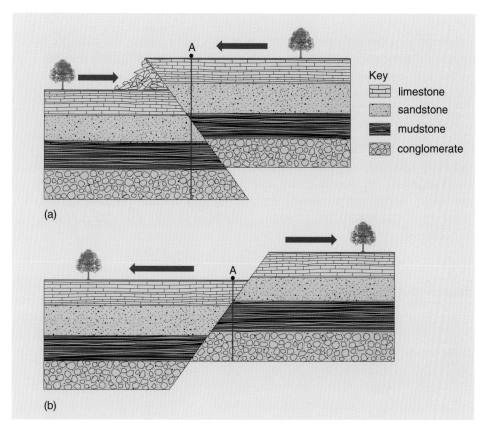

Figure 5.14 A repeat of Figure 5.9, with arrows to show the direction of horizontal movement.

(b) The sandstone and the mudstone are repeated in the sequence in Figure 5.9a, whereas the sandstone is missing from the sequence in Figure 5.9b.

(c) The separation of the trees in Figure 5.9a is less than in Figure 5.9b; therefore, compression results in overall shortening and tension results in overall extension.

Question 5.2

Mudstone is converted to slate, to schist or to gneiss at progressively higher grades of metamorphism. The rocks produced at higher grades are increasingly coarse-grained. The minerals formed are progressively more anhydrous (like feldspars and garnets) as water is liberated when hydrous minerals (like clays and micas) break down. The texture changes from the smooth, even texture of a mudstone with fine clay mineral grains to that of slate, with very fine-grained aligned mica flakes, allowing the rock to split into thin flakes along smooth, perfectly parallel surfaces; schist, with roughly aligned, coarser-grained platy minerals, so that the rock splits along uneven, roughly parallel surfaces; and gneiss, with crude mineral banding and fewer platy minerals, so it does not split as easily.

Question 5.3

The presence in rock exposures of folds and faults, formed in response to either compression or tension, are signs of movements in the Earth. The presence of regional metamorphic rocks with visible metamorphic minerals and textures formed at considerable depth also demonstrate that burial and uplift have taken place as a result of tectonic activity.

Question 5.4

Metamorphic belts are formed by regional metamorphism of pre-existing rocks encountering high pressures and temperatures during mountain building, which generally involves collision and crustal thickening at convergent plate boundaries. Erosion of mountains and the buoyant uplift of thickened crust are largely responsible for raising metamorphic belts to the surface so exposing their interiors.

Question 5.5

Figure 5.15 shows a completed version of the rock cycle.

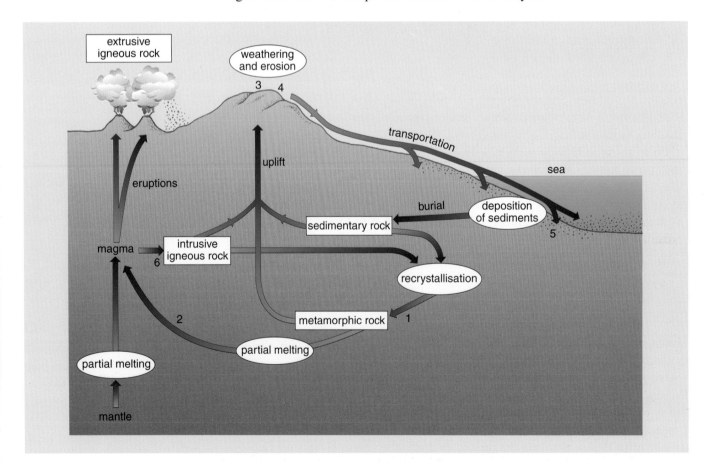

Figure 5.15   The completed rock cycle.

Question 6.1

The volume of Etna is given in km^3 but you have calculated the rate of growth in $m^3 \, y^{-1}$. You therefore need to convert the growth rate to $km^3 \, y^{-1}$, or, alternatively, to convert the volume to m^3.

There are 10^9 cubic metres in a cubic kilometre. Imagine a cube $1 \, km \times 1 \, km \times 1 \, km$; each side is 1000 m long and so the cube has a volume of $1000 \times 1000 \times 1000 \, m^3 = 10^9 \, m^3$.

Therefore the rate of growth is:

$$\frac{5.0 \times 10^6}{10^9} \, km^3 \, y^{-1} = 5.0 \times 10^{-3} \, km^3 \, y^{-1}$$

The age of Etna is now calculated by dividing the volume by the growth rate:

$$\text{age} = \frac{350 \, km^3}{5.0 \times 10^{-3} \, km^3 \, y^{-1}} = 70\,000 \, y$$

Question 6.2

The half-life of ^{235}U is 704 Ma. From Table 6.4 in the comments on Activity 6.2, a D/P value of 3.0 corresponds to 2.0 half-lives. For the ^{235}U to ^{207}Pb decay scheme, that is equivalent to an age of $2.0 \times 704 \, Ma = 1408 \, Ma$. Thus the zircon, and hence the granite, are 1400 Ma old, to two significant figures.

Question 6.3

The lower layered rocks (C) were deposited and then folded by a tectonic event (G). After the folding, magma cut through the layered rocks and across the folds, to form a large igneous intrusion (A). Erosion wore down the mountains that had formed during the tectonic event. That left the surface (D), maybe as a plain or a marine erosion surface, which defines an unconformity. Sediments (F) then accumulated above the unconformity. At a later stage, another tectonic event fractured and displaced all the older rocks along a fault (Ef). The last geological event represented by rock was another injection of magma that cut across the fault and all other features to form a narrow igneous intrusion (B). Since then, erosion has produced the present land surface. [*Note:* because the section does not show a relationship between the granite intrusion A and the unconformity, their ages relative to one another are uncertain, but both are older than the fault and the basalt intrusion.]

Question 7.1

(a) (i) The microscopic view shows a large range of grain sizes, from pebbles around 3 mm to fine sand grains of 0.1 mm and perhaps smaller in size – therefore, it is poorly sorted. (ii) The grains range from moderately to poorly rounded, the smaller ones being angular. (iii) Whatever the environment in which they were deposited, the pebbles indicate it was high energy.

(b) The sediment's poor sorting rules out an origin as a wind-blown dune sand or on a beach. The most likely environment was water flowing on land.

(c) Because the rock contains feldspar grains, the influence of chemical weathering in liberating grains to be transported must have been minimal (the presence of feldspar also suggests rapid transport in water).

Question 7.2

The irregular but roughly N–S trending belt of Carboniferous rocks coincides with the uplands of the Pennines. It is surrounded to the east, west and south by younger sedimentary rocks occupying lowland areas. This is most easily explained by a broad upfold trending N–S along the line of the Pennines.

Question 7.3

From around 90 Ma, the animation shows Africa slowly moving towards Europe. The seaway between them was clearly experiencing the tectonic effects, developing a series of slivers of land in the frames for 65 and 50 Ma. At some time between 50 and 20 Ma, the two continents collided, to form the Alps. In fact, that major orogenic event began around 30 Ma ago, to form the E–W mountain belt. The structures in southeastern England are parallel to that trend, and affect both Cretaceous and Cenozoic rocks, so they are the outermost ripples of the Alpine Orogeny.

Comments on activities

Activity 2.2

The answer is shown in Figure 2.25. The reasoning behind the answer is as follows.

The metamorphic rocks A1 and B1 may or may not be of approximately the same age, but they must certainly be much older than the sedimentary (i.e. unmetamorphosed) beds A2 and B2. Schist and slate are both metamorphic rocks (Book 2) produced when rocks are buried deeply and subject to increased pressures and temperatures. They have clearly been metamorphosed, uplifted and eroded before the deposition of the overlying strata. There must therefore be an unconformity (indicated by U) between these metamorphic rocks and the overlying shales.

Beds 2, 3 and 4 in both A and B match in both fossil content and in rock type, so are likely to have been deposited at similar times. The presence of trilobites in beds A2 and A4, and B2 and B4 means that beds A2, A3 and A4 and B2, B3 and B4 must be of Palaeozoic age, as trilobites are confined to the Palaeozoic Era. (The age ranges of trilobites and other fossil groups were given in the Activity.)

The presence of ammonites in B5 and B6 means that these beds must be Mesozoic, as ammonites were confined to the Mesozoic Era. In addition, plesiosaurs were also confined to the Mesozoic, so this is additional evidence that B5 cannot be Palaeozoic or Cenozoic. There may be an unconformity (indicated by U?) between B4 and B5, although bed B4 might happen to be the latest Palaeozoic and bed B5 the earliest Mesozoic; more detailed identification of fossils present would reveal if this was the case.

Bed A5 (and the overlying bed, A6) must be of Cenozoic age, as A5 contains whale vertebrae, and whales originated only in the early Cenozoic (Figure 2.22 and Box 2.4). No Mesozoic rocks are therefore represented in A, so with Cenozoic rocks lying on Palaeozoic rocks there must be an unconformity between A4 and A5. Bed B7 (and the overlying bed B8) must also be Cenozoic as bed B7 contains whale vertebrae. There may therefore be an unconformity between B6 and B7 although bed B6 might happen to be the latest Mesozoic and bed B7 the earliest Cenozoic; again, more detailed identification of fossils present would reveal if this was the case.

In practice, the strata above and below an unconformity often dip at different angles (in addition to being of very different ages) because the underlying beds have been tilted, uplifted and eroded before the deposition of the overlying beds.

Note that each of the other fossil groups mentioned in columns A and B (i.e. brachiopods, crinoids, corals, bivalves and echinoids) occur in all three Phanerozoic eras (as stated in the Activity), and are thus not diagnostic of any one era. Individual species, however, do have a much more restricted time-range.

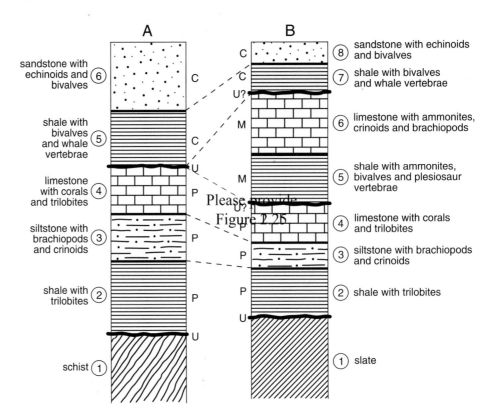

Figure 2.25   Completed version of Figure 2.24. P stands for Palaeozoic, M for Mesozoic, C for Cenozoic and U for unconformity.

Activity 3.1

Table 3.2   Completed Table 3.1.

Mineral	Classification	Composition	Colour	Lustre	Cleavage	Shape	Hardness
Quartz	Silicate (framework)	SiO_2	Mainly colourless – can be coloured	Glassy	None (irregular fracture)	Prismatic	7.0
Feldspar	Silicate (framework)	Alkali $(K,Na)AlSi_3O_8$ Plagioclase, from $NaAlSi_3O_8$ to $CaAl_2Si_2O_8$	Mainly white – can be pinkish	Glassy to dull	Two good	Prismatic	6.0–6.5
Mica	Silicate (sheet)	Pale (muscovite) $KAl_3Si_3O_{10}(OH)_2$ Dark (biotite) $K(Fe,Mg)_3AlSi_3O_{10}(OH)_2$	Silvery (muscovite) or brown to black (biotite)	Pearly	One perfect	Tabular	2.5
Pyroxene	Silicate (single chain)	$(Ca,Mg,Fe)_2Si_2O_6$	Dark green to black	Dull to glassy	Two at 90°	Stubby prismatic	5.5–6.0
Olivine	Silicate (isolated group)	$(Mg,Fe)_2SiO_4$	Pale to dark green. Weathers reddish brown	Glassy	None	Stubby prismatic	6.5–7.0

Activity 3.2

Task I

Grains do not break away easily from Specimens 5 and 6, nor do broken surfaces tend to pass around grains, as is common in many sedimentary rocks. In fact, where the rock is broken, some individual grains reveal cleavage planes of mineral crystals. Characteristically for igneous rocks, the individual grains in both basalt and granite are crystals held together tightly, being intergrown and interlocking, so they are irregular in shape.

Grains in the granite sample are randomly oriented and randomly distributed. This is characteristic of an igneous texture, rather than that of a metamorphic rock (a tendency for interlocking crystals to be aligned, or to be arranged in a banded structure). A few flat crystals in the basalt sample may show some alignment, but that does not affect the entire sample as it would in a metamorphic rock. In the basalt (Specimen 5) a few flat crystals became aligned because the magma was flowing before it became completely solid (see Section 3.2.1).

Task 2

(a) The basalt is very dark throughout; the granite is generally paler, but more variable in the colour of its constituent grains (white, grey and black). Much of the basalt is fine-grained, most crystals being too small to measure by eye, but some (long thin ones and broad chunky ones) are up to 10 mm long. The granite, by contrast, is coarse-grained throughout, most grains being 2–5 mm across, and a few up to 20 mm.

(b) The overall colour of a rock depends on its mix of different minerals. Almost all of the minerals in the basalt are dark grey or dark green to black (although there are some paler crystals on and close to weathered surfaces). By contrast, most of the minerals in the granite are white or pale grey, only a few being black.

The grain size depends on the rate of cooling during crystallisation; an indication of the way crystallisation occurred (Book 2, Activity 5.1). Thus the mainly fine-grained basalt cooled rapidly as an extrusive rock and crystallised at the Earth's surface. (The few larger crystals in the basalt are explained in Section 3.2.1.) The coarse-grained granite cooled slowly as an intrusive rock, crystallising deep beneath the Earth's surface.

Activity 3.3

Task I

The three types of mineral in granite have the following properties, which match consistently with those in Table 3.2 in the comments on Activity 3.1:

Quartz: grey, glassy, irregular, 1–4 mm diameter, no cleavage.

Feldspar: white, more box-shaped, 2–10 mm across, with reflecting cleavage planes.

Mica: black (some silvery) flakes, 1 mm across, shiny surfaces, which represent cleavage planes.

Task 2

(a) The chemical formulas for the main minerals in granite and basalt are as follows.

Granite:	alkali feldspar	$(K,Na)AlSi_3O_8$
	plagioclase feldspar (Na-rich) quartz	$NaAlSi_3O_8$ SiO_2
	dark mica (biotite)	$K(Fe,Mg)_3AlSi_3O_{10}(OH)_2$
Basalt:	plagioclase feldspar (Ca-rich)	$CaAl_2Si_2O_8$
	pyroxene	$(Ca,Mg,Fe)_2Si_2O_6$

(b) On the basis of the proportions of these minerals and their compositions, granite will contain more potassium (K, in alkali feldspar and dark mica) and sodium (Na, in alkali feldspar) than the basalt. Silicon (Si) is present in all the silicate minerals but granite contains 30% quartz (SiO_2) whereas basalt does not contain any, so silicon must be more abundant in granite. Basalt will contain more calcium (Ca, in plagioclase feldspar and pyroxene). There is abundant pyroxene (50%) in the basalt, so it will contain much more iron (Fe) and magnesium (Mg) than granite. The dark mica (10%) is the only mineral in the granite containing iron and magnesium.

Activity 4.1

Task 1

The soil (a mixture of sediment grains) begins to settle as soon as the water comes to rest. The largest grains settle almost immediately, and obvious but smaller grains soon after. The finest grains need a few hours to settle from murky water.

Task 2

The types of grain will depend on the nature of your soil sample. Some soils are stony or sandy, others are muddier. The following description is of a fairly typical soil.

Larger grains at the bottom of the jar are succeeded by layers of progressively finer material. The coarsest material contains pebbles (>2 mm). Immediately above it is sand (<2 mm, >0.063 mm). The next grains are just visible but not easily measurable. The finest material at the top is too fine to see with the unaided eye.

If the soil has a high organic content, there will be fragments floating on or suspended in the water.

Figure 4.15 is a simple sketch, with labelling conveying the important information in the description above. Your diagram, and the way it is labelled, will differ from this one because your soil is different, but you should check that you have labelled the important features.

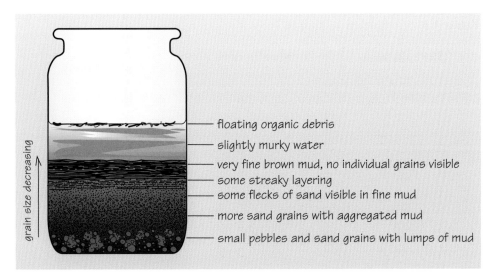

Figure 4.15 Sketch of settled sediment in a jar.

Task 3

The topmost sediment is like sludge and feels slimy. It is probably clay- to silt-sized mud (4–63 μm) and the grains cannot be seen using the hand lens. Below that are increasingly coarse sands. The coarsest material may include rounded or angular pebbles made of rock and/or mineral fragments. Some of the sand-sized grains may be recognisable minerals. Translucent glassy grains of quartz are common in soil. Pale-coloured but opaque grains of feldspar or silvery flakes of mica sometimes occur. There may also be dull, dark-coloured grains of unidentifiable minerals – probably iron minerals or bits of charcoal.

Activity 4.2

Task 1

(a) Physical and chemical weathering break down exposed rocks to produce sediment grains.

(b) Grains move downstream by rolling, bouncing or in suspension.

(c) River sediments typically contain a wide range of grain sizes and minerals. Beach sediments contain a much narrower range of grain sizes and fewer minerals, and quartz frequently dominates. The range of grain sizes expresses the degree of sorting in the sediment; the narrower it is, the better sorted are the grains.

(d) Wind-blown grains are normally well-rounded and their surfaces are very finely pitted. Grains deposited by water are more angular and have a glassy appearance.

Task 2

The calculated mass percentages for each sieve are shown in Table 4.3.

Table 4.3   Completed version of Table 4.1.

Sieve size/mm	Mass in sieve/g	Proportion of total mass/%
4	1.0	2.1
2	1.4	2.9
1	4.8	10.1
0.5	7.1	14.9
0.25	14.5	30.4
0.12	9.4	19.7
0.06	7.3	15.3
pan	2.2	4.6
Total	47.7	100.0

The histogram for these data is shown in Figure 4.16. Because the sand is distributed over a large number of sieves, this histogram represents a poorly sorted sediment.

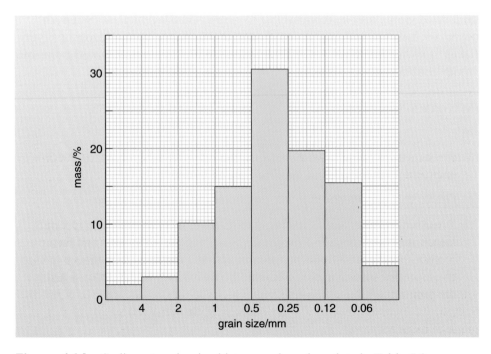

Figure 4.16   Sediment grain-size histogram based on data in Table 5.3.

Task 3

(a) In Figure 4.7a: (i) has a poorly sorted distribution and is likely to be river sand; (ii) is very well-sorted and likely to be desert sand; (iii) is fairly well-sorted and likely to be beach sand.

(b) Matching Figure 4.7a with Figure 4.7b: (a)(i) and (b)(iii) represent poorly sorted distributions (a river sand); (a)(ii) and (b)(i) are very well-sorted (a desert sand); and (a)(iii) and (b)(ii) are fairly well-sorted (a beach sand). Note that the narrow spread of well-sorted sand on the histogram (all the sand ends up in two or three sieves) results in a steep graph of cumulative frequency. Conversely, poorly sorted sand has a broader spread on the histogram, and the cumulative frequency graph is less steep.

Task 4

A steel nail removes grains from the sandstone more easily than from the igneous rocks, but most are too tightly held for a fingernail to work. The grains range from almost 2 mm in diameter to a size that is too small to be measured (<0.1 mm). (Note: some samples are coarser than others.) The sand grains are glassy and are mostly quartz. The finer material is soft and crumbly; probably clay. There is not a wide range of coarse grains, as very few have a diameter greater than 2 mm, but there is a considerable amount of very fine material. Overall, the sediment has a greater spread of grain sizes than is found in a desert sand, or even a beach sand; it resembles a river sand.

Through a hand lens, most individual quartz grains are glassy and angular, much like those transported by water in the video sequence. They are not well-rounded and 'frosted' wind-blown grains. In places the grains are closely packed, but in others soft, pale powdery material (largely clay) surrounds them. You can also see lots of holes in the rock, especially on a cut surface. Water soaks rapidly into the rock, so there is a lot of open space between the grains.

Activity 5.1

Task 1

Table 5.2 shows the results of comparing the properties of slate, gneiss and schist. Note: your sample of schist may differ slightly in grain size, colour and degree of banding from the typical example described here.

Task 2

The grain sizes of the three rocks vary, and so does the nature of the layering. The order of increasing grain size is slate – schist – gneiss. In the same order, the layering becomes more uneven: flat in the slate (Figure 5.3a), uneven in the schist (Specimen 4), and undulating in the gneiss (Figure 5.3b). There is also greater separation between layers along which the rocks would tend to break. (In Section 5.1.2 you will see how these changes in character reflect an increase in grade of metamorphism.)

Table 5.2   Completed version of Table 5.1.

Property	Slate	Gneiss	Schist
Grain size	Very fine; surfaces are smooth and most grains are too small to distinguish; only larger dark flecks (0.5 mm max.) are visible	Coarse; easy to see grains. Average size 3–5 mm. Some individual 1–2 mm grains of a dark mineral. Also tightly packed in layers	Medium; easy to see granular minerals (mostly 0.5–2 mm); difficult to distinguish platy minerals in tightly packed layers
Colour	Pale grey with dark flecks, fairly uniform	Pale (creamy/grey) bands and dark (black) layers	Silvery grey-brown, mottled cream, black and pinkish brown on cut surfaces. Rusty brown colour on broken surfaces. (Staining from iron compounds released on weathering.)
Texture	A scaly effect is apparent where lighting highlights edges to thin layers with flat surfaces. Not possible to see arrangement of fine grains. (Breakage is along parallel surfaces running through the rock, caused by aligned platy minerals.)	Irregular, sometimes lens-shaped bands of pale granular minerals, and dark sinuous and discontinuous bands of platy minerals	Uneven surfaces, sometimes crinkly, but fairly smooth, with a reflective sheen from planar alignment of medium- to coarse-grained platy minerals. In some samples, layers of dark and light minerals may be present (as in gneiss)
Minerals	Minerals unrecognisable. (Mainly fine-grained mica that you would see as a slightly reflective sheen in a hand specimen.)	Grey quartz, white feldspar, dark (biotite) mica	Mainly silvery and dark mica flakes, similarly sized glassy quartz grains and a few pinkish-brown garnet grains (*Minerals Gallery*)

Activity 6.1

Task 1

The cumulative volume data are shown in Table 6.3. Each cumulative volume is the sum of the volume of lava produced that year and the previous value of the cumulative volume.

Task 2

A graph of the cumulative volumes is shown in Figure 6.10, with a best-fit line drawn through the data points.

The gradient of the best-fit line was determined using the construction lines drawn on the graph, and is

$$\text{gradient} = \frac{\text{rise}}{\text{run}} = \frac{(970 - 220) \times 10^6 \text{ m}^3}{(1950 - 1800) \text{ y}}$$

$$= \left(\frac{750}{150} \right) \times 10^6 \text{ m}^3 \text{ y}^{-1} = 5.0 \times 10^6 \text{ m}^3 \text{ y}^{-1} \text{ to two significant figures}$$

Table 6.3 Completed version of Table 6.1. Volumes of lava flow from eruptions of Etna, 1766–1951.

Year of eruption	Volume of lava flow/10^6 m^3	Cumulative volume/10^6 m^3
1766	106	106
1780	15	121
1793	80	201
1809	19	220
1812	25	245
1819	31	276
1832	50	326
1843	50	376
1853	128	504
1865	46	550
1879	36	586
1886	56	642
1892	100	742
1908	3	745
1910	34	779
1911	36	815
1923	45	860
1928	30	890
1942	2	892
1947	4	896
1949	3	899
1951	50	949

The gradient has units of volume per unit time; in other words it is a measure of the rate of growth between 1758 and 1951. So, averaged over the period between 1758 and 1951, Etna grew at a rate of about 5.0×10^6 m^3 y^{-1}, or 5.0×10^{-3} km^3 y^{-1}.

Figure 6.10 Cumulative volume of lava flows from Etna, 1766–1951.

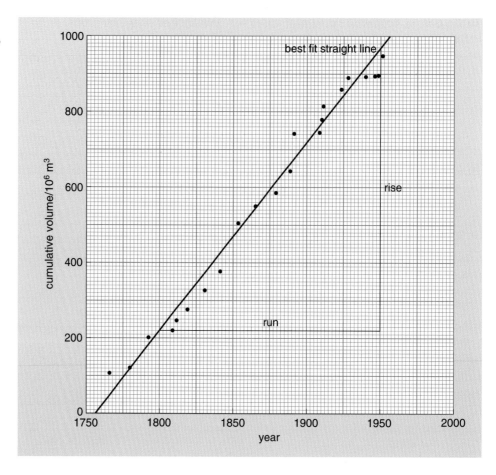

Activity 6.2

Task 1

Table 6.4 shows the results for (a) and (b), which are plotted in Figure 6.11.

Table 6.4 Completed Table 6.2.

Time/days	0	3	6	9	12	15	18	21	24	27	30
Half-life (n)	0	1	2	3	4	5	6	7	8	9	10
Atoms of parent isotope (P)	1024	512	256	128	64	32	16	8	4	2	1
Atoms of daughter isotope (D)	0	512	768	896	960	992	1008	1016	1020	1022	1023
D/P ratio	0	1	3	7	15	31	63	127	255	511	1023
D/P ratio by Eqn 6.7	0	1	3	7	15	31	63	127	255	511	1023

(c) The black (solid line) graph (Figure 6.11) for atoms of the parent isotope shows numbers of atoms decreasing rapidly for the first few half-lives, and then the decrease in numbers slows until only one is left. Since there is no such thing as 'half an atom', all atoms of the parent isotope have decayed by the eleventh half-life. In reality, the number of atoms of even a rare isotope in a small sample of a mineral will be enormous, and some will still exist after a great many more than 10 half-lives. The red (dashed line) graph for atoms of the daughter isotope is an exact mirror image of that for its parent.

Task 2

Table 6.4 shows that the values of D/P calculated by using Equation 6.7 are the same as by simple division.

Figure 6.11 shows the plot of D/P changing with time in blue (dotted line); again, it is a mirror image of the decay curve for the parent isotope.

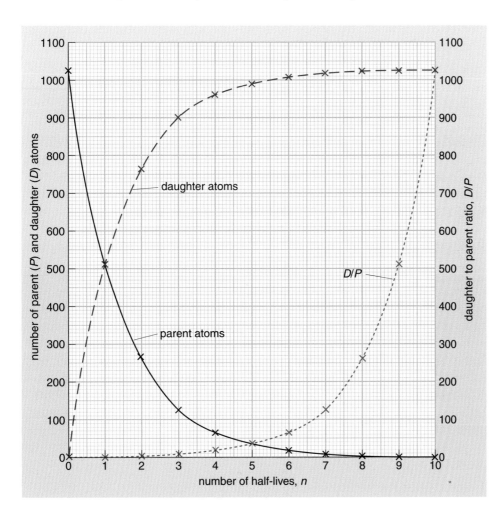

Figure 6.11 Plots from Task 1 (a) and (b) and Task 2. The black (solid) line shows the change in the number of radioactive parent atoms with time (Task 1a); the red (dashed) line shows the change in the number of daughter atoms with time (Task 1b) and the blue (dotted) line the change in the daughter to parent ratio (D/P) with time (Task 2).

Activity 7.1

Task 1

The Devonian upper rocks are reddish to pink and layered on a scale of centimetres to tens of centimetres, suggesting a sedimentary origin. The layering is dominantly parallel, although small-scale cross-bedding can be seen in Figure 7.5b. They are moderately sorted sandstones (but note the conglomerate layer in Figure 7.5b). Like the Torridonian Sandstones, the Devonian upper sedimentary rocks are red-beds laid down in a strongly oxidising environment, i.e. on land, under moderate- to high-energy conditions. Being poorly sorted, they too were probably deposited by flowing streams.

Task 2

The grey Silurian lower rocks are also layered on a scale of tens of centimetres, but grains are not visible. They are fine-grained sedimentary rocks deposited under low-energy conditions. No cross-bedding is visible. Their grey colour suggests that the environment was non-oxidising. The presence of fossil trilobites (see the comments on Activity 2.1) indicates that they were deposited on the Silurian sea floor. These rocks are deep-water, marine mudstones.

Task 3

The bedding in the Silurian sedimentary rocks is almost vertical. This suggests extreme tilting, probably as a result of intense folding and crustal thickening through tectonic compression at some time between 420 and 380 Ma. The unconformity is almost planar, which implies that the mountains produced by crustal thickening had been eroded to an almost flat land surface by the time the Devonian red-beds were deposited. Both the unconformity and the Devonian beds dip gently northwards (Figure 7.5a), which suggests later, slight tilting of the crust.

Activity 7.2

Task 2

Figure 7.21 shows a sketch based on Figure 7.7a; it is useful to compare the two figures. Note that the student who produced this sketch has correctly concentrated on the main features, including the boundaries between the main beds of sandstones and the large-scale, high-angle cross-bedding within them that is typical of desert dunes. To save time, and to avoid unnecessary detail, only a few of the individual layer boundaries have been sketched in, as more-or-less continuous lines. The vertical feature near the centre is of little significance; the beds are not displaced across it (at least at this scale of view). So it is not a fault plane but merely a natural crack or joint.

Activity 7.3

Towards the end of the Precambrian (600 Ma), all continental crust was locked together in a supercontinent that extended from high northern latitudes to the South Pole, where glaciation was in progress. Northern Britain was close to the South Pole, and experienced this glaciation. Southern Britain was also at low southern latitudes, but several thousand miles away, to the east. At 560 Ma, glaciation had finished and sea-floor spreading had split three substantial

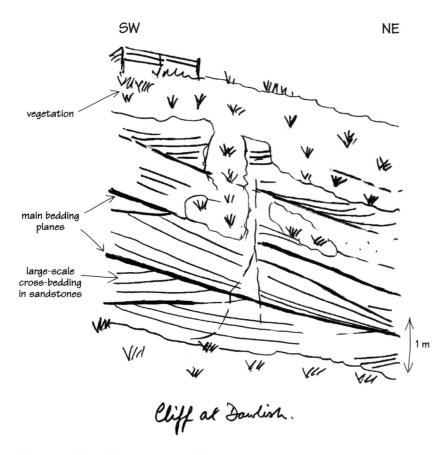

SW   NE

vegetation

main bedding
planes

large-scale
cross-bedding
in sandstones

1 m

Cliff at Dawlish.

Figure 7.21   Sketch of the cliff section in Figure 7.7a.

continents from the supercontinent. The westernmost of these was to become modern North America, including the northern British Isles crust, at the northern side of the Iapetus Ocean. Spreading also resulted in oceanic volcanic arcs at subduction zones, where new continental material was evolving.

This break-up continued through the Cambrian, northern parts of the British Isles moving northwards, while their southern segment drifted over the South Pole, as a part of the remaining supercontinent. Between the Upper Cambrian (500 Ma) and the Middle Ordovician (470 Ma) one of the volcanic arcs collided with the westernmost of the isolated continents. This resulted in the first stage of the Caledonian Orogeny in the northern British Isles. At the same time, the southern segment broke away from the supercontinent to drift northwards.

By the Upper Ordovician (450 Ma), the Iapetus Ocean separating the northern and southern British Isles had begun to close. This happened by southward subduction beneath the southern segment, causing volcanism in Wales and the English Lake District. By the Middle Silurian (430 Ma), the Iapetus Ocean had almost vanished, and two of the main drifting continents had begun to collide in what is now western Scandinavia. By the Lower Devonian (400 Ma), the two main continents had welded together, including both parts of the British Isles. From this time until the Triassic, the British Isles drifted steadily northwards. During the 450–400 Ma period, other small fragments of continental crust had split from the northern margin of the southern supercontinent. Sea-floor spreading to their south was driving them northwards too.

By the Upper Devonian (370 Ma), two main clusters of continental material had developed, separated by a closing linear ocean (called the Rheic Ocean). By Lower Carboniferous times this ocean was almost closed, a complex cluster of small continental blocks jostling in the east. From Upper Carboniferous to Lower Permian times (300–280 Ma), the final collision of the North America–Scandinavia and southern continents took place, which drove the Variscan Orogeny. This added the final parts to the British Isles: the Precambrian metamorphic rocks and Carboniferous oceanic crust on the two major, south-facing headlands of southwestern England (Figures 7.10 and 7.16). In the Carboniferous, the British Isles were at tropical latitudes, yet major glaciation was beginning at high southern latitudes, to linger until 260 Ma. By the Triassic (240 Ma), Pangaea was complete, running almost from pole to pole, the British Isles being trapped well within its northern part, at a northern latitude similar to that of the present-day Sahara desert. The last 'stitch' in the formation of Pangaea occurred when Asia collided with Europe along the line of the present Ural Mountains (260 Ma).

Activity 7.4

(a) The first sign – which is easily missed – that Pangaea's time was ending is a string of enclosed lakes running ENE–WSW through its central parts in the Upper Triassic (220 Ma). These are signs of a series of huge rift valleys that began to develop roughly along the join between what would become North and South America and Africa. Great thicknesses of evaporites formed in them. Through the Lower to Middle Jurassic (200–170 Ma) the rifts had joined to produce a seaway reminiscent of the modern Red Sea, but much bigger. Similar signs appear, at lower centre, of a split developing between Africa and the united India, Australia and Antarctica.

By the Upper Jurassic (150 Ma), both lines of rifting had formed narrow linear oceans, so that Pangaea had become three separate entities: North America–Europe–Asia, South America–Africa and India–Australia–Antarctica. It is interesting to note that the last two masses had been united continuously since the late Precambrian, a supercontinent with the memorable name Gondwana (named after the aboriginal Gonds of the Indian subcontinent). The Lower Cretaceous (120 Ma) marked the beginning of the separation of Africa and South America and India from Australia–Antarctica, which themselves separated at the end of the Cretaceous (65 Ma). India's course is dramatic, as seen in the animation frames up to 20 Ma. It drifted north and eventually met Asia at around 50 Ma, the collision creating the Himalaya and Tibetan Plateau, which continue to grow as Indian crust drives beneath that of Asia. Africa's slower northward drift, during roughly the same time, had a similar orogenic effect: the Alps and the Caucasus.

The other large tectonic feature of the Cenozoic is the final separation of North America from Eurasia from about 65 Ma. For much of the Mesozoic and to the present there were far more smaller continents and surrounding shallow seas than at any previous time since 600 Ma ago – perhaps a major factor in encouraging the very rapid evolution and diversification of Mesozoic and Cenozoic faunas (Section 2.5).

(b) The proportion of shallow seas is the key to visualising global sea-level changes. In the Triassic to Lower Jurassic (240–200 Ma), they form a fringe around Pangaea. Once break-up was under way (170 Ma) there are signs of marine incursions in North America and Europe. These become progressively larger through the Jurassic and Cretaceous (to 90 Ma), and affect Africa and South America with huge inland seaways. During the Upper Cretaceous, into the Cenozoic and up to the present these gradually shrink. By 20 Ma, modern continental outlines are roughly as they are today.

The conclusion is that, accompanying the decisive break-up of Pangaea, some long-term process caused global sea level to rise (by as much as 300 m). The volume of the ocean basins must have decreased. That may have happened because of a combination of massive outpourings of flood basalts on the sea floor (this did happen in the West Pacific) and heating and therefore expansion of increasing zones of oceanic lithosphere along the growing length of mid-ocean ridges. From the Middle Cretaceous, the ocean-basin volume increased, so that sea level fell globally. The recent changes (since 2.5 Ma) in sea level are mainly due to the growth and melting of ice caps. Interestingly, during the previous ice age of the Carboniferous and Permian (frames from 340 to 260 Ma), although there is evidence that sea level did fluctuate in a similar manner, overall it must have been much higher than in the Cenozoic because vast areas of continent were flooded.

Appendix

The Geological Time Scale agreed by the International Commission on Stratigraphy (published in 2004) is repeated here for easy reference. It is available online at http://www.stratigraphy.org/ (last accessed November 2011).

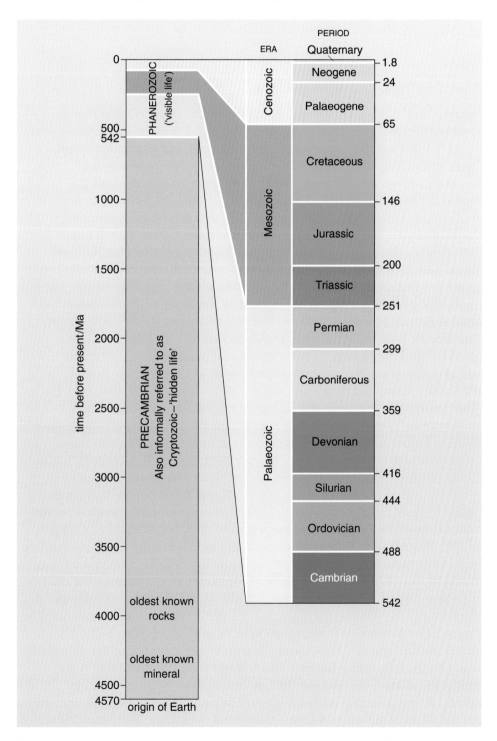

Figure A1 The main divisions of the International Geological Time Scale. (A repeat of Figure 2.7.)

Acknowledgements

The S104 module team gratefully acknowledges the contributions of the S103 *Discovering science* course team and of its predecessors.

Grateful acknowledgement is made to the following sources for permission to reproduce material in this book.

Figures

Cover: Eric Heller/Science Photo Library;

Figure 2.1a: © J. Chester Farnsworth, Princeton University Natural History Museum; Figure 2.1b: © Martin Lockley; Figure 2.2: Courtesy of Peter Sheldon; Figure 2.3: © Frank M. Carpenter; Figures 2.4a and 2.6a: © Heather Angel; Figure 2.4b: Clarkson, E. N. K. (1993) *Invertebrate Palaeontology and Evolution*, 3rd edition, Chapman and Hall, by permission of the author; Figures 2.5 and 2.6b: Fish, J. D. and Fish, S. (1989) *A Student's Guide to the Seashore*, Unwin Hyman, © Cambridge University Press; Figure 2.8a: Donald R. Lowe; Figure 2.8b: Courtesy of Professor Andrew Knoll; Figure 2.8c: Earth Science World Image Bank http://www.earthscienceworld.org/images; Figure 2.8d: © Society for Sedimentary Geology/www.earthscienceworld.org; Figure 2.9: Schopf, J. W.(1992) 'The oldest fossils and what they mean', *Major Events in the History of Life*, Jones & Bartlett. Reprinted with permission from Jones & Bartlett Learning, Sudbury, MA, www.jdlearning.com; Figure 2.10a: Reprinted by permission from Macmillan Publishers Ltd: *Nature*, vol. 391, pp. 553–558, Xiao, S. et al. 'Three-dimensional preservation of algae and animal embryos in a Neoproterozoic phosphite', © 1998; Figures 2.10aiii and 2.10aiv: Reprinted from *Earth Science Review*, vol. 77, McCall, G. J. H., 'The Vendian (Ediacaran) in the geological record: Enigmas in geology's prelude to the Cambrian Explosion', pp. 1–229, © 2006, with permission from Elsevier; Figure 2.10av: From Glaessner, M. F. (1984) *The Dawn of Animal Life*, Cambridge University Press; Figure 2.10avi: Sprigg, R. C. (1947) 'Early Cambrian jellyfish from the Flinders Ranges, South Australia', *Transactions of the Royal Society of South Australia*, The Royal Society of South Australia; Figure 2.10avii: Brasier, M. D. et al. (1997) 'Ediacarian sponge-spicule clusters from southwestern Mongolia and the origins of the Cambrian fauna', *Geology*, vol. 25, © Geological Society of America; Figure 2.10b: Chip Clark, National Museum of Natural History, Smithsonian Institution; Figure 2.11: Plates 1–3 of Matthews, S. and Missarzhevsky, V. V. (1975) *Journal of the Geological Society of London*, vol. 131, London; Figures 2.12a–e: © Professor Simon Conway Morris and H. B. Whittington; Figures 2.12f and 2.17: Courtesy of John Sibbick; Figure 2.13a: National Museums and Galleries of Wales; Figure 2.13b: © Wendy Webb; Figure 2.13c: © Jason Dunlop; Figure 2.14: Daeschler, Edward B. et al. (2006) 'A Devonian tetrapod-like fish and the evolution of the tetrapod body plan', *Nature*, vol. 440, no 7085, p. 761; Shubin, Neil H., Daeschler, Edward B. and Jenkins, Farish A. (2006) 'The pectoral fin of *Tiktaalik roseae* and the origin of the tetrapod limb', *Nature*, vol. 440, issue 7085, April 2006. Nature Publishing Group. Reprinted by permission from Macmillan Publishers

Limited; Figure 2.15: National Museum of Natural History, Smithsonian Institution; Figure 2.16: Benton, M. J. (1997) *Vertebrate Palaeontology*, 2nd edn, Chapman and Hall, by permission of the author; Figure 2.18a: Courtesy of Peter Sheldon; Figure 2.18b: Richard Grieve, Geological Survey of Canada; Figure 2.18c: Bruce F. Bohor, United States Geological Survey; Figure 2.19a: Benton, M. J. (1993) 'Dinosaur summer' *The Book of Life*, Ebury Hutchinson, Random Group (UK) Ltd; Figure 2.19b: Geological Society of Canada; Figure 2.19c: Courtesy of Dr Mike Widdowson; Figure 2.20: Stanley, S. M. (1993) *Exploring Earth and Life through Time*, W. H. Freeman & Co. Publishers; Figure 2.21: © George Gaylord Simpson, Oxford University Press; Figure 2.22: Thewissen, J. G. M., Hussain, S. T. and Arif, M. (1994) 'Fossil evidence for the origin of aquatic locomotion in archaeocete whales', *Science*, vol. 263, 14 January 1994, American Association for the Advancement of Science; Figure 2.23: W. B. Hamilton/US Geological Survey;

Figure 3.2a: Courtesy of Marc Davies; Figure 3.2b: Courtesy of the Northern Ireland Tourist Board; Figure 3.3a: Press, F. and Siever, R. (1994) *Understanding Earth*, W. H. Freeman & Co. Publishers; Figures 3.3b and 3.4b: Courtesy of Andy Tindle; Figure 3.3c: Angus Miller, Geowalks; Figure 3.4a: Dunning, F. W., Mercer, I. F. et al. (1978) *Britain Before Man*, Crown copyright material is reproduced under Class Licence No C01W0000065 by permission of Controller of HMSO and the Queen's Printer for Scotland; Figures 3.14a and 3.14b: Courtesy of Dr Steve Drury;

Figure 4.1a: Courtesy of Chris Wilson; Figure 4.1b: Courtesy of J. G. Ogg; Figure 4.1c: Angela Coe; Figure 4.4: Courtesy of Evelyn Brown; Figure 4.5a: Courtesy of Andy Tindle; Figure 4.5b: Courtesy of Dr Steve Drury; Figure 4.12a: Dr Andy Sutton, www.andysuttonphotography.com; Figure 4.12b: DigitalGlobe Inc; Figure 4.13a: Courtesy of Professor Bill Church, University of Western Ontario; Figure 4.13b: Courtesy of NASA;

Figure 5.6a: From www.rocksforkids.com. Original source unknown; Figure 5.6b: From www.und.nodak.edu, University of North Dakota; Figure 5.7b: Courtesy of J. G. Ogg; Figure 5.7c: Courtesy of Professor Chris Hawkesworth; Figure 5.8a: Courtesy of M. S. Paterson; Figure 5.8b: Manuel Marques Lopez, www.nimbar.net; Figure 5.8c: From www.uwsp.edu, Kevin P. Hefferan; Figures 5.10a and 5.10c: Courtesy of Dr Steve Drury; Figure 5.10b: Courtesy of Rodney Gayer;

Figure 6.1: © English Heritage Photographic Library; Figure 6.2: © Hazel Rymer;

Figure 7.1: © British Geological Survey; Figure 7.2a: Courtesy of Dr Simon H. Lamb; Figures 7.2b, 7.3a, 7.3b, 7.4a and 7.4b: Courtesy of Department of Earth Sciences, Oxford University; Figures 7.5a, 7.5b, 7.5c, 7.6b, 7.7a and 7.14: Courtesy of Dr Steve Drury; Figure 7.6a: Courtesy of Martin Stokes; Figure 7.8: Miller Victor, C. (1961) 'Identification and interpretation: approach and criteria', *Photogeology*, McGraw Hill; Figure 7.17: Mac Niocaill, C., van der Pluijm, B. A. and Van der Voo, R. (1997) 'Ordovician paleography and the evolution of the Iapetus ocean geology', *Geology*, vol. 25(2), February 1997, Geological Society of America; Figure 7.18: © J. S. Watson; Figure 7.19: © Natural History Museum, London; Figure 7.20a: Angela Coe; Figure 7.20b: Taken from Teacher Resource Exchange. Original source unknown; Figure 7.20c: Courtesy of Peter Skelton;

Index

Entries and page numbers in **bold type** refer to key words that are printed in **bold** in the text and that are defined in the glossary. Where the page number is given in *italics*, the index information is carried mainly or wholly in an illustration or table.